My Inspirational Quotes That Can Change Your Life

INSPIRE A BILLION

KAUSHIK MAHAPATRA

INDIA • SINGAPORE • MALAYSIA

Contents

Meet Me – Kaushik Mahapatra 😊   *vii*

Acknowledgement   *ix*

Author's Inspirational Quotes that can change your Life

1. We Tend To Like People Who Are Like Us.
   However, the Beauty Is in Liking People Who Are
   Unlike Us   1

2. The Way to Life Is To Find Out Your Own Way
   of Living   7

3. True Mastery Is Not Just About What We Do
   but Also How We Feel, Think, and Respond   14

4. We Are All Separated by Boundaries but United
   by Wisdom. Keep Leading with Wisdom   22

5. Small Corrections Often Lead to Great
   Transformations   31

6. Be Comfortable, Being Uncomfortable   39

7. Fear and Negativity Spreads Faster than Illness   48

8. Freedom from Negativity Is the Greatest Freedom   55

9. Seek Permission from Yourself and No One Else   64

10. Human Beings Can Never Be Useless, They Are
    Just Used Less   73

11. It Is Not Change but Sustainable Change That
    Can Transform Us in the Long Run   84

12. Past Made You, Present Can Destroy You,
    Future Can Mould You — 93

13. The Extra in the Ordinary Is Mastery — 101

14. If It Is to Be, It Is by Us — 117

15. Leadership Is the Love for Humanity — 125

16. The First Step for Attaining Wisdom Is Curiosity — 133

17. Spirituality Is the Only Answer to the Unanswered — 140

18. Knowledge, Talent and Potential Is of No Use,
    If It Is Unused — 147

19. Making a Contribution in Anything You Do,
    Is the Biggest Devotion — 155

20. Leading Life Both Queen Size and King Size Is the
    Ultimate Inclusion — 162

21. There Is So Less We Know About Ourselves.
    Self-Realization Leads to True Glory — 172

22. Me and We Are Incomplete Without Each Other.
    It Is Always You and Around You — 181

23. Embracing Your Ignorance Is the First Step
    Towards Wisdom — 189

24. The Rich Always Go the Wise. Being Wise Is the
    Greatest Richness — 197

25. The Journey Towards Spirituality Is Through
    Simplicity — 204

26. The Best Possible Gift to Your Child as a Parent
    Is Not to Interfere Much — 212

27. Youth Should Get a Degree in Life Management
    Before They Get Any Other Management Degree — 220

28. You Can Rewrite the Script of Your Life Through
Dedication, Determination and Devotion (3D)   229

29. The Biggest Failure in Life Is to Succeed at Things
Which Don't Really Matter to You   236

30. Where There Is Life, There Is Light   244

31. Resisting Change Is like Resisting a Better Version
of Yourself   251

32. The Best Moments in Life Are Lived and Not Just
Captured   260

33. Keep Your Plans Private, Your Move Silent;
Live Life Low Key but Recite Your Prayers
Aloud and Free   268

34. Drop the Baggage Before You Run   276

35. Love Your Problems; They Make You the
Solution Master   283

36. The Journey Towards Smart Work Is Hard Work   292

37. Bad Day ≠ Bad Life   301

38. The Start Always Takes Care of the End   309

About the Author   *317*

Meet Me – Kaushik Mahapatra 

Kaushik is an Award winning Influencer, International speaker, a Top-selling Author, Asia's most promising Corporate Coach and Trainer, Leadership Coach, Business coach, Renowned Mindfulness & Neuroscience Guru, Spiritual Teacher and an Emotional Health Educator in Asia.

🎯 He has been mentored by the World's Best Leaders - John Mattone - World's No.1 Executive Coach & Steve Jobs Coach) and Tony Robbins - World's No. 1 Speaker and Motivator), Blair Singer - The Master of Masters, Jack canfield - The man who modernized formulas for success, Gurudev Sri Sri Ravi Shankar - Most sought after Spiritual Leader and Founder of Art of Living.

🎯 Kaushik founded Indian Leadership Academy(ILA), and serves as the president with over 150,000 Alumnus in Multiple countries. These certified coaches, Leaders and trainers have created a leadership movement within their own communities. He also works as an advisor to Skill Central UK. His motto is to Lead with Wisdom and create oneness in the world through unconditional sharing and wisdom.

🎯 27 years of rich experience in running multi million business units as a Leader. As a Facilitator and a Coach, he has worked with 100000 + leaders in world-class companies, including IBM, Amazon, Bosch, Deutsche, Ericsson, PayPal, Flipkart, Softcrylic, GE, Alcon, DHL (Philippines), Amadeus(France), Unity(Dubai), Virtusa (US), MASHREQ Bank (UAE), Makino (Japan).

🎯 Specializations: Leadership Interventions, Leadership Coaching, Inclusive Leadership, Quantum Leadership, Millennial Leadership, Leadership development through Sports, Career Switch Coaching, Return to work Coaching, CXO coaching, Emergenetics, Neuroscience, Neuroleadership, Neurosales, NLP & Mindfulness, Corporate Spirituality, Agile, Design Thinking, DISC, Thomas DISC Assessments, Retreats, Worldcafe facilitation, Keynote Speaking.

His Previous Books- "Are we Leading" (TOP SELLER), "Minibook of Mindfulness", Coffee Tea or Coaching.

Recipient of Philipe Award for community leadership by GE.

Dream Project - ILA - Indian Leadership Academy

International Venture - KMG - Kaushik Mahapatra Global

Global Voluntary Organization : Inspire a Billion

Community Venture : 60+ - India's first play school for 60+, Female Founders program

🎯 WORK Locations: His Workshop Locations: India, Singapore, UK, UAE, Philippines, Vietnam, Spain, Indonesia, Mauritius, Qatar

Acknowledgement

Inspiration fuels the world. Like a ripple in a pond, its effect is contagious: one person ignites another, sparking a chain reaction of motivation and change.

The word "BILLION" in the book's title - INSPIRE A BILLION, conveys an extraordinary scale—far beyond the realm of everyday life. It represents a vast, almost boundless multitude of individuals, emphasizing the sheer magnitude of influence.

However, The journey to inspiring a billion often begins with just one or two—perhaps by igniting a spark within yourself, your team, your family, or your community.

In this book, I have distilled the essence of my inspirations into powerful quotes—my Mantras. These words encapsulate the wisdom drawn from people, experiences, and practical insights, shaping my journey while resonating deeply with those around me

The Book is dedicated to:

- to my Mom- Sudeshna Mahapatra and Dad - Prabhas Mahapatra for being the greatest of Coaches and without whom this book would not have come into existence. Truly blessed tohave you as my parents.

- to my mother-in-law and father-in-law Shantilata Mishra and Nilambara Mishra for your constant guidance and always making me feel so special.

- to my wonderful wife Linki Mishra for her unconditional love and support despite my shortcomings. No greater light illuminates my path than the positive changes you have brought into my life.

- to my Children Rounak and Ronit for your profound love and caring. My children are my best role models.

- •to my Loving sister and Brother Sobhna and Kausam for all those sweet childhood memories.

- to my teachers and mentors for always keeping the faith.

- to Indian Leadership Academy and thousands of colleagues, employees, executives, parents, youth, and teachers who has inspired and encouraged me to pen down my thoughts.

- to my dearest colleague Ishani Mishra for helping me to to edit this book from end to end and coming up with unique ways to convey my thoughts which helped me to pen down my thoughts. Without you this book would have taken ages to complete.

- to my friends and relatives for all the good advice, support and love.

- to my wonderful readers for picking up this book and giving your valuable time. Love you all.

We Tend To Like People Who Are Like Us. However, the Beauty Is in Liking People Who Are Unlike Us

Despite how aggressively diversity and inclusivity gets marketed throughout the globe, favouritism and preferentiality continues to rule personal and professional realms. Strangely, the more it is being marketed, the lesser it is being followed. True to the saying, birds of a feather flock together!

It is an age old adage that holds true even to this date. The proverb essentially hints towards those humans having similar mind-set, personalities, cultural backgrounds and ethnicities. However, the catch here is, practicing and following such a social norm tends towards projecting a monochromatic palette.

A very old popular lore comes to mind when we address this issue.

The scene unfolds with a fluffy mother duck, warming six shiny eggs in her nest. At regular intervals, she keeps turning the eggs one by one with her beak. Eventually, with loud cracks the eggs begin to hatch one by one. Five eggs hatch, and emerging from them were five fluffy wobbling yellow ducklings ready to quack with their mama. But the sixth egg; which was the biggest of them all, didn't show any signs of hatching. The mother duck was heartbroken. The egg wasn't moving, not even a single sign of life. Yet, the mother duck kept the egg and the ducklings warm under her wings. She was hopeful, that the sixth egg would hatch too. And true to her hope, the egg hatched after two days.

However it was rather shocking to see that instead of yellow downy feathers, a grey head with no feathers poked out of the broken shell. For a split second, the mother was devastated, but soon recovered from the shock and cleaned the chick of remaining shell bits. The chick looked rather ugly with a grey wrinkly body sans feathers and crooked legs, that wobbled while it walked. It was no surprise that the chick was immediately ousted from the community. His own siblings wouldn't include him. This hurt the little duckling deeply. The duckling fled the farm and reached the end of the forest where he saw another flock of wild ducks. The wild ducks refused to acknowledge and mingle with him, instead they made him feel even more miserable. Heartbroken, the duckling flew and reached a hut with many pets. The owner of the pets saw the duckling and salivated at the thought of the eggs that it could lay. However after realising it was a drake, and a rather ugly looking one, the owner threw him out.

Nowhere to go now, the duckling swam in a lake and stayed there for a long time; alone and isolated without anyone to talk to. The seasons rolled by, and winter fell upon the land. The little duckling was hiding behind a tuft of grass, shivering and huddled amongst its own feathers. A farmer was passing nearby, who noticed the duckling. Feeling pity towards the poor creature, he took him home, fed him and took good care of him. The duckling spent its winter happily fed and warm under the farmer's roof. Eventually, winter came to an end and summers returned. On one such fine morning, the duckling went swimming to the lake.

The duckling started swimming and enjoying the warm rays of the sun, when suddenly something caught its eye. A couple of children, by the lakeside were cheering pointing at its direction. The duckling couldn't believe what it saw. Never in his life, did it feel appreciated, other than the kindness shown by the farmer. Unable to understand the situation, it tried to steer away from the crowd.

Upon trying to decipher this weird reaction, the duckling started looking at all directions to find a clue. Frantically searching its eyes fell upon its reflection. On the clear lake surface, was the reflection of the duckling, all white pristine feathers with a beautifully sculpted orange beak. Oh how surprised it felt. He wasn't a duck after all, he was a swan.

All along, it wasn't his fault, he wasn't ugly after all. He was just misunderstood by the company he came across and that made all the difference in its traumatic experience. But thanks to the kind farmer, who despite its looks nursed and nurtured him back to health.

Like this kind farmer, we need start being more open and kind to what we perceive differently from our regular drill.

Why do we stick to our flock?

The obvious answer to this question is judgement and fear of the unknown. People are fearful of what might be in store for them if they associate with something that is entirely different from what they have seen, experienced and believed so far.

All human beings enjoy the comfort of their own space. A well curated personal, professional and social circle surrounds us all. The reason behind creating this bubble is to ensure security. Anything foreign to this, is subject to threat and fear.

We have to perceive the unknown as an opportunity rather than as a threat. This alone makes the difference throughout.

So what is the problem with sticking to your flock?

It is observed that every individual creates parallel social circles around himself. Sometimes, these social circles overlap, sometimes they don't. We have raised boundaries globally for petty reasons. From religion to culture or from ethnicity to principles; from morality to ethics or from personality to language we have always established grounds to justify our fear of unknown.

In a fiercely competitive world, finding a familiar soul is one of the best things that can happen to you. A kindred spirit is an endless source of reinforced support and appreciation. Despite how appealing that might sound, it does not provide you with the imperative challenges and criticism required for you to grow. The more you run in your own circles, the more you tend to keep returning to the same spot from where you started. You fail to reach new destinations. Like a flock of birds you keep migrating from one destined point to another, unbothered to look for a new adventure.

What should you do to rectify the situation?

Years and years of social conditioning has made us prone to ignoring people whom we don't know or have no business with. We need to abandon this and try to mingle with as many people possible. We humans are equipped with the world's best expression – a smile. It is a simple curve but is potent enough to crack locks of the toughest hearts. Greet people with a smile. Acknowledge and regard them with respect and dignity.

Try to find subtle clues and hints of friendliness and likeability in their personalities. Once you start looking at the bright side, the dark side will just be a mere shadow. Apart from this, start accepting that both light and dark are complimentary, one comes with the other. And most importantly, both are necessary for the other to survive.

Additionally, one should also strive to see the positive in every situation. Most humans are taxed and stressed, thanks to the challenges that come with situations. And eventually, they lose interest towards making the good out a person. It is a common practice amongst people to asses and judge people as per the mood they are in. Always remember, just because you are wearing red glasses, the town isn't painted red. Every human has a color of their own, unique in its own accord. Try to have a palette full of vibrant colors that fills your life with joy and ecstacy.

It is known that affirmations have the capacity to code and decode outcomes from our subconscious mind. Affirmations are positive statements that help you look at the brighter side of life, motivate you and ensure outcomes from your daily practices. Repeating affirmations, such as writing them repeatedly or reading them aloud is a great exercise that one should practice everyday.

Let us read this affirmations aloud to have an open mind and welcome more friends.

- Kind and productive actions make a person beautiful.

- I see the best in people.

- People see the best in me.

- The world is full of beautiful people.

- I love everyone.

- I am patient with everyone.

- I look for the best in every situation.

- I make friends quickly wherever I go.

Words have power over our mind. Positive words tend to feed our subconscious with energy, positivity and vigour. Similarly, positivity of attitude fills our world with positive outcomes. Eventually, such practices attract people to us, who become an inherent part of our circle. The more diversely we connect amongst people, the more productive we become.

Needless to say, a human is best known for its capability to turn the impossible into possible. Practices of global inclusion have already kick started and it is not long that we will have a globe connected via communality of friendship, rather than divided via boundaries of differences.

The Way to Life Is To Find Out Your Own Way of Living

L et us begin with an interesting tale.

Once there was a father son duo; farmers by profession, living in a quaint and quiet village. On one fine sunny day, they loaded their produce on the family donkey to visit the nearby farmer's market that was just a village away. The donkey was no ordinary donkey though. He was an elite breed with a robust muscular structure. Something the farmer took pride in, and took good care of it. Always gave him the best grass, best quality grams and clean cool water from the well behind the house.

The father and son walked beside the donkey, gossiping away their worries and discussing the quality of their produce while they went. The weather was amicable and the market had a suitable footfall that day. The duo spent the day selling their produce and mingling with customers alike.

By the end of the day, they had sold almost all of their produce and were ready to pack for the day. They expected to sell the rest of the produce while they were on their way home. They fed the donkey and offered it water, which it lapped away happily. Since most of the load was gone, the son packed the rest of it and let it hang by the donkey's saddle. The trio went ambling away through the streets announcing their leftover produce.

It was a tradition between the father and son to sing songs of their folklore and enjoy the scenic beauty of the setting sun while they went home. They sang especially loud songs to cheer themselves from a day long work and drown the din and noise of their surroundings. However, not all sounds can be ignored.

While on their journey back home, the father seemed tired and stumbled on his way. However, the donkey's back was free hence the son offered his father to sit on the donkey's back. Appreciating the son's help gracefully, the father climbed up the back of the donkey and they went on their way. The son began singing a joyous melody of filial love and devotion.

Soon they were stopped by a lady by the corner of the street. She bought a few fresh veggies from them and casually commented.

"Such a bright boy you have there mister! What a melodious voice. Kids are our lifelines though. Had it been my kid, I would have given a cushion too, for a comfortable journey. And such a long journey too, ought to give those little feet some rest! Just a thought!"

"Father's these days, so cruel!" she commented while she shut the door on their face.

The father's face burnt with shame at the fastidious comment. He nimbly climbed down the back of the donkey and asked his son to cover the rest of the journey on the donkey's back.

"I have rested enough son, the lady is right! You need rest too. Ride your way home son!"

"She doesn't know you are old and injured father, I would rather walk than let you injure yourself anymore. Moreover you have toiled enough today, with the sales and deliveries. Let me walk by your side!"

"Its ok; here, climb and take the reins."

Reluctantly, the son climbs the donkey and takes them forward. On the way home, they stopped at a grocery store to unload some last of their potatoes. A group of elderly were sitting at the store, playing cards and having tea. The shopkeeper offered some tea to the father son duo, while writing up the bill.

"Had it been my son, I would have felt ashamed for calling him mine. Such ungrateful chap! For God's sake, the father is old. The nerve of him to let his father walk!" said one of the old men.

"Westernisation has killed our culture. The young generation has forgotten their roots! Poor father!" said another.

"Good lord, forbid my son from going rogue like this" – added another old man.

All the while the father and son were listening to these sceptical comments. It was now the son's turn to be humiliated. The son was so shame faced that he didn't dare touch the reins again. He simply stood up and walked ahead of the donkey, leaving the father to decide for the next stop. This time, they were crossing a bridge. The sun was nearing the horizon and the duo seemed tired. Yet, the donkey walked idle and the father-son duo went by foot. There was a peal of laughter bursting at the end of the bridge. On nearing the scene the son overheard.

A throng of young mercenaries were riding their horses laughing at them.

"What a waste of precious resource, and such a handsome donkey too! Those fools could have ridden on it! Ha Ha Ha!"

The comments felt like salt to their wound, more like insult to injury!

Infuriated, the son asks the father to climb back on the donkey and climbs on it too. Now both father and son are riding the poor donkey. They crossed the bridge without any further comments and made their way into the entrance of the village. They wouldn't have gone another mile, when a concerned neighbour greets them.

"Good day at the market I see, no goods left. By any chance did you get rid of your wits too you pair?"

"Why would you say so?" – chimed the father.

"Why would I not? Look at the poor donkey, carrying the load of both the father and son! Have you gotten rid of your humanity too? Poor animal! Had I been the master of such a fine beast, I would carry the load myself and kept it mighty fine for tougher times."

The confused duo got down from the animal and took away its load too! They carried it through the village to their hut. Peals of ridicule rained on them at their idiocy for carrying the load, when there was a perfectly fine donkey trailing behind them.

Now as the father and son return back to their humble hut, tired and spent; the mother awaits them with water and supper. They narrate their rather odd day to her, while she cleans and feeds the donkey. The astonished mother exclaims,

"From when did you start listening to what people have to say? It's your donkey, your son and your decision."

"Can't believe I married such a dork!" she murmurs as she stomps away into the house, while the father and son look at each other perplexed and annoyed at their own foolishness.

Why make your own life rules?

At times, we forget that we are individuals of our own making. No two minds can work alike. We are unique and diverse and that makes the world a better place. No doubt, constructive and rational inputs make us better human beings; but always remember, your shoes will only fit you. You need to be conscious and cautious while accepting and rendering advices. While some advices can transform your lives, some can lead to transgression as well. And above all, make sure that you accept advices that benefit you and your situation.

Constructive advices have power to create bonds. An advice is not just a random statement thrown at somebody. Through an advice, a person tries to assist another person through reasoning and experience. We should always consider advices as gems, since the person has taken personal interest in assisting us, by investing time and utilising their thoughts to handcraft a life lesson for us. Any person giving an advice has an intention behind it. Usually positive in nature, advices are often linked towards personal growth and welfare. An advice drafted correctly has the ability to drive a person towards success and prosperity.

What is not an advice?

However, there are so called advices that are harmful. Such statements are not advices, but carefully crafted manipulative devices. Any advice made with the intention to slow you down, cause you harm or block your progress is not an advice at all. It is sheer manipulation to bring you down. Most manipulative people pose as your avid well-wishers. Pay heed to advices with utmost scrutiny, it is never known when the knife cuts you. Statements served to you on a silver platter, coated with sugary syrup are often made with an attempt to misguide you.

What are our affirmations?

Let us vow to be more careful when it comes to safeguarding our life interests. Here are some affirmations that will make you confident with your own decisions.

- I am capable of making productive and positive decisions for myself.

- I graciously accept advices.

- I am careful before implementing advices.

- I give advices with a clean heart.

- I give advices out of goodwill, concern and experience.

- I give advices for the betterment of others.

- I have the ability to make the right choices for myself.

- I am grounded and have faith in my capabilities.

- I care for myself and for others.

- I am always learning.

From whom should you take advices?

There are a few principles one should always follow when advices are concerned.

- Always follow advices only when they come from a trusted source. Your trusted source can be someone from your inner circle, such as friends, family, confidante or a close associate.

- Advices are best judged and implemented when your gut gives you a thumbs-up. Your gut feeling is usually the most accurate of signals that you can get. If you feel that something is amiss, it is because it usually is amiss. Trust your gut feeling. Its always right.

- Have faith in your own intuition, knowledge and experience. before jumping into implementing an advice run through the coarse and its consequences, you will generally get a clear picture of the outcome.

And above all, believe in yourself. You have the power to make the right decision. Just close off all your senses, let the din and noise of the background fade away and you will find the path ahead.

True Mastery Is Not Just About What We Do but Also How We Feel, Think, and Respond

Emotional control, often referred to as emotional intelligence, encompasses the ability to recognize, understand, and manage one's own emotions, as well as the emotions of others. While it might seem counterintuitive to prioritize emotional control before skill mastery, this approach carries significant advantages. Emotional control provides the psychological groundwork for effective learning, fostering a mind-set conducive to focused attention, resilience, and adaptability.

By tending to the emotional landscape of those they guide, coaches create an environment where individuals can flourish both as skilled practitioners and as well-rounded, emotionally intelligent human beings.

The journey of a prodigy who prioritizes emotional control before skill mastery is underpinned by several psychological mechanisms. One key mechanism is the regulation of the brain's stress response system. When emotions run high and stress takes hold, cognitive resources are diverted away from skill acquisition, impeding effective learning. Emotional control empowers prodigies to modulate their stress response, ensuring that their cognitive faculties remain attuned to the task at hand.

Furthermore, emotional control nurtures the development of metacognition, the ability to reflect on and regulate one's own cognitive processes. This metacognitive awareness enables prodigies to identify unproductive patterns of thinking and emotional responses that hinder skill acquisition. By pre-emptively addressing negative emotions such as frustration, impatience, or self-doubt, prodigies can maintain a growth-oriented mindset and approach challenges with tenacity.

Do we know someone who won over their emotions, to reach their desired skill set?

In the annals of Olympic history, one name shines with a brilliance that transcends time: Jesse Owens. The year was 1936, and the world had converged on Berlin for the Summer Olympics. Amidst the towering expectations and the looming political tensions, Owens, a young African-American athlete, embarked on a journey that would not only redefine his life but also send ripples of change through the fabric of history.

Jesse Owens, a prodigious sprinter and long jumper, had captured the attention of the sporting world with his unparalleled speed and extraordinary agility. His journey to the 1936 Olympics was not only a personal quest for excellence but also a statement against the racial prejudices that plagued his era.

As the Games unfurled in the heart of Berlin, Adolf Hitler's Nazi regime sought to assert their twisted ideology of Aryan supremacy. Amidst this tumultuous backdrop, Owens emerged as a symbol of defiance—a living testament to the fallacy of such supremacist beliefs.

Jesse Owens came all the way from his home town to Berlin to take part in the Olympics. Determined to debunk Hitler's theories, he embarked on a relentless six-year journey of self-improvement and discipline. His goal: to prove that the power of determination and human spirit could triumph over oppressive ideologies.

A year before the grand event, he astounded everyone by setting a world record of 26 feet 8-1/4 inches in the running board jump at his university. Expectations were sky-high for his Olympic performance. However, in the world of sports, even the most seasoned athletes can stumble. Owens found himself in for an unexpected surprise. As the time approached for the broad-jump trials, he was taken aback by the sight of a tall young man effortlessly clearing the pit at nearly 26 feet during his practice leaps. This athlete turned out to be a German by the name of Luz Long. It was rumoured that Hitler had high hopes of victory with Long, intending to use it as a propaganda tool to support the Nazi ideology of "master race" or Aryan superiority. Fully aware of his own African American heritage, he couldn't help but feel anger towards Hitler's intentions. This anger fuelled his determination to prove to Der Fuhrer and the proponents of the "master race" theory that true superiority knows no race or ideology.

However, he also understood that an athlete consumed by anger often makes costly mistakes, a fact coaches frequently emphasize. Regrettably, he became no exception to this rule. During the first of his three qualifying jumps, he leaped from a position several inches beyond the take-off board, resulting in a foul. The second jump was even worse, and he couldn't help but bitterly question himself, "Did I come 3,000 miles for this? To foul out of the trials and make a fool of myself?" In his frustration, he walked a few yards from the pit and kicked the dirt, wrestling with the mix of anger and disappointment within him.

Frustration consumed him, and in his exasperation, he kicked the ground. But then, a friendly hand landed on his shoulder. It was none other than his German rival, Luz Long. Long had effortlessly qualified for the finals on his first attempt. Their eyes met, and instead of hostility, a warm, friendly connection was formed. Luz offered a firm handshake and words of encouragement. He advised Jesse to take off from a few inches behind the board, a simple yet transformative suggestion that helped Jesse qualify for the finals.

That night, Jesse sought out Luz to express his gratitude for the invaluable advice. Their conversation transcended sports, touching upon their personal lives, global events, and the state of the world. Jesse was relieved to learn that Luz didn't subscribe to notions of racial superiority. Their friendship blossomed, and Luz proved to be a broad-minded individual who wanted nothing more than to see Jesse succeed, even if it meant winning the event himself.

The following day, Luz shattered his own record, providing Jesse with a remarkable source of inspiration. When Jesse executed his performance, it was Luz who first offered his congratulations, a gesture made even more remarkable by the fact that Hitler himself was observing them. Luz's sportsmanship was a shining example of integrity and humility. Jesse went on to win four gold medals in the event, but he often said that the true prize was his friendship with Luz. It was a bond that would endure until Luz's tragic death in the Second World War.

Jesse Owens would later reflect that Luz Long embodied the true spirit of sportsmanship. To Luz, participating and giving one's all mattered more than victory or defeat. His legacy was a reminder that in the realm of sports, the ultimate triumph lies not in medals but in the enduring friendships forged through the pursuit of excellence.

What do we learn from this?

Even though Owens understood that anger could undermine an athlete's focus and lead to mistakes, his rage was ignited by

Hitler's manipulative introduction of Luz Long to demonstrate Aryan supremacy. As an African American, Owens resented this, and his anger towards Hitler's tactics momentarily overshadowed his determination to succeed in the Olympics. This anger clouded his thoughts and resulted in fouls during his initial two trial attempts. In Jesse's case, he fouled in his first two trial leaps, primarily due to his take-off from several inches beyond the line. He was devastated, feeling as though he had travelled 3000 miles only to fail miserably.

Keeping one's emotions in check, especially in high-stakes situations like athletic competitions or other significant endeavours, is highly essential. Firstly, emotions, particularly intense ones like anger or frustration, can cloud judgment and impair one's ability to think clearly. When emotions are in control, it becomes challenging to make rational decisions and execute tasks effectively. Secondly, Emotional turmoil can physically affect the body, causing tension, nervousness, and stress. These physical manifestations can hinder an individual's ability to perform at their best. In sports, for example, maintaining emotional control can help an athlete execute their techniques and strategies with precision.

Moreover, emotional outbursts or unchecked emotions can lead to impulsive actions, which often result in mistakes. Therefore, keeping emotions in check fosters resilience, allowing individuals to bounce back from setbacks and challenges. Emotional stability helps maintain focus and determination even in the face of adversity.

Moistly maintaining composure is seen as a sign of professionalism. It demonstrates that an individual can handle pressure and maintain their integrity even in challenging circumstances. However, emotional outbursts can hinder effective communication with others, whether it's with teammates, coaches, or colleagues. Keeping emotions in check promotes constructive and productive interactions. Additionally, focusing on long-term goals often requires setting aside momentary emotional reactions. When individuals prioritize their overarching objectives over temporary emotional responses, they are more likely to stay on course and achieve their goals.

In summary, controlling one's emotions is crucial for maintaining clarity, optimal performance, preventing mistakes, building resilience, displaying professionalism, fostering effective communication, and staying committed to long-term goals. It allows individuals to navigate challenges more effectively and make better decisions in high-pressure situations.

How do you manage your emotions?

Balancing our emotions in day-to-day life requires a blend of spirituality and practicality. On a spiritual level, it's about cultivating inner awareness and mindfulness. It's the art of recognizing emotions as transient visitors, acknowledging their presence without judgment, and gently guiding them towards peaceful shores. Through meditation and deep reflection, we can create a sanctuary within, a place where emotional storms dissipate, and clarity emerges.

Practically, emotional control involves honing our response mechanisms. It's the conscious choice to pause before reacting, to breathe in the midst of chaos, and to empathetically consider the perspectives of others. It's the realization that emotional intelligence is not about suppressing feelings but understanding and channelling them constructively. We need to practice active listening, seek healthy outlets for expression, and prioritize self-care to bolster emotional resilience.

Ultimately, the synergy of spirituality and practicality forms a sturdy bridge to emotional equilibrium. By harmonizing our inner landscapes with the demands of the external world, we find ourselves not as slaves to emotion but as skilled navigators of the human experience. In this union, we discover the profound wisdom of keeping emotions under control in our day-to-day journey.

Let's repeat some affirmations to keep our emotions in check.

- "I am the master of my emotions, and I choose to respond with calm and composure."

- "I embrace my emotions as valuable messengers, but I don't let them control me."

- "I have the power to pause and choose my response wisely in any situation."

- "I release any negative emotions that no longer serve me, making space for positivity."

- "I am in control of my reactions, and I choose peace and serenity over chaos."

- "I practice mindfulness daily, allowing me to observe my emotions without judgment."

- "I am resilient, and I bounce back from challenging emotions with grace."

- "I communicate my feelings effectively and empathetically, fostering understanding."

- "I prioritize self-care, knowing that a balanced mind leads to balanced emotions."

- "I am grounded and centered, even in the midst of life's emotional storms."

In the realm of coaching and personal development, the mantra 'coach the emotion before you coach the skill' underscores the profound importance of addressing the inner world of individuals to unlock their full potential. This philosophy emphasizes that emotions are the driving force behind performance, and by nurturing emotional well-being, coaches can lay a strong foundation for skill development and success. In adopting this approach, coaches not only enhance skill acquisition but also empower individuals to navigate life's challenges with poise and a deeper understanding of themselves. Ultimately, 'coach the emotion before you coach the skill' serves as a reminder that true growth and excellence spring from a place of emotional balance, resilience, and self-awareness.

We Are All Separated by Boundaries but United by Wisdom. Keep Leading with Wisdom

In a world that seems increasingly divided by physical, political, and ideological boundaries, the power of wisdom emerges as a unifying force that transcends these divisions. Wisdom, a quality often associated with deep understanding, empathy, and sound judgment, has the potential to bridge gaps and foster unity among individuals and nations. In this inspirational essay, we will explore the idea that while we may be physically separated by boundaries, we are ultimately united by the wisdom that resides within each of us. Through the lens of wisdom, we can find common ground, work towards shared goals, and lead ourselves and others to a brighter future.

Boundaries, whether they are physical, political, or conceptual, have been a part of human existence since time immemorial. They serve various purposes, from demarcating territories and protecting individual rights to delineating cultural and social norms. However, boundaries can also be divisive, leading to conflicts, misunderstandings, and isolation.

- Physical Boundaries

Physical boundaries are perhaps the most tangible form of separation. These boundaries can be natural, such as oceans, mountains, and rivers, or artificial, like walls, fences, and borders. Physical boundaries can create a sense of distance between people and can be a source of tension when they are contested or used as tools of exclusion.

- Political Boundaries

Political boundaries, including national borders, represent the limits of a government's jurisdiction and control. These boundaries determine citizenship, legal rights, and access to resources. While they are essential for the functioning of modern societies, political boundaries can also contribute to conflicts, discrimination, and inequalities.

- Conceptual Boundaries

Conceptual boundaries are those that exist in our minds, separating us based on ideologies, beliefs, and perceptions. These boundaries can be just as impactful as physical or political ones, as they influence how we interact with others and shape our worldviews.

The Power of Wisdom:

Wisdom, on the other hand, is a quality that defies these boundaries. It is not confined to a particular location or group but is accessible to all who seek it. Wisdom is often associated with the following characteristics:

- Deep Understanding: Wisdom involves a profound comprehension of the world and human nature. It goes beyond surface-level knowledge and delves into the complexities of life, society, and the human psyche.

- Empathy and Compassion: Wisdom is accompanied by a sense of empathy and compassion. Wise individuals understand the perspectives and feelings of others, leading to more harmonious relationships and cooperation.

- Sound Judgment: Wisdom allows for sound judgment and decision-making. Wise individuals are adept at evaluating situations, considering long-term consequences, and making choices that benefit both themselves and their communities.

- Emotional Regulation: Wisdom is often associated with emotional intelligence, enabling individuals to manage their emotions effectively and respond to challenging situations with equanimity.

- Lifelong Learning: Wisdom is a lifelong pursuit. Wise individuals are committed to continuous learning and self-improvement, recognizing that wisdom is not a destination but a journey.

Wisdom as a Unifying Force:

When we view the world through the lens of wisdom, we begin to see how it can serve as a unifying force that transcends boundaries and divisions.

- Wisdom Transcends Physical Boundaries: While physical boundaries may separate us geographically, wisdom knows no such limits. Wisdom can be shared across continents and cultures, connecting individuals who may never meet in person. Through the exchange of ideas and experiences, wisdom can bridge the gap created by physical distance.

- Wisdom Transcends Political Boundaries: Political boundaries may dictate our legal rights and affiliations, but wisdom can influence how we interact with individuals from other nations and cultures. Wise leaders and diplomats have historically played crucial roles in resolving conflicts and fostering international cooperation.

- Wisdom Transcends Conceptual Boundaries: Conceptual boundaries, often rooted in differing ideologies and beliefs, can be some of the most challenging to overcome. However, wisdom encourages us to seek common ground, engage in meaningful dialogue, and find solutions that transcend ideological divisions.

Leading with Wisdom:

To harness the unifying power of wisdom, we must not only recognize its importance but also strive to lead with wisdom in our own lives. Here are some ways in which we can do so:

- Cultivate Self-awareness: Wisdom begins with self-awareness. We must take the time to reflect on our thoughts, emotions, and actions, seeking to understand ourselves better. By gaining insight into our own motivations and biases, we can make wiser choices in our interactions with others.

- Practice Empathy: Empathy is a cornerstone of wisdom. It involves stepping into the shoes of others and genuinely trying to understand their perspectives. When we practice empathy, we build stronger connections and foster a sense of unity with those around us.

- Embrace Lifelong Learning: Wisdom is not a static state but a continuous journey of learning and growth. We should be open to new ideas, diverse viewpoints, and experiences that challenge our existing beliefs. By embracing lifelong learning, we expand our wisdom and our capacity to connect with others.

- Lead by Example: As individuals, we can lead by example in our families, workplaces, and communities. By demonstrating wisdom through our actions, we inspire others to do the same. Leading with wisdom means making decisions that consider the well-being of both ourselves and those around us.

- Promote Dialogue and Understanding: In a world marked by division and polarization, promoting dialogue and understanding is crucial. Wisdom encourages us to engage in constructive conversations, even with those who hold different viewpoints. By seeking common ground and finding areas of agreement, we can work towards solutions that benefit everyone.

Support Wise Leadership:

Wise leaders have the potential to bring about positive change on a larger scale. We should support and elect leaders who demonstrate wisdom, empathy, and a commitment to unity. Wise leadership can help bridge divides and create a more harmonious and equitable society.

India, a diverse and culturally rich nation, has a long history of leaders who have exhibited wisdom in their governance, decision-making, and contributions to society. Here are some examples of India leading with wisdom in various domains:

- Mahatma Gandhi's Nonviolent Resistance: Mahatma Gandhi, one of the most revered leaders in history, demonstrated profound wisdom through his philosophy of nonviolent resistance. His advocacy for peaceful protests and civil disobedience against British colonial rule not only led to India's independence but also inspired similar movements worldwide, promoting the idea that wisdom can triumph over brute force.

- Dr. A.P.J. Abdul Kalam's Visionary Leadership: Dr. A.P.J. Abdul Kalam, India's Missile Man and former President, was known for his visionary leadership in the field of science and technology. His wisdom lay in harnessing the power of science for the benefit of society, emphasizing education, research, and technological innovation to propel India into the 21st century.

- Jawaharlal Nehru's Commitment to Education: India's first Prime Minister, Jawaharlal Nehru, recognized the importance of education as a means of empowering the nation. His wisdom was evident in his commitment to establishing institutions of higher learning, including the Indian Institutes of Technology (IITs) and Indian Institutes of Management (IIMs), which continue to contribute significantly to India's development.

- Mother Teresa's Compassion and Selflessness: Mother Teresa, an Albanian-Indian nun and missionary, exemplified wisdom through her selfless dedication to serving the poor and marginalized in society. Her Missionaries of Charity organization continues to provide care and assistance to those in need, reminding us of the wisdom in compassion and kindness.

- C.K. Prahalad's Business Insights: Management guru C.K. Prahalad, an Indian-American scholar, contributed significantly to the field of business management. His wisdom was evident in concepts like the "bottom of the pyramid," which emphasized that businesses could create value by serving low-income populations. This perspective has influenced corporate social responsibility initiatives globally.

- Amartya Sen's Work on Human Development: Nobel laureate Amartya Sen's wisdom is reflected in his groundbreaking work on human development and the capability approach. His research has contributed to a deeper understanding of human well-being beyond economic indicators and has influenced global policies on poverty reduction and social justice.

- Dr. Verghese Kurien's White Revolution: Dr. Verghese Kurien, often called the "Father of the White Revolution," demonstrated wisdom through his leadership of the cooperative dairy movement in India. His efforts in organizing farmers and modernizing dairy production not only transformed India into the world's largest milk producer but also improved the lives of millions of rural families.

- Aruna Roy's Grassroots Activism: Social activist Aruna Roy, through her work with the Mazdoor Kisan Shakti Sangathan (MKSS), showcased wisdom in grassroots activism. Her advocacy for transparency and accountability in governance led to the Right to Information Act in India, empowering citizens with the tools to combat corruption and hold authorities accountable.

- Ratan Tata's Ethical Business Leadership: Ratan Tata, former Chairman of the Tata Group, is known for his ethical and socially responsible approach to business. His wisdom in maintaining high ethical standards within the conglomerate and his commitment to philanthropy have set an example for corporate leaders worldwide.

- Ela Bhatt's Empowerment of Women: Ela Bhatt, the founder of the Self-Employed Women's Association

(SEWA), displayed wisdom by empowering women in India's informal sector. Her organization provides support and resources to women workers, helping them achieve economic independence and social recognition.

These examples demonstrate that India has a rich tradition of leaders who have led with wisdom in diverse fields, leaving a lasting impact on the nation and the world. Their actions and insights continue to inspire and guide individuals and organizations toward a more compassionate, inclusive, and equitable future.

To follow their footsteps, here are some affirmations to help you gain knowledge and lead with wisdom. These affirmations can be used as daily reminders to focus your mind and intentions on your pursuit of knowledge and wise leadership:

- "I am a lifelong learner, constantly seeking knowledge and wisdom in all aspects of my life."

- "I am open to new ideas and experiences, allowing them to expand my understanding and wisdom."

- "I approach challenges as opportunities to learn and grow, applying wisdom to find solutions."

- "I trust my intuition and inner wisdom to guide me in making sound decisions."

- "I am committed to self-improvement, dedicating time each day to acquiring new knowledge."

- "I am a wise and empathetic leader, inspiring others through my actions and words."

- "I lead with integrity, making ethical choices that reflect my wisdom and values."

- "I embrace diversity of thought, recognizing that different perspectives contribute to greater wisdom."

- "I am patient with myself and others, understanding that wisdom often comes with time and experience."

- "I radiate positive energy and inspire those around me to pursue knowledge and wisdom."

- "I use my wisdom to create a harmonious and productive environment in my personal and professional life."

- "I am a source of guidance and support for others, sharing my wisdom to help them achieve their goals."

- "I trust in the journey of acquiring knowledge, knowing that each step brings me closer to wisdom."

- "I am grateful for the wisdom I have gained and excited about the wisdom that awaits me."

- "I lead by example, demonstrating the power of wisdom in making a positive impact on the world."

In a world filled with boundaries that can separate us physically, politically, and conceptually, wisdom emerges as a unifying force that transcends these divisions. It is the thread that connects us all, reminding us of our shared humanity and the potential for cooperation and understanding. As we navigate the challenges of the modern world, let us remember the words: "We are all separated by boundaries but united by wisdom. Keep leading with wisdom." In doing so, we can build a more compassionate, just, and united world for ourselves and future generations.

Small Corrections Often Lead to Great Transformations

In the grand tapestry of life, it is the seemingly insignificant threads that often weave the most remarkable stories. "Small corrections often lead to great transformations" is a profound truth that resonates with individuals, communities, and societies alike. The cumulative impact of minor adjustments can result in profound and inspiring transformations.

How can we embrace making corrections?

A very small technique comes into play when we talk about incorporating small corrections in our day to day lives. brain rewiring is a marvellous technique, that helps you incorporate small corrections in your day to day lives. before delving into the techniques, it is important to know what productivity output does the technique present?

Rewiring the brain is not about changing who you are fundamentally but about optimizing your cognitive and emotional processes to improve various aspects of your life. The brain's ability to rewire itself, also known as neuroplasticity, allows you to adapt to new situations and challenges. It enables you to learn new skills, cope with changes, and recover from injuries or trauma. Moreover, rewiring the brain enhances your capacity to acquire knowledge and skills. It helps you absorb information more effectively, which can lead to better academic or professional performance. By engaging in activities that stimulate memory, you can strengthen your recall abilities. This is particularly important for learning, problem-solving, and everyday tasks. Additionally, brain rewiring can help improve mental health by promoting positive thought patterns, reducing stress and anxiety, and combating conditions like depression and post-traumatic stress disorder.

By adapting your brain to work more efficiently can boost productivity. This includes better time management, concentration, and task organization. Rewiring can enhance creativity by encouraging innovative thinking, breaking free from mental blocks, and fostering a willingness to explore new ideas. Developing emotional intelligence through brain rewiring can improve your ability to manage emotions, build healthier relationships, and handle stress more effectively. Neuroplasticity can be harnessed to overcome addictions and change unhealthy habits. It allows you to create new, positive neural pathways that replace old, destructive ones. The brain can be rewired to modulate pain perception, which is especially valuable for individuals dealing with chronic pain conditions. Engaging in activities that promote brain health and neuroplasticity can potentially delay cognitive decline and reduce the risk of age-related neurological diseases like Alzheimer's and dementia.

Brain rewiring can be a catalyst for personal growth, helping you become a better version of yourself by breaking through limitations and building on your strengths. In essence, rewiring the brain is a means of optimizing your mental and emotional processes to lead a more fulfilling and successful life. It's a way of unlocking your brain's full potential and adapting to the ever-changing demands and opportunities that life presents.

What are the corrections needed?

The Power of Early Rising

Waking up early in the morning is a practice that has the potential to transform your life. It offers you a precious gift - the gift of time. In those quiet, undisturbed hours before the world awakens, you can find a sense of serenity and productivity that sets the tone for the rest of your day. Early mornings offer tranquillity. The world is still and calm, providing an ideal environment for reflection, meditation, or simply enjoying a moment of solitude. With fewer distractions, your mind is at its sharpest. Early morning hours can be incredibly productive, allowing you to focus on tasks, set goals, and plan your day. Early risers often have more time for exercise and healthy routines. A morning workout can boost your energy, metabolism, and overall fitness. Whether it's reading, writing, or pursuing a hobby, early mornings provide uninterrupted time for personal development and self-improvement. Establishing a consistent wake-up time can contribute to better sleep patterns, which in turn can improve mental health and reduce stress. In essence, waking up early is a simple yet transformative habit that can set the stage for a more peaceful, productive, and fulfilling life.

Remember, the key to successfully waking up early is to establish a consistent routine and prioritize getting enough rest at night to support your early rise. With dedication and practice, you can unlock the many benefits of starting your day with the rising sun.

Clean and Healthy Eating: Nourish Your Body, Elevate Your Life:

In the hustle and bustle of our modern lives, it's easy to overlook one of the most precious gifts we have—our health. Clean and healthy eating isn't just a dietary choice; it's a powerful act of self-love and self-care. It's a conscious decision to honour your body, mind, and spirit. When you choose clean and healthy foods, you're not only nourishing your body with essential nutrients but also sending a powerful message to yourself: "I am worth it."

Clean eating fills you with energy, making you feel vibrant and alive. Nutrient-rich foods provide the fuel your body needs to thrive, allowing you to seize each day with enthusiasm. A diet rich in fruits, vegetables, whole grains, and lean proteins supports your brain health. You'll experience improved focus, sharper memory, and enhanced cognitive function. Clean eating strengthens your immune system, helping your body ward off illnesses and recover more swiftly. You'll find yourself better equipped to face life's challenges head-on. Food isn't just fuel; it's also a source of comfort and joy. Clean and healthy eating can lead to a more stable mood, reduced stress, and an overall sense of well-being. By making mindful choices about what you put on your plate, you're investing in a long and healthy life. You're reducing the risk of chronic diseases and embracing a future filled with vitality.

Choosing clean and healthy eating is an act of self-respect. It's a way of telling yourself that you deserve the very best—nutrient-dense, whole foods that support your well-being. Remember that clean and healthy eating is not about deprivation or perfection. It's about finding balance and savouring the abundance of delicious, wholesome foods that nature provides. It's about treating your body with kindness and making choices that align with your vision of a thriving, joyful life. So, with each bite you take, know that you're nourishing more than just your body—you're nurturing your dreams, your aspirations, and your potential. Clean and healthy eating is an invitation to elevate your life, one mindful choice at a time.

Journaling and planning your day:

In the whirlwind of daily life, it's easy to feel overwhelmed by tasks, responsibilities, and goals. This is where the simple yet transformative practices of journaling and planning come into play. They are your compass in the bustling sea of life, guiding you toward success, fulfilment, and personal growth.

Journaling is a mirror to your thoughts, emotions, and aspirations. It provides a safe space to pour your heart onto paper, untangling the complexity of your mind.

Journaling allows you to express your feelings, reducing stress and promoting emotional well-being. It's your confidant, listening without judgment. Secondly, writing down your thoughts and experiences fosters self-awareness. It helps you recognize patterns, strengths, and areas for improvement, facilitating personal growth. A journal is where dreams become tangible goals. When you put your ambitions on paper, you're more likely to take concrete steps toward achieving them.

Additionally, writing about challenges and dilemmas can lead to clarity and innovative solutions. It's like having a brainstorming session with yourself. Moreover, keeping a gratitude journal can shift your focus toward the positive aspects of life. It cultivates contentment and an appreciation for the present.

The next step is planning. Planning your day is like setting the sails of your ship—it determines your direction and pace. Here's why it's crucial: Planning helps you identify your most important tasks and allocate time to them. This ensures that you focus on what truly matters. It's all about making the most of your time. A well-structured day minimizes procrastination and maximizes productivity.

Knowing what to expect and having a plan in place reduces stress. You're less likely to feel overwhelmed when you have a roadmap. Moreover, Planning encourages efficient use of resources, including time and energy. You avoid unnecessary detours and stay on course.

When you plan, you're committing to your goals. This sense of responsibility increases your chances of follow-through.

Incorporating journaling and planning into your daily routine isn't just about time management; it's about life management. It's about taking charge of your narrative, refining your purpose, and making each day count. Embrace the power of your journal and the structure of your plan. They are the tools that empower you to navigate life's waters with purpose and intention, helping you to reach your desired destination—one thoughtful entry and one well-planned day at a time.

Extending a Helping Hand: The Compassion that Binds Humanity:

In the intricate web of life, there exists a universal truth - our collective well-being is intricately connected. When we extend a helping hand to those in need, we not only uplift them but also strengthen the bonds that tie us all together. Here's why offering assistance to those less fortunate is a profound act of humanity.

Helping others fosters empathy and understanding. It allows us to step into someone else's shoes, gaining a deeper appreciation for their struggles and triumphs. It has been observed that acts of kindness and support build stronger, more resilient communities. By assisting one another, we create a safety net that ensures no one is left behind. Moreover, helping those in need can rekindle hope. It reminds individuals facing adversity that they are not alone and that brighter days are possible.

Also, there's a unique sense of fulfilment in knowing you've made a positive impact on someone's life. It nourishes your own spirit and reinforces the goodness within you. It is said that when you help someone, you inspire a cycle of generosity. The person you assist may, in turn, help another, creating a ripple effect of kindness. Such acts of assistance deepen the connections between people. They create bonds built on trust, gratitude, and shared experiences. Collectively, our acts of kindness might shape a better world. By addressing societal issues and supporting vulnerable populations, we contribute to positive global change.

Afterall, compassion is a beautiful sentiment, but when transformed into action, it becomes a powerful force for good. Helping others turns compassion into tangible results. We must remember that our world is a tapestry woven with diverse threads. When we help those in need, we strengthen the entire fabric, ensuring it remains resilient and vibrant. Remember, the act of helping need not be grand or extravagant. It can be as simple as lending a listening ear, offering a warm meal, or providing a comforting presence. Every small gesture has the potential to create significant impact.

Here are some affirmations to start off with:-

- I am a compassionate being, capable of empathy and understanding.

- I embrace my imperfections, knowing they make me uniquely human.

- I choose kindness and love as my guiding principles in all interactions.

- I appreciate the beauty of the present moment and savour life's simple pleasures.

- I connect with others on a deep, authentic level, fostering meaningful relationships.

- I acknowledge my emotions and allow myself to feel and express them without judgment.

- I am open to learning from my mistakes and growing as a person.

- I practice gratitude daily, recognizing the abundance of blessings in my life.

- I value diversity and celebrate the richness it brings to our human experience.

- I am a source of positivity and support, lifting others up in times of need.

- I strive to make a positive impact on the world, no matter how small it may seem.

- I am connected to the natural world and respect the environment that sustains us.

- I am open to new experiences and adventures, embracing the journey of life.

- I trust in my intuition and inner wisdom to guide me on the path of authenticity.

- I recognize that my humanity is a gift, and I cherish every moment of this precious life.

These affirmations can help you connect with your humanity, fostering self-acceptance, empathy, and a deeper appreciation for the shared human experience.

Be Comfortable, Being Uncomfortable

Magic happens outside your comfort zone!

Comfort is a delightful sensation. It envelops us in warmth, security, and familiarity. Yet, like any good thing in life, too much of it can lead to a paradoxical state known as "comfort addiction."

Comfort addiction refers to the tendency to seek comfort to excess, often at the expense of personal growth, challenge, and adventure. While comfort itself is not inherently negative, when it becomes an obstacle to progress, it can limit our potential and hinder our pursuit of a fulfilling life. To be precise, comfort is an innate human desire. It's natural to seek solace and relaxation, especially in a fast-paced world filled with stress and uncertainty. The comfort zone feels safe, predictable, and soothing. However, when comfort becomes a way of life, it can lead to complacency. We become resistant to change, avoid challenges, and stagnate in our personal and professional development. Achieving a balance between comfort and growth is key. It's about enjoying the comforts of life while also embracing discomfort when necessary. Stepping outside of your comfort zone can lead to incredible personal growth, new experiences, and expanded horizons.

It is no secret — "Discomfort is where growth happens." It's where you stretch your limits, acquire new skills, and discover your resilience. Embracing discomfort doesn't mean shunning comfort but rather finding a harmonious blend of both in your life. Every time you venture outside your comfort zone, you're on a learning curve. It may be challenging, but it's also immensely rewarding. It's where you discover your untapped potential. Moreover, a life solely focused on comfort may feel empty in the long run. A fulfilling life often involves purpose, growth, and meaningful challenges that stretch you to become the best version of yourself.

In essence, it's vital to recognize the allure of comfort, but also to be mindful of its potential to hold us back. A life well-lived is one that balances the comfort of the familiar with the exhilaration of new experiences and challenges. It's a journey that embraces both comfort and discomfort as essential parts of the human experience, leading to a richer, more satisfying life.

Our history and mythology both teach us the importance of discomfort being the path to success. Be it Ramayan or Mahabharat or any other epic none have gained success without penance. One such account is of the great Gautama Buddha. The great soul, who got enlightenment under the Bodhi tree at Bodh Gaya.

Having it all is not enough – The journey of Siddhartha Goutama:

The life of Siddhartha Gautama, who would later become known as Gautama Buddha, is a profound journey from worldly comfort to spiritual enlightenment. Central to this transformative journey were the austerities practiced by Siddhartha in his quest to unravel the mysteries of existence and alleviate human suffering.

Siddhartha Gautama was born in Lumbini, in what is now Nepal, around 563 BCE. He belonged to the Shakya clan and grew up in princely luxury, shielded from the harsh realities of the world. Raised in opulence, he enjoyed a life of comfort, surrounded by indulgence and splendour. However, Siddhartha's exposure to the 4 great sights - suffering, disease, and old age outside the palace walls ignited his profound curiosity about the nature of human existence.

At the age of 29, Siddhartha made a momentous decision that would change the course of his life. He chose to renounce his princely privileges, including his wife Yasodhara and their infant son Rahula, and embark on a spiritual journey. This radical step, known as the "Great Renunciation," marked the beginning of Siddhartha's engagement with austerities as a means of self-purification.

To begin with, Siddhartha joined a group of ascetics and embraced a life of extreme self-discipline and austerities. Siddhartha subjected himself to prolonged fasting, often going without food for extended periods. His emaciated form became a testament to his dedication to self-mortification. He even renounced the comforts of clothing and shelter, choosing to live in the most austere conditions. Exposure to the elements and the rigors of the ascetic life became a daily reality. On top of it, Siddhartha engaged in intense meditation, often for hours on end, seeking to transcend the limitations of the physical body and attain higher states of consciousness. Additionally he embraced a minimalist lifestyle, possessing only the bare essentials and eschewing all forms of material wealth and possessions. Siddhartha's such rigorous austerities took a profound toll on his physical health. He became emaciated, weak, and near the brink of death due to extreme fasting and deprivation. His body, once robust and princely, was now a mere shadow of its former self. This physical discomfort was a crucial aspect of his journey, symbolizing his willingness to endure tremendous hardships in the pursuit of spiritual awakening.

While meditating under the Bodhi tree in Bodh Gaya, Siddhartha faced temptations that tested his resolve. The demon Mara, symbolizing desire and delusion, tempted him with worldly pleasures, distractions, and doubts. Siddhartha's ability to resist these temptations was a testament to his unwavering commitment to overcome discomfort and attain enlightenment. After six years of relentless striving and self-purification through austerities, Siddhartha came to a profound realization—the extreme asceticism he had practiced was not the path to enlightenment. He recognized that a balanced approach, known as the Middle Way, was necessary. This realization marked a significant shift in his journey, demonstrating his capacity to adapt and evolve.

Under the Bodhi tree, Siddhartha Gautama attained the ultimate breakthrough—the state of Nirvana or enlightenment. He realized the Four Noble Truths, which explained the nature of suffering and the path to liberation from it. This transformative moment marked the end of his personal discomfort and the beginning of his mission to teach others the path to enlightenment.

Enough of spirituality now. Do we know any present age example demonstrating this? Yes of course.

Mary Kom: Punching Through Adversity to Greatness:

Mary Kom, a name synonymous with Indian boxing and a symbol of female empowerment, faced numerous difficulties and hardships on her remarkable journey to becoming a global boxing icon. Born in the north-eastern Indian state of Manipur in 1982, Mary's life story is a testament to her indomitable spirit and unwavering determination. This real-life Indian story reveals the adversities she overcame to reach the pinnacle of success.

Mary Kom was born into a modest family in Kangathei, Manipur. Her parents, Mangte Tonpa Kom and Mangte Akham Kom, were agricultural laborers, struggling to make ends meet. Growing up, she experienced the financial constraints of her family and the lack of resources in her hometown. In Manipur, as in many parts of India, pursuing sports, let alone boxing, was not considered a viable career option for girls. Mary had to confront deeply ingrained gender biases and societal stereotypes. Her decision to become a boxer defied conventional norms and drew scepticism from her community. This went to such extents that she was almost disowned by her own father.

During her formative years in boxing, Mary Kom had access to rudimentary training facilities. She often trained in makeshift boxing rings and had limited access to professional coaches and equipment. Despite these limitations, her determination to succeed never wavered. Mary's family faced significant financial challenges, making it difficult to support her boxing ambitions. Her journey to competitions, purchasing equipment, and meeting training expenses required considerable financial sacrifices. Mary often had to rely on the generosity of well-wishers and local supporters. In 2001, Mary Kom became a mother, a role that added a new layer of complexity to her life. Balancing the responsibilities of motherhood with the rigorous demands of boxing training and competitions was an additional hurdle. Yet, she managed to find a way to excel in both areas of her life. At the start of her career, women's boxing in India was not as recognized or supported as it is today. Mary had to compete in international competitions with limited exposure and resources. The path to gaining international recognition was challenging and often involved self-funding her participation in tournaments.

Like all athletes, Mary faced injuries and setbacks during her career. These injuries required rehabilitation and mental resilience to bounce back and continue her training and competitive journey. One of Mary's dreams was to compete in the Olympics, but women's boxing was not included in the Olympics until 2012. She had to wait for years to realize her Olympic dream while continuing to compete in other international competitions.

Despite these formidable challenges, Mary Kom's unyielding dedication, relentless hard work, and the unwavering support of her family propelled her to unprecedented heights in the world of boxing. She went on to become a six-time world champion, an Olympic bronze medallist, and an inspiration to countless young Indian athletes, especially women, who aspire to break barriers and pursue their dreams. Mary Kom's story embodies the spirit of resilience and determination. It is a narrative of punching through adversity to achieve greatness and a testament to the power of unwavering self-belief. Her journey is a source of inspiration for individuals not only in India but around the world, proving that with passion, perseverance, and an unshakable spirit, one can overcome even the most formidable obstacles. Mary Kom, the "Magnificent Mary," is not just a boxing legend; she is a symbol of triumph over adversity and a beacon of hope for aspiring athletes everywhere.

Throughout history and across diverse fields, countless individuals have demonstrated that embracing discomfort is the key to achieving greatness. Their stories, like guiding stars in the night sky, illuminate the transformative power of resilience, determination, and the ability to navigate through life's challenges.

The triumph of enduring discomforts:

In the world of sports, figures like Mary Kom, who rose from humble beginnings and overcame financial constraints, societal norms, and gender biases, remind us that pursuing one's passion often involves stepping out of one's comfort zone. Their achievements inspire future generations to shatter barriers, setting new standards of excellence.

In the realm of business and innovation, luminaries like Elon Musk and Steve Jobs have shown us that disruptive progress is rarely born from complacency. These visionaries challenged convention, embraced uncertainty, and endured countless setbacks, ultimately reshaping industries and changing the way we live.

In literature, figures like J.K. Rowling and Nelson Mandela used the power of words and resilience to overcome personal trials and systemic injustices. Their stories illustrate that enduring discomfort is not just about personal gain but can also be a catalyst for societal transformation.

The common thread that weaves through these narratives is the understanding that enduring discomfort is not a destination but a crucial phase of the journey. It is the forge where resilience is tested, character is honed, and greatness is achieved. By confronting challenges head-on, we stretch our boundaries, discover hidden strengths, and tap into the wellspring of our potential.

The benefits of enduring discomfort are manifold. It cultivates a tenacious spirit that refuses to yield in the face of obstacles. It fosters adaptability, teaching us to thrive amidst uncertainty and change. It nurtures empathy, as we gain a deeper understanding of the struggles of others. Most importantly, it fuels the fires of innovation and creativity, pushing us to explore uncharted territories and redefine what is possible.

Certainly, affirmations can be powerful tools to motivate and push yourself beyond discomforts. Here are some affirmations that can encourage you to embrace challenges and grow through discomfort:

- "I welcome discomfort as a sign of growth and opportunity."

- "I am resilient, and I thrive in the face of adversity."

- "I embrace discomfort as a stepping stone to success."

- "I trust my ability to overcome challenges and emerge stronger."

- "I am not defined by my comfort zone; I am defined by my willingness to step outside of it."

- "I see discomfort as a chance to learn, adapt, and evolve."

- "I am in control of my response to discomfort, and I choose to respond with courage and determination."

- "I find strength in discomfort, and it propels me toward my goals."

- "I believe in my ability to push through discomfort and achieve greatness."

- "I am the master of my own growth, and I embrace every challenge with an open heart."

As we embark on our own journeys, let us remember that discomfort is not a foe to be feared but a friend that propels us forward. It is a reminder that the pursuit of success is not a smooth path but a winding, arduous trail. When we embrace discomfort with open arms, we harness its transformative energy, turning challenges into stepping stones and setbacks into stepping stones to scale greater heights.

In the end, success is not merely the destination; it is the culmination of a journey enriched by the discomforts endured, the lessons learned, and the indomitable spirit that refused to yield. As we follow the footsteps of those who have gone before us, may we find solace in the knowledge that the path to success is not about avoiding discomfort but about embracing it as the crucible where dreams are forged into reality.

Fear and Negativity Spreads Faster than Illness

One of the most unpleasant feelings known to human – FEAR.

Fear is created as a response to perceived threat or danger. This threat or danger can be real or imaginary, depending on the person concerned. Fear in humans is originated and created mentally, but its effects are physically visible. Not only does it revs up a surge of emotions, but also prepares your body for fight or flight. For some there might be a wave of Goosebumps, while to some others there might be a flash of heat throughout the body. Many would sweat streams while others might completely shut down. And, then there will be daredevils amongst you seeking thrill out of fear.

Today it has got a bad name due to the negativity associated with it. Usually, fear indicates something ominous. However, fear is a survival instinct. It alerts the brain and body to take a quick action. But fearing the unknown and unnecessary is actually – unnecessary! Yes, you will be afraid of a lot of things, as long as you face and overcome them, its fine. The moment we let fear overtake us and create a panic situation, we are doomed, that very moment.

Fear propagates via panic. We are social beings; it is in our nature to pick up signals and alarms from our fellow beings. Once on alert, it is not long that we immediately connect and ask our near and dear ones to be careful. Usually, the communication of which is exaggerated with each passing call. And this creates a chain of panic and fear propagation throughout the community. Instead of propagating fear, we must concentrate on transferring facts and solutions. And if there are no solutions, we must together strive to find one.

When did we realise the terrifying potency of fear?

In the mid-19th century, a quiet village nestled within the sprawling city of London became the epicentre of a harrowing tale that would forever transform the way we understand and combat infectious diseases. The events that unfolded during the cholera outbreak of 1854, chronicled in "The Ghost Map," authored by Steven Johnson, stand as a testament to the intertwined narratives of fear, death, scientific inquiry, and human resilience.

As the outbreak unfurled, fear cast a suffocating shadow over the village. Cholera, a ruthless waterborne disease, materialized as an invisible specter, snatching lives without warning and leaving communities in a state of bewilderment. Panic surged through the population, as the true cause of the disease remained shrouded in mystery, and authorities struggled to devise an effective strategy to quell its deadly advance. The pervasive sense of vulnerability served as a stark reminder of the fragility of human existence in the face of an implacable adversary.

At the heart of the unfolding tragedy was Dr. John Snow, a maverick physician driven by an unrelenting desire to decipher the enigma of cholera. Contrary to prevailing beliefs, Dr. Snow doubted the miasma theory, which attributed diseases to foul odours emanating from decaying matter. Instead, he postulated that contaminated water was the vector of the disease, a notion that placed him at odds with the established medical orthodoxy. With methodical determination, he embarked on a quest to uncover the truth.

Central to Snow's investigation was his mapping of cholera cases—a groundbreaking endeavour that connected the dots between disease distribution and water sources. Through meticulous analysis, he identified a cluster of cases around the infamous Broad Street water pump. The correlation between these cases and the pump was a revelation that would shape the trajectory of the outbreak.

Snow's findings crystallized a pivotal moment in the narrative. Armed with evidence that defied convention, he engaged in a spirited battle to convince authorities of the necessity to remove the pump handle, effectively severing the connection between contaminated water and the spread of cholera. The decision was met with resistance, as fear of change and scepticism about the new theory held sway. However, Snow's steadfast conviction and the irrefutable logic of his argument ultimately prevailed, leading to the pump's closure.

The aftermath of this intervention marked a turning point in the outbreak's trajectory. Death's stranglehold on the village began to loosen as the incidence of cholera cases diminished. Snow's dedication to scientific rigor, his visionary use of mapping, and his audacious challenge to conventional wisdom had led to a breakthrough that saved lives and sowed the seeds of modern epidemiology.

"The Ghost Map" is not just a historical account—it is a timeless parable that reverberates through the corridors of science and society. It underscores the profound implications of fear and death in shaping the human response to disease. Fear, a potent force, can paralyze and obstruct progress, as it did in the initial stages of the outbreak. The specter of death, with its indiscriminate reach, serves as a chilling reminder of our vulnerability, driving us to seek understanding and mastery over the forces that threaten our existence.

The narrative also spotlights the transformative power of scientific inquiry and the audacity to challenge established paradigms. Dr. John Snow's journey from scepticism to revelation is a testament to the potential of a single individual to challenge the prevailing wisdom and reshape our understanding of reality. Snow's approach, anchored in empirical evidence and rigorous analysis, showcases the ability of scientific inquiry to dispel the shadows of uncertainty and ignorance.

Furthermore, "The Ghost Map" highlights the critical role of data visualization and mapping in elucidating complex patterns. Dr. Snow's use of maps as a tool to visualize the geographic distribution of cholera cases was a pioneering endeavour that laid the foundation for modern epidemiology. The ability to visually represent data enabled him to discern patterns, identify clusters, and pinpoint the source of the outbreak, demonstrating the power of data-driven insights.

Ultimately, the cholera outbreak of 1854 and its unravelling through "The Ghost Map" serve as a poignant reminder that the convergence of fear, death, science, and human determination can forge an indelible path toward progress. As humanity faces contemporary challenges posed by infectious diseases, the lessons embedded within this historical narrative—of questioning assumptions, embracing evidence-based approaches, and harnessing the power of data—continue to illuminate the way forward. Just as Dr. John Snow's unyielding pursuit of truth altered the trajectory of an outbreak, so too can our collective commitment to knowledge and resilience lead us to triumph over the forces that threaten our well-being.

How do we overcome fear?

The first step towards conquering fear lies in acknowledging its presence. Avoidance often magnifies fear, but by confronting it head-on, we begin to strip away its power. This confrontation demands introspection—understanding the source and nature of our fear. Is it rooted in past experiences, uncertainties, or the fear of failure? Identifying these underlying causes empowers us to address them directly.

Facing fear demands embracing discomfort. Growth seldom occurs within the comfort zone, and confronting fear necessitates stepping into the unknown. This discomfort is a crucible for strength, fostering resilience and adaptability. As we repeatedly confront our fears, they begin to lose their potency, gradually transforming from insurmountable obstacles into manageable challenges.

Seeking support is another pivotal aspect of overcoming fear. Sharing our fears with trusted friends, family, or professionals can provide valuable insights and perspectives. Additionally, witnessing others who have triumphed over similar fears can inspire and embolden us.

Visualizing success is a potent technique in the arsenal against fear. By vividly imagining a positive outcome, we rewire our minds to focus on possibilities rather than limitations. Visualization instils confidence, creating a mental blueprint for success that helps ease anxiety.

Ultimately, embracing fear as a catalyst for growth is a triumph of the human spirit. It is a declaration of our autonomy, a refusal to be confined by our anxieties. Overcoming fear requires us to harness our inner strength, cultivate resilience, and embrace discomfort. With each triumph over fear, we emerge stronger, more confident, and open to a world of boundless opportunities.

Let us repeat a few affirmations together!

Since fear is a touchy subject, we have listed a number of affirmations, that would awaken your subconscious and help you battle through fearful situations.

- I am strong and capable, unshaken by fear.

- Fear is only a temporary obstacle, and I have the courage to overcome it.

- I release my worries and embrace the present moment with confidence.

- Every challenge I face is an opportunity to grow and learn.

- I am the master of my thoughts, and I choose to cultivate positivity.

- I trust myself to navigate through uncertainty with grace and resilience.

- I am empowered by my past victories over fear, and I carry that strength forward.

- Fear is a passing cloud; my inner light shines through regardless.

- I approach challenges with a fearless heart and an unwavering spirit.

- I welcome fear as a chance to prove my strength and determination.

- I believe in myself and my ability to conquer any fear that stands in my way.

- My inner peace and courage silence the whispers of doubt and fear.

- I am a warrior of fearlessness, armed with positivity and self-assurance.

- My potential is limitless, and fear cannot restrict my journey.

- I choose to focus on possibilities rather than succumb to fear's illusions.

- I am bold, resilient, and fully equipped to overcome any challenge.

- Fear may knock, but I answer with unwavering faith in my strength.

- I embrace the unknown with curiosity and the belief that I can handle anything.

- With each breath, I release fear and inhale confidence and empowerment.

- My heart is a sanctuary of courage, dispelling fear's shadows with each beat.

- Repeat these affirmations daily to reinforce your mindset of fearlessness and cultivate a resilient attitude in the face of challenges.

Freedom from Negativity
Is the Greatest Freedom

The origins of negativity are as mysterious as they are deeply rooted in the human experience. Negativity often sprouts from the seeds of doubt and fear, taking root in the fertile soil of our minds. It can be nurtured by past disappointments, watered by self-criticism, and thrive in the shadows of uncertainty. Like a dark cloud that looms on a sunny day, negativity can descend upon us unexpectedly. It may begin as a single thought, a solitary doubt, and then multiply like a virus, infecting our outlook on life. It feeds on our insecurities, finding strength in our vulnerabilities. Yet, despite its origins, negativity need not be a permanent fixture in our lives. It is within our power to recognize its presence, to confront it with positivity and resilience. In acknowledging its existence, we can trace its roots back to their source and unearth the strength to overcome it.

The shackles of negativity are invisible, yet they are more constricting than any physical chains. They wrap themselves around our hearts and minds, binding us to a bleak and suffocating world. Imagine, for a moment, that our hearts are magnificent castles, built to house dreams, love, and boundless possibilities. These castles are surrounded by lush gardens of hope, tended to by the light of optimism.

But the shackles of negativity creep in like stealthy shadows, encircling our castles.

They are made of whispers, each one carrying the weight of doubt and fear. These whispers crawl through the cracks in our castle walls, infiltrating our inner sanctum. They coil themselves around the chambers of our hearts, constricting the flow of joy and love. Our minds, once vast and open landscapes, become overgrown with thorny vines of self-doubt. These vines twist around our thoughts, choking out creativity and confidence. They create a labyrinth of negativity, where every path leads to despair.

The shackles of negativity plague our hearts and minds with insidious thoughts:

"You're not good enough."

"No one cares about you."

"You'll never succeed."

With each thought, the chains grow tighter, imprisoning us in a world of despair. We become trapped in a cycle of negativity, where every failure, every setback, reinforces our belief that we are unworthy.

But here's the beauty of the human spirit: even in the darkest dungeons of our minds, there is a flicker of hope. Like a lone candle in a pitch-black room, it refuses to be extinguished. It reminds us that we have the power to break free. With courage and determination, we can shatter the shackles of negativity. We can summon the strength to challenge those whispers of doubt. We can nurture the gardens of hope within our hearts, allowing them to flourish and push back the darkness. As the chains of negativity fall away, our castles open up to the boundless sky of possibility. Our minds become fertile fields, where the seeds of creativity and confidence can grow without hindrance. We find ourselves free, liberated from the shackles that once held us captive. In the end, we realize that the only true chains were the ones we allowed to form within our hearts and minds. We have the power to release ourselves, to break free from the suffocating grip of negativity, and to embrace a world where our castles stand tall, bathed in the radiant light of hope and positivity.

Let's learn how Tommy broke through the chains of negativity!

Tommy sat on the front porch; his eyes fixed on the gleaming red bicycle that stood before him. The summer sun beat down on the pavement, warming the air around him. It was a perfect day to learn how to ride, but Tommy's heart was heavy with doubt. He was dyslexic, and that constant feeling of not being good enough had seeped into every part of his life. Learning to ride a bicycle seemed like an insurmountable challenge.

"Come on, Tommy, you can do this," his father encouraged, a bright smile on his face. "I believe in you."

Tommy's internal dialogue began to churn, a cacophony of self-doubt and negativity. "I'll never get this. I always mess things up. Why even bother?" Those thoughts raced through his mind, threatening to suffocate his enthusiasm.

His father, sensing Tommy's hesitation, knelt down and looked him in the eyes. "You see, Tommy, the bicycle represents more than just learning how to ride. It's about freedom. Freedom from self-doubt, freedom from negativity. Once you conquer this, you'll know that you can overcome anything."

Tommy absorbed his father's words, letting them sink in. He realized that his father was right; he needed to break free from the chains of negativity that held him back. With renewed determination, he approached the bicycle.

As Tommy mounted the bike, his internal dialogue continued its relentless assault. "You're going to fall. Everyone's going to laugh at you. You'll never learn this." But Tommy clenched his teeth and gripped the handlebars, determined to silence those destructive thoughts.

"You're going to fail, Tommy. You always do."

His fingers trembled as he gripped the handlebars. The first pedal pushed him forward, but his unease grew:

"You're never going to get the hang of this. You'll make a fool of yourself."

Tommy's father held onto the back of the bicycle seat, offering support and balance. Tommy's anxiety surged:

"I can't do this. I'm going to fall. Why even try? It's gonna hurt like shit!"

Despite his inner turmoil, he continued to pedal. The bicycle wobbled dangerously, and his confidence slipped:

"This is impossible. I'm not like other kids. Dyslexic, remember?"

Tommy's father encouraged him, but his own thoughts weighed him down:

"Is he just pretending to believe in me? He must be so disappointed."

And then, it happened. Tommy's concentration faltered for a split second, and the bicycle tilted to one side. He lost his balance and tumbled to the ground. It was a painful reminder of his struggle:

"I knew it. I'm a failure. I can't even ride a stupid bike."

His father rushed to his side, helping him back up. Tommy's internal dialogue was relentless:

"I can't do this. I'll never do this. I should just give up."

But Tommy's father refused to let him surrender. He helped Tommy get back on the bicycle, his determination stronger than ever. But Tommy pedalled forward, still trembling with doubt:

"I'll probably fall again. I always mess things up."

And then, it happened once more. Tommy's control slipped, and he hit the pavement. This time, it stung even more. He could feel the tears welling up:

"I can't take this. Maybe I'm just not meant to ride a bike."

But this time, his father's encouraging words echoed in his mind, urging him to try again. Tommy wiped away his tears, the internal dialogue now shifting:

"I can't let negativity win. I have to keep trying."

With renewed determination, he mounted the bicycle once more. Despite the falls and the persistent negativity, Tommy kept pushing forward. He coaxed himself that falling down was just a part of the process, and with each fall, he grew stronger, more resilient. Eventually, he picturised himself riding the bicycle, effortlessly and in doing so, he conquered the negativity that had held him back for so long.

His father held onto the back of the bicycle seat, offering support and balance. Tommy took a deep breath and began to pedal. At first, the bicycle wobbled precariously, and he felt a surge of panic. But he didn't give in to his fear. He kept pedalling, one rotation at a time.

As he pedalled forward, Tommy started to experience something remarkable. The more he focused on the present moment, the less room there was for negativity to creep in. The wind tousled his hair, and the world around him began to blur as he gained speed. He was riding, really riding, and for the first time in a long time, he felt an overwhelming sense of freedom.

"I'm doing it!" Tommy exclaimed; his voice filled with astonishment.

This time his father let go of the seat, and Tommy continued to pedal on his own. He felt like he was flying, free from the weight of self-doubt and negativity. With each passing moment, he grew more confident. As he rode around the block, Tommy's internal dialogue had transformed. It now whispered words of encouragement. "You can do this. You are capable. You are free."

When he returned to the front porch, Tommy dismounted the bicycle with a triumphant smile. His father beamed with pride.

"See, Tommy, you did it! You broke free from those negative thoughts, and now you know what real freedom feels like."

Tommy nodded, tears of joy in his eyes. He had not only learned to ride a bicycle, but he had also discovered that freedom from negativity was indeed real freedom. It was a lesson he would carry with him throughout his life, a reminder that he could conquer any challenge as long as he believed in himself and banished the negativity that held him back.

What do we learn from this?

The origins of negativity may be elusive, but our capacity to dispel it and cultivate a more positive mindset is a testament to the resilience of the human spirit. In the fertile soil of our hearts, we can choose to plant seeds of hope, kindness, and optimism, and watch as they grow into a garden that banishes negativity and allows positivity to bloom.

Combatting negativity is like embarking on a journey to cleanse the soul and restore the inner harmony that negativity disrupts. In the intricate web of life, where shadows of doubt and despair often lurk, the spirit yearns for a beacon of light to guide it through the darkness. To combat negativity spiritually is to embark on a sacred quest, an inner odyssey that seeks to rekindle the divine flame within. Here are a few practices that might help you break free from chains of negativity.

Meditation: The Inner Sanctuary: Begin by entering the sanctuary of your own mind. Close your eyes and breathe deeply, allowing your thoughts to settle like ripples on a serene pond. In this tranquil space, you will discover the power to silence the cacophony of negativity that often rages within.

Self-Reflection: The Mirror of Truth: Look into the mirror of your soul without judgment. Confront your fears, doubts, and insecurities honestly. Acknowledge them, for only in recognizing the shadows can you begin to dispel them.

Positive Affirmations: The Chants of Transformation: Whisper to yourself words of affirmation like sacred mantras. Remind yourself of your worth, your strength, and your limitless potential. Each affirmation is a note in the symphony of self-love.

- "I release all negativity from my life, and I welcome positivity with open arms."

- "I am the master of my thoughts, and I choose positivity over negativity every day."

- "Negativity has no power over me; I am the captain of my own ship, steering towards a brighter horizon."

- "I am free from the chains of self-doubt, and I believe in my abilities to overcome any challenge."

- "I let go of past grievances and embrace the present with a heart full of positivity and forgiveness."

- "My mind is a sanctuary of peace and optimism, where negativity finds no refuge."

- "I am worthy of love, success, and happiness, and I release any negative beliefs that suggest otherwise."

- "Every setback is an opportunity for growth, and I choose to see the silver lining in every situation."

- "I attract positivity, abundance, and joy into my life like a magnet, repelling negativity effortlessly."

- "I am free to live a life filled with hope, gratitude, and optimism, leaving behind the shadows of negativity."

Gratitude: The Elixir of Contentment: In the temple of your heart, cultivate gratitude. Offer thanks for the simple blessings that surround you. Gratitude is a balm that soothes the wounds inflicted by negativity.

Connection: The Weaving of Souls: Seek the company of kindred spirits on this journey. Share your struggles, your triumphs, and your wisdom. Together, you will forge a spiritual shield against negativity.

Nature: The Sacred Cathedral: Venture into the embrace of nature. Amidst the rustling leaves and the song of birds, you will find solace and inspiration. Nature is a manifestation of the divine, a reminder of the beauty that exists beyond negativity.

Acts of Kindness: The Offering of Light: Extend your hand to others in acts of compassion and kindness. In lifting others, you will elevate your own spirit. Negativity withers in the presence of love and benevolence.

Forgiveness: The Healing Elixir: Forgive not only others but also yourself. Release the chains of resentment that bind you to the past. Forgiveness is a divine alchemy that transmutes negativity into inner peace.

Prayer: The Conversation with the Divine: Enter the sacred dialogue with the divine, however you conceive it to be. In prayer, you surrender your burdens and find strength in the belief that you are not alone on this journey.

Mindfulness: The Art of Presence: Finally, practice the art of mindfulness. Be fully present in each moment, for it is in the now that the spirit finds its truest form. Let go of the past, cease worrying about the future, and savor the beauty of the present.

As you undertake this spiritual voyage, remember that combating negativity is not a battle against external forces but an inner transformation. The spirit is a resilient flame, and with the right practices and intentions, it can burn brightly, dispelling the shadows of negativity, and illuminating the path to a more profound and fulfilling existence.

Seek Permission from Yourself and No One Else

In the labyrinthine journey of life, often obscured by societal expectations and external pressures, there emerges a profound spiritual truth: the need to seek permission from oneself and no one else. It is a concept that challenges the conventional narratives of conformity and approval-seeking, inviting us to embark on a journey of self-discovery and inner sovereignty. In a world that often clamours for our compliance, it's easy to forget that we are the architects of our own destinies, the masters of our own souls. Seeking permission from oneself is not an act of rebellion; it is an act of reclamation—an affirmation that our lives are our own to shape, mould, and define.

The journey begins with introspection, a deep and honest conversation with oneself. It's a process of peeling back the layers of conditioning and societal expectations, exposing the raw essence of our authentic selves. In this sacred space of self-exploration, we confront our fears, acknowledge our desires, and uncover the dreams that have long lain dormant within us. To seek permission from oneself is to grant oneself the freedom to dream unapologetically, to aspire without restraint, and to carve a path that resonates with the deepest chambers of the heart. It is an act of self-compassion, an acknowledgment that our happiness and fulfilment matter, that our dreams deserve to be nurtured and pursued.

But the journey is not without its challenges. It requires courage—the courage to defy the judgments and opinions of others, the courage to say "no" when our hearts and souls urge us to do so, and the courage to stand firm in our authenticity, even when it feels like the world may not understand. It's about recognizing that seeking permission from oneself is not an act of selfishness; it's an act of self-love. It's an acknowledgment that we must tend to our own well-being, honour our own aspirations, and prioritize our own growth and evolution. In doing so, we become better equipped to contribute positively to the world around us.

In this journey of self-permission, we embrace the power of choice. We choose the paths that align with our values, the relationships that nourish our souls, and the endeavors that resonate with our purpose. We grant ourselves the freedom to say "yes" when it feels right and "no" when it doesn't, recognizing that our inner compass is our truest guide. Ultimately, seeking permission from oneself is an act of reclaiming our sovereignty. It is a declaration that we are the authors of our own stories, the captains of our own ships. It is an invitation to live life authentically, to honour our unique journeys, and to trust that the universe conspires in our Favor when we align with our true selves.

As we navigate the complexities of existence, let us remember the liberating truth that seeking permission from oneself and no one else is a profound act of spiritual sovereignty. It is an affirmation that our lives are sacred canvases, waiting for the strokes of our own authentic expression. It is an invitation to embrace the beauty of our uniqueness, honor our inner wisdom, and step boldly into the world as the empowered creators of our own destinies.

Let us meet a few people who sought permissions only from themselves!

Ritesh Agarwal's journey from a small town in India to becoming the founder and CEO of OYO Rooms, a prominent hotel chain, is a remarkable story of resilience and entrepreneurial spirit. Born in Bissam Cuttack, a small town in the eastern state of Odisha, Ritesh Agarwal displayed a keen interest in entrepreneurship from a young age. His ambitious dreams extended beyond the boundaries of his hometown, and he was determined to make a mark on the world.

However, Ritesh's journey was not without its challenges. When he expressed his desire to venture into entrepreneurship and start a business, his parents were understandably concerned. In India, where traditional career paths often prioritize stability and established professions, the prospect of their son pursuing an unconventional path was met with resistance. Ritesh's parents, like many others in similar situations, worried about the uncertainties and risks associated with entrepreneurship. They had expectations of a more traditional career for their son and were initially apprehensive about his decision to forge a different path. Despite the resistance from his parents, Ritesh Agarwal remained undeterred. Armed with his vision and a determination to redefine the hospitality industry in India, he set out on his entrepreneurial journey. His ambition was to create a platform that would provide standardized and affordable accommodations for travellers, especially in budget segments.

In 2013, at the age of 19, Ritesh founded OYO Rooms. He started small, working tirelessly to build the platform and secure hotel partnerships. In the early days, he faced numerous challenges, including financial constraints and the scepticism of potential investors. As OYO Rooms began to gain traction and offer a solution to a pressing need in the Indian hospitality sector, Ritesh's hard work and dedication began to pay off. The platform expanded rapidly, transforming the budget accommodation landscape in India.

Today, OYO Rooms is one of the world's largest hotel chains, with a global presence. Ritesh Agarwal's entrepreneurial journey serves as an inspiration, not only for his success but also for his ability to persevere and prove the sceptics wrong. Over time, as OYO Rooms achieved remarkable success, Ritesh's parents and society at large began to acknowledge and support his entrepreneurial endeavours. His story exemplifies how determination, vision, and the willingness to face resistance can lead to extraordinary entrepreneurial achievements, ultimately redefining entire industries.

The story of **Steve Jobs**, co-founder of Apple Inc. and a pioneer in the world of technology and innovation, is marked by remarkable determination and vision. However, his journey was not without significant resistance, both from his parents and society, as he embarked on the path of entrepreneurship. Steve Jobs, born in San Francisco in 1955, developed a fascination with electronics and technology at an early age. His early experimentation with electronics led to him collaborating with his friend Steve Wozniak to build and sell "blue boxes" that allowed people to make free long-distance phone calls.

Steve's parents, Clara and Paul Jobs, had high hopes for their son's future. They had aspirations for him to attend college and pursue a traditional career. When Steve decided to drop out of Reed College after just six months, his parents were deeply concerned. They were wary of his unconventional choices and unsure about the potential for success in his pursuits. They worried that his choice to forgo college was a reckless decision that might jeopardize his future. However, despite his parents' apprehensions and societal pressures to follow a more conventional path, Steve Jobs continued to pursue his passion for technology and entrepreneurship. He and Wozniak co-founded Apple Computer, Inc. in a garage in Cupertino, California, in 1976. They introduced the Apple

I, a personal computer, which marked the beginning of a transformative journey.

The early days of Apple were marked by struggles, financial challenges, and the uncertainty of success. The groundbreaking Apple II, released in 1977, began to change the personal computing landscape. However, Steve's unconventional management style and strong-willed personality often clashed with his colleagues and investors, leading to his removal from the company he had co-founded in 1985. After a period of exile, Steve Jobs returned to Apple in 1996. The company he once co-founded was facing difficulties, but his vision and leadership led to a remarkable resurgence. Under his guidance, Apple introduced groundbreaking products such as the iMac, iPod, iPhone, and iPad, revolutionizing multiple industries.

Steve Jobs' relentless pursuit of innovation and perfection left an indelible mark on the world. His creations not only transformed Apple into one of the most valuable companies globally but also changed the way people interact with technology. In hindsight, Steve Jobs' decision to follow his own path, despite the resistance he faced from his parents and societal expectations, underscores the importance of staying true to one's vision and passion. His story serves as a testament to the power of individual determination and the potential to redefine industries and shape the future.

How to seek permission from yourself?

Seeking permission from yourself and no one else is a deeply personal and introspective process that involves making decisions based on your own values, desires, and authentic self. Here are steps to help you in this journey of self-permission:

- **Self-Reflection**: Take time to reflect on your goals, dreams, and aspirations. What is it that truly matters to you? What do you want to achieve in your life?

- **Identify Your Values**: Understand your core values and principles. What are the principles that guide your decisions and actions? Knowing your values will help you make choices aligned with your authentic self.

- **Trust Your Intuition**: Learn to trust your gut feelings and intuition. Your inner voice often knows what's right for you. Listen to it, and have confidence in your own judgment.

- **Distinguish External and Internal Expectations**: Differentiate between societal or external expectations and your own desires. Recognize when you're making choices based on what others expect of you, and question whether these align with your true self.

- **Set Boundaries**: Establish clear boundaries in your life to protect your time, energy, and well-being. Say "no" when necessary, and prioritize your own needs and goals.

- **Self-Compassion**: Be kind and compassionate toward yourself. Understand that it's okay to make mistakes or change your mind. Self-compassion allows you to grant yourself permission to be imperfect.

- **Practice Self-Acceptance**: Embrace who you are, including your strengths and weaknesses. Accept yourself fully and without judgment, recognizing that you are worthy of pursuing your own path.

- **Visualize Your Ideal Life**: Create a vision of your ideal life based on your values and desires. Use this vision as a guide for making decisions that align with your true self.

- **Take Ownership of Your Choices**: Understand that you are responsible for the decisions you make. Take ownership of your choices, whether they lead to success or challenges.

- **Learn from Experience**: Embrace the lessons that come from your choices and experiences. Use both successes and failures as opportunities for growth and self-discovery.

- **Surround Yourself with Supportive People**: Seek out a supportive network of friends, family, or mentors who encourage and respect your autonomy and decisions.

- **Practice Mindfulness**: Mindfulness meditation and self-awareness practices can help you stay attuned to your inner thoughts and feelings, making it easier to make choices that reflect your true self.

- **Stay Committed**: Commit to the process of seeking permission from yourself. It may require ongoing effort and self-reflection, but the rewards of living authentically are worth it.

Remember that seeking permission from yourself is a lifelong journey of self-discovery and self-empowerment. It's about living in alignment with your true self and making choices that reflect your own values and aspirations, rather than seeking external validation or approval.

Let us repeat some affirmations:

Affirmations can be a powerful way to reinforce the idea of seeking permission from yourself and no one else. Here are some affirmations to help you embrace this mindset:

- I trust my inner wisdom to guide my decisions and choices.

- I am the author of my own life, and I give myself permission to pursue my dreams.

- I release the need for external approval and validation; my self-approval is enough.

- I honor my values and desires, making choices that align with my authentic self.

- I have the right to set boundaries that protect my well-being and happiness.

- I am free from the opinions and expectations of others; I live my life on my terms.

- I grant myself permission to make mistakes, knowing they are opportunities for growth.

- I choose self-compassion and self-acceptance over self-judgment and criticism.

- I am the ultimate authority in my life, and I trust my decisions wholeheartedly.

- I let go of the fear of judgment and embrace the courage to be myself.

- I create my own path, unburdened by societal norms or external pressures.

- I deserve to live a life that reflects my true passions and desires.

- I am resilient and empowered, capable of overcoming challenges and setbacks.

- I celebrate my uniqueness and embrace my individuality with pride.

- I am the captain of my own ship, navigating life's journey with confidence.

Repeat these affirmations regularly, internalizing their messages to reinforce your commitment to seeking permission from yourself and no one else. They can serve as a powerful tool for cultivating self-empowerment and living authentically.

Human Beings Can Never Be Useless, They Are Just Used Less

In a small, dimly lit classroom of the Ludwigsfeld Primary School in Ulm, Germany, a young boy named Albert Einstein sat hunched over his desk, his eyes filled with curiosity and brilliance that seemed to shine brighter than the rest. It was the late 19th century, a time when conformity and rote learning were the norm. One day, the teacher, a stern figure with a thin mustache and a sharp glare, posed a challenging question to the class. The room fell silent, except for the scratching of pens against paper. Albert, lost in his thoughts, failed to register the question immediately. The teacher's patience wore thin as he repeated the question, his voice dripping with condescension, "Einstein, are you even paying attention? What's the answer?" Albert looked up, his brow furrowing in concentration. He stammered, searching for the words to articulate his thoughts. But before he could respond, the teacher sneered, his tone laced with ridicule, "You'll never amount to anything, Einstein. You're a dreamer, not a scholar. Perhaps your head is in the clouds because your feet can't touch the ground."

The classroom erupted into laughter, a chorus of mocking voices that seemed to echo off the walls. Students pointed fingers and exchanged knowing glances, revelling in their teacher's derisive words.

"Inquiring about the year of the Prussian victory at Waterloo, the history teacher's voice dripped with impatience. "When did the Prussians defeat the French, Einstein?"

"I'm not certain, sir," Albert replied hesitantly, feeling the weight of his teacher's expectation.

"Why don't you know? You've been told often enough," the teacher snapped sharply, his frustration palpable.

"I must have forgotten," Albert admitted, his eyes fixed on the floor.

"Have you ever made an effort to learn?" Mr. Braun questioned; his disbelief evident.

"No, sir," Albert replied, his honesty undiluted.

"Why not?" Mr. Braun persisted, his eyebrows furrowing in confusion.

"I can't see the point in memorizing dates. They can be looked up in a book," Albert stated matter-of-factly.

Mr. Braun fell silent for a moment, trying to comprehend Albert's perspective.

"You astound me, Einstein," he finally managed, a mixture of frustration and incredulity in his voice. "Don't you realize most things can be found in books? That applies to all the facts you learn at school."

"Yes, sir," Albert acknowledged, undeterred.

"Then you don't believe in learning facts," Mr. Braun concluded, his tone one of disappointment and resignation.

"Frankly, sir, I don't," Albert replied earnestly.

"Then you don't value education at all?" the teacher asked, disbelief tainting his voice.

"Oh, yes, sir, I do. I just don't think learning facts is education," Albert explained, his conviction unwavering.

"In that case," the history teacher sneered with heavy sarcasm, "perhaps you can enlighten the class with the Einstein theory of education."

Albert flushed, his cheeks burning under the scrutiny of his teacher. "I believe it's not facts that matter, but ideas," he asserted, his voice unwavering despite the tension in the room. "Learning the dates of battles, or which army killed more men, holds little interest for me. Understanding why those soldiers were trying to kill each other seems far more valuable."

"That's enough," Mr. Braun's eyes turned cold and cruel. "We don't need a lecture from you, Einstein. You will stay in for an extra period today, although I doubt it will be of any benefit. It won't do the school any good either. You are a disgrace. I can't fathom why you continue to attend."

"It's not my choice, sir," Albert pointed out, his frustration barely contained.

"Then you are an ungrateful boy and ought to be ashamed of yourself. I suggest you ask your father to take you away."

Albert felt despondent as he left school that afternoon, not because it had been a particularly terrible day — most days were miserable by now — but because he had to return to the loathsome place the next morning. He longed for his father to take him away, but there was no point in asking. He already knew the answer: he had to stay until he had earned his diploma.

Returning to his lodgings did not bring him comfort. His father's finances were so limited that Albert had been assigned a room in one of Munich's poorest quarters. He endured the meagre food, the lack of comfort, even the dirt and squalor, but he detested the atmosphere of violence that pervaded the slum. His landlady regularly beat her children, and every

Saturday her husband returned home drunk, subjecting her to even more brutality.

"At least you have a room of your own, which is more than I can say," Yuri observed when he visited in the evening.

"At least you live among civilized human beings, even if they are all poor students," Albert responded, trying to find a silver lining.

"They are not all civilized," Yuri remarked grimly. "Didn't you hear? One of them was killed last week in a duel."

"And what happened to the one who killed him?" Albert inquired.

"Nothing, of course. He's even proud of it. His only concern is that the authorities have forbidden him from fighting more duels. He's upset because he won't have a scar on his face to wear as a badge of honour for the rest of his life."

"Ugh!" exclaimed Albert. "And these are supposed to be students."

"Well, you'll be a student one day," said Yuri, his tone heavy with irony.

"I doubt it," Albert sighed, his frustration palpable, as he spoke to his cousin Elsa during her visit to Munich. Elsa, attempting to offer encouragement, remarked, "I'm sure you could pass if you tried, Albert. Many boys less intelligent than you manage it. They say you don't have to understand the material, just repeat it in the exams."

"That's the problem," Albert replied, his voice heavy with dissatisfaction. "I can't simply memorize facts."

"You don't need to comprehend it fully. Anyone can learn by rote. You just need to make an effort. But I always see you with a book under your arm," observed Elsa. "What are you reading?"

"A book on geology," Albert confessed.

"Geology? Rocks and such? Is that even part of your curriculum?" Elsa inquired, puzzled.

"No, we have hardly any science at school," Albert explained.

"Then why study it?" Elsa questioned, trying to understand his motivation.

"Because I enjoy it. Isn't that reason enough?" Albert responded.

Elsa sighed, sympathizing with his passion but concerned about his future. "You're right, Albert," she acknowledged. "But it won't help you with your diploma."

Music was his only solace, but even that was cut short when his irritated landlady demanded he stop playing the violin.

"That wailing irritates me," she complained. "There's enough noise in this house, with all the kids howling."

While tempted to point out her role in the noise, Albert kept silent.

"I need to leave this place," he confided in Yuri, weary after six months in Munich. "It's absurd to continue like this. Eventually, it will turn out I've wasted my father's money and everyone's time. It would be better for everyone if I stopped now."

What do we learn from this?

Albert Einstein's teachers failed to appreciate his intelligence in various ways, neglecting to nurture his extraordinary talents and curiosity, which perfectly aligns with the quote "humans are not useless but are used less."

In the rigid classroom of Ludwigsfeld Primary School, Albert's teachers were bound by traditional teaching methods, emphasizing memorization over understanding. When he questioned the value of memorizing historical dates and instead expressed a desire to delve into the reasons behind historical events, he was met with impatience and frustration. The teachers failed to recognize his thirst for knowledge, dismissing his approach as unorthodox.

Furthermore, the school system's narrow focus on rote learning meant Albert's unconventional thinking and innovative ideas were often ignored. His teachers, perhaps influenced by societal norms, couldn't see beyond the confines of the curriculum. His passion for subjects like geology, which weren't part of the standard syllabus, was seen as irrelevant, leading to his interests being sidelined.

Emotionally, this neglect was profoundly disheartening for young Albert. His enthusiasm for learning, fuelled by genuine curiosity and a hunger for understanding the world, was stifled. The dismissive attitude of his teachers left him feeling unappreciated, undervalued, and disconnected from the educational environment. The system failed to harness his potential, leaving him "used less" in the context of his remarkable intellectual capabilities.

In this way, Albert Einstein's teachers tragically failed to recognize the profound intellect and curiosity within him, exemplifying how humans, especially gifted individuals, can be underutilized and unappreciated within systems that don't acknowledge and nurture their unique talents and perspectives.

How do we apply this to our own lives?

Imagine a bustling city where every person is like a star in the night sky, each one with their unique glow and brilliance. In this city, people are not confined by rigid molds; instead, they are celebrated for their diversity, for the myriad of talents, passions, and dreams that make them who they are. This city thrives on the creative energy of its inhabitants, where the streets echo with the laughter of those who have found their true calling, their authentic selves.

In this vibrant city of life, there is a little bakery nestled in a quiet corner. The owner, Mrs. Thompson, is not just a baker; she is a storyteller. Her cookies and cakes are not just confections; they are canvases for her tales. With each creation, she weaves a story, and people don't just come for the taste; they come for the experience. Mrs. Thompson's ability to blend her passion for baking with her love for storytelling has turned her bakery into a haven of enchantment. In this city, her unique approach to her craft is not just appreciated; it's cherished.

Down the street, there's a man named Samuel, an unassuming janitor in the city's grand museum. To the casual observer, he might seem ordinary, but Samuel possesses an extraordinary gift – he has an uncanny ability to notice the subtlest of details. While cleaning the museum, he notices the way sunlight dances on the ancient artifacts, the intricate brushstrokes of forgotten masterpieces, and the faintest whispers of history that linger in the air. Samuel's keen observation skills have not only kept the museum spotless but have also unearthed hidden stories, transforming the museum into a living tapestry of the past.

In a nearby park, there's a group of friends who have turned their love for music into something magical. Each of them plays a different instrument, and when they come together, their melodies create a symphony that resonates with the very soul of the city. They don't just play for themselves; they play for the community. Their music becomes the heartbeat of the city, reminding everyone that life is a harmonious blend of different notes, tones, and rhythms.

In this city of endless possibilities, people find fulfilment not by conforming to norms but by embracing their uniqueness. They understand that being 'normal' doesn't mean being identical; it means being authentically themselves. Every quirk, every passion, every dream is celebrated. Just like the stars in the night sky, each person shines in their own way, adding to the brilliance of the universe.

And so, in the streets of this ordinary yet extraordinary city, every thread is a reminder that embracing one's uniqueness, valuing diverse talents, and nurturing individual passions can turn a routine existence into an extraordinary adventure. In this city of endless creativity and acceptance, the ordinary becomes extraordinary, and the mundane transforms into magic, proving that in the grand story of life, it's the unique characters and their exceptional journeys that truly make the tale unforgettable.

From a social perspective, the concept of "humans being used less" reflects the unfortunate reality where individuals are often pigeonholed and undervalued due to societal stereotypes, biases, and prejudices. These stereotypes, deeply ingrained in cultures and societies, categorize people based on their gender, race, ethnicity, age, abilities, or socioeconomic background.

These preconceived notions not only limit opportunities but also create barriers for personal and professional growth, perpetuating a cycle of underutilization.

One prevalent stereotype is gender bias, where women have historically been confined to certain roles and professions, undermining their potential in various fields. Similarly, racial and ethnic stereotypes marginalize minority groups, restricting their access to education, employment, and social opportunities. Ageism affects both the young and the elderly, with younger individuals often seen as inexperienced and older individuals as less adaptable, limiting their contributions to society. People with disabilities often face prejudice, overlooking their abilities and potential, relegating them to the sidelines.

These stereotypes not only hinder individual progress but also impede societal advancement. By underestimating the capabilities of individuals based on these biases, societies are depriving themselves of diverse perspectives, innovative ideas, and unique talents. It's akin to having a library full of books but only reading a few, missing out on the vast knowledge and wisdom the rest can offer.

How do we stop this?

Imagine a garden, lush with diverse and vibrant flowers, each with its unique color, fragrance, and beauty. Yet, in this garden, there's one flower that hides its petals, doubting its own vivid hues and subtle fragrance. This flower represents a person, underestimating their own worth and potential, despite the brilliance within.

The sun rises, casting a warm glow over the garden, and a gentle breeze rustles the leaves. This is a moment of self-reflection for the hesitant flower. It realizes that, just like every other bloom, it too possesses unique qualities that make it extraordinary. It has the strength to stand tall, the resilience to weather storms, and the ability to bring joy to those who appreciate its splendour. With newfound confidence, the flower starts to acknowledge its previous blooms - the moments of resilience, the times it stood tall in adversity, and the subtle victories it achieved. Each of these experiences is a petal, forming a vibrant, blooming testament to its potential. As the sun's rays touch its leaves, the flower begins to glow with a newfound radiance.

In this garden, there's a wise old tree, its roots deep within the earth, symbolizing knowledge and growth. The tree shares its wisdom with the hesitant flower, teaching it the art of setting realistic goals. Like a wise mentor, the tree advises the flower to start small, nurturing itself with positive thoughts and achievable milestones. "Just as a tiny seed grows into a mighty tree," the tree whispers, "your dreams, too, can blossom into reality."

Embracing the tree's guidance, the flower begins to unfurl its petals, one at a time. Each petal represents a new skill learned, a fear overcome, or a goal achieved. The garden witnesses this transformation, applauding the flower's bravery. The once hesitant bloom, now confident and bold, stands tall amidst the other flowers, its vibrant colors now a beacon of inspiration for others.

At night, when the stars blanket the sky, the flower gazes at them in awe. Each star represents a dream, a possibility waiting to be explored. With a heart full of courage, the flower decides to reach for the stars, stepping out of its comfort zone. As it ventures into the unknown, it discovers new talents, passions, and strengths, each one adding a new sparkle to its petals.

In this blooming journey, the flower encounters fellow blooms - kindred spirits who encourage and support its growth. Together, they form a tapestry of colors and fragrances, celebrating each other's uniqueness. The garden, once a place of self-doubt, is now a sanctuary of self-discovery and acceptance.

And so, the hesitant flower, once underutilized and underestimated, now stands as a testament to the power of self-belief. Its transformation inspires others, reminding them that within every soul lies a universe of untapped potential. The garden, once a metaphor for self-doubt, is now a canvas of endless possibilities, where every bloom, including the hesitant flower, thrives, embraces its uniqueness, and dances in the sunlight, a living testament to the boundless power of self-belief.

What do we know now?

Let this quote be a poignant reminder of the vast reservoir of untapped potential within every individual. It challenges societies to break free from limiting stereotypes and biases, encouraging them to recognize and harness the diverse talents, skills, and passions that each person possesses. Embracing this philosophy fosters a world where every individual is valued, where their unique contributions are acknowledged and celebrated. By unlocking the full spectrum of human capabilities, we pave the way for a future where creativity, innovation, and compassion reign, transforming the world into a tapestry of endless possibilities, each thread woven from the extraordinary talents that reside within us all.

It Is Not Change but Sustainable Change That Can Transform Us in the Long Run

In the ever-dynamic era of globalisation, the concept of sustainability emerges as a beacon guiding humanity through the intricate maze of progress. It is not merely a buzzword or a trend; it is a fundamental ethos that defines our relationship with the planet we call home. As I reflect on the pressing need and immense importance of sustainability in today's world, I cannot help but ponder the profound cost we, as a species, have incurred due to our historical negligence.

Why do we need to be sustainable?

Sustainability, at its core, is the harmonious coexistence of nature and human civilization. It embodies a delicate equilibrium where our ambitions do not plunder the Earth's resources faster than they can replenish, ensuring a legacy for future generations. The need for sustainability resonates with a clarity that cuts through the complexities of our modern lives. Our planet, adorned with breathtaking biodiversity and intricate ecosystems, has endured the weight of our demands for centuries. Yet, in the relentless pursuit of progress, we have often overlooked the silent cries of the environment. Therefore, the consequences of our collective oversight are stark and undeniable. Climate change, the most conspicuous manifestation of our unsustainable practices, has ushered in a new era of uncertainty. Rising temperatures, melting ice caps, erratic weather patterns, and catastrophic natural disasters serve as haunting reminders of our past follies. The loss of biodiversity, another casualty of our insatiable hunger for resources, disrupts the intricate web of life, leading to unforeseen repercussions for both nature and humanity. Pollution, deforestation, and depletion of vital resources have scarred the Earth, altering landscapes and endangering countless species.

The price we have paid for our lack of attention to sustainability is measured not just in ecological terms but also in human suffering. Vulnerable communities, often the least responsible for environmental degradation, bear the brunt of climate-related disasters. Droughts, floods, and extreme weather events displace millions, triggering conflicts over dwindling resources. The very foundations of our societies are shaken as we grapple with the consequences of our past actions.

However, in acknowledging the cost we have paid, there lies a glimmer of hope. The awareness of our past mistakes can serve as a catalyst for change. It compels us to re-evaluate our priorities, to adopt sustainable practices, and to nurture a profound respect for the planet that sustains us. Sustainability is not a choice; it is a responsibility, a pact we must honor with the Earth and with future generations. In this introspective moment, let us recognize that the path to a sustainable future is not merely a course correction; it is a collective journey of redemption. It calls for innovation, collaboration, and a deep reverence for the social structure that envelops our world.

Although many organisations, self-help groups, governments and congregations have come up with ideas for global sustainable developmental changes relating to nature and earth, less is known about social sustainability.

Is social sustainability really required?

The social fabric that binds us together is woven with the delicate threads of compassion, empathy, and understanding. In the tapestry of human existence, social sustainability stands as the cornerstone upon which the well-being of future generations rests. It is not merely a lofty ideal but an urgent necessity, a vibrant hue in the intricate design of our shared future. At its essence, social sustainability embodies the promise of a just society, where every individual is afforded dignity, respect, and equal opportunities. It champions inclusivity, embracing diversity in all its forms, be it cultural, economic, or ideological. In a world often marred by division and discord, social sustainability is the bridge that connects us across the chasms of prejudice and discrimination.

The importance of social sustainability resonates deeply in the context of nurturing future generations. As we embark on this introspective journey, we must recognize that the world we create today is the legacy we bequeath to our children and their children. A socially sustainable society provides a nurturing environment where young minds can flourish, unburdened by the shackles of inequality. It fosters education that enlightens, healthcare that heals, and communities that nurture the spirit.

The urgency of social sustainability cannot be overstated. In a rapidly changing world, marked by technological advancements and global interconnectivity, the need for social cohesion is more pressing than ever before. The challenges we face, whether they be economic disparities, political upheaval, or environmental crises, necessitate collaborative solutions rooted in empathy and understanding. Social sustainability is the compass that guides us, reminding us of our shared humanity and the collective responsibility we bear for the world we inhabit.

Imagine a world where kindness is currency, where understanding is our common language, and where the well-being of one is intertwined with the well-being of all. This vision is not utopian; it is the promise of social sustainability. It calls upon us to transcend the boundaries of self-interest and embrace the broader tapestry of human existence. It challenges us to be architects of a society where every individual is not just a beneficiary but an active participant, contributing their unique thread to the vibrant mosaic of humanity. As we reflect on the urgent need and immense importance of social sustainability, let us do so with a sense of purpose and determination. In nurturing social sustainability, we nurture the very essence of our shared humanity, ensuring that the generations yet unborn inherit a legacy of compassion, equality, and boundless opportunity.

Fulfilling Dreams: The Tale of Sanjaynagar's Transformation:

In the heart of Ahmednagar, there existed a community known as Sanjaynagar, a place where hope persevered amidst adversity. Four decades ago, this two-acre settlement was a far cry from the vibrant community it has become today. Back then, the land was marshy and weed-infested, forcing the residents to navigate through knee-high waters daily. Yet, the people of Sanjaynagar possessed a collective spirit that refused to succumb to their challenging circumstances. In the face of adversity, the residents took a stand. Fuelled by their determination, they demanded better living conditions, compelling the government to take notice. Fortunately, their settlement fell under the purview of government-owned land, making them eligible for transformative programs like the Pradhan Mantri Awas Yojana (Urban) Mission (PMAY). This initiative aimed to provide homes to the economically weaker sections of society, offering a glimmer of hope to Sanjaynagar.

This journey toward transformation was not a solitary one. The design studio Community Design Agency (CDA) joined forces with the local NGO Snehalaya, a stalwart presence in the community for over two decades. Together, they embarked on a mission to reimagine Sanjaynagar, empowering its residents to shape their own destiny.

Crucial to this transformation was the participatory design process. Every resident had a voice; every family shared their dreams. Building consensus was the cornerstone, and the community members became the decision-makers, while architects and social workers acted as facilitators. The families in Sanjaynagar, deeply rooted in their land, had specific visions. They envisioned a better future for their children, safe and healthy housing that could create opportunities for generations to come. Light and ventilation became more than architectural elements; they became symbols of hope. The residents emphasized social interaction, wanting to foster a sense of community. They sought spaces where they could engage with neighbours, where their children could play freely, and where their animals could thrive. This vision was not just about buildings; it was about creating a sanctuary for life to flourish.

Amidst the challenges of the pandemic, the project named 'Swapnapurti' (meaning 'Fulfillment of Dreams') began to take shape. The very first families volunteered to undergo the process of redevelopment without a precedent to guide them. Challenges emerged, as they often do, but the spirit of Sanjaynagar prevailed. The lack of a prior example meant that creativity and adaptability were their guiding stars. The architects, social workers, and residents collaborated, finding innovative solutions to every hurdle.

With each brick laid and each dream realized, Swapnapurti emerged as a testament to human resilience. It was more than a housing project; it was a beacon of hope. Amidst a pandemic and economic uncertainty, the people of Sanjaynagar proved that dreams, when nurtured collectively, could indeed come true. As Swapnapurti stood tall, it not only provided homes but also inspiration. It became a reminder to all: the power of community, creativity, and determination could transform even the most challenging of circumstances into a thriving, vibrant reality. And in Sanjaynagar, dreams were no longer distant visions but tangible, fulfilling realities.

As we tread this path, let us do so with humility, mindful of the past, and with unwavering determination to build a future where sustainability is not just a concept but a way of life.

What do we learn from this?

The transformation of Sanjay Nagar slum goes beyond mere change; it embodies the essence of sustainable change, a concept that holds the key to transformative progress in the long run.

- Empowerment Through Participation: Sanjay Nagar's journey taught us that sustainable change is not a top-down imposition but a participatory endeavour. When residents become active participants in the decision-making processes of their own community, they feel a sense of ownership. This sense of ownership is what fuels long-term commitment and sustainable development. In Sanjay Nagar, the community's active involvement in the redevelopment process became the driving force behind the transformation.

- Preserving Cultural Identity: Sustainable change respects and preserves the cultural identity of a community. Sanjay Nagar's residents were not just given new homes; they were given spaces that respected their way of life. By integrating the community's values, traditions, and preferences into the redesign, Sanjay Nagar became a place where the residents could maintain their identity, fostering a sense of belonging that is essential for any sustainable change.

- Building Resilient Communities: Sustainable change builds resilience. It equips communities to face challenges and adapt to new circumstances. In Sanjay Nagar, the participatory approach and the community's active engagement meant that they were not just beneficiaries but also problem solvers. When unforeseen challenges arose, the community and its support networks found innovative solutions. This adaptability is a hallmark of sustainable change.

- Fostering Economic Stability: Sustainable change promotes economic stability by creating opportunities for skill development and employment within the community. In Sanjay Nagar, the redevelopment not only provided housing but also encouraged entrepreneurship. By understanding the community's needs and aspirations, sustainable change fosters economic growth from within, ensuring that the benefits are self-sustaining.

- Strengthening Social Bonds: Sustainable change strengthens social bonds. When communities actively engage in their own development, it fosters a sense of solidarity and mutual respect. In Sanjay Nagar, the collaborative efforts created a tight-knit community where individuals supported each other. These social bonds are the fabric that holds communities together during times of adversity, ensuring the sustainability of the positive changes achieved.

- Environmental Consciousness: Sustainable change is environmentally conscious. It incorporates eco-friendly practices and encourages responsible use of resources. In Sanjay Nagar, the redevelopment project took into account not just the needs of the residents but also the surrounding environment. This mindfulness ensures that the changes made do not come at the cost of the environment, thus guaranteeing a sustainable legacy for future generations.

In the story of Sanjay Nagar's transformation, we find a blueprint for sustainable change. It's a reminder that true progress is not about quick fixes or superficial alterations. Instead, it's about fostering deep-rooted, lasting change that respects the people it aims to help, preserves their cultural heritage, and creates a foundation for a brighter, more sustainable future. Sanjay Nagar teaches us that it's not just about changing lives; it's about empowering communities to sustain those changes, ensuring a transformative impact that stands the test of time.

Let us repeat these affirmations together to bring about a similar change in our community as well.

- I embrace sustainable change, knowing it transforms my life in profound and lasting ways.

- Every positive change I make is a step toward a more sustainable and fulfilling future.

- I am committed to making changes in my life that are not only transformative but also enduring.

- I am resilient and open to adapting, allowing sustainable change to shape my journey.

- I am the architect of my life; I create changes that stand the test of time.

- With every sustainable change, I grow stronger, wiser, and more compassionate.

- I welcome challenges as opportunities for sustainable growth and transformation.

- My willingness to embrace sustainable change empowers me to overcome any obstacle.

- I trust in the process of sustainable change, knowing it leads me to my highest potential.

- I release resistance and allow sustainable change to flow naturally, bringing positivity into my life.

Past Made You, Present Can Destroy You, Future Can Mould You

People usually ask us to focus on the present, but I say, past is of as much importance. Giving undue importance to present can be both dangerous and destructive. Albeit, it's the past and future that hold all the power; while present is just a concept of fleeting time.

"The past is not a burden; it is a scaffold which brought us to this day, a foundation upon which we build our future, and a gallery of memories that paints the canvas of our soul."

In the quiet recesses of our minds, the past resides as a tapestry woven with threads of experiences, memories, and emotions. It is within this intricate mosaic that the foundation of our personality, behaviour, decision-making, and selfhood finds its roots. The past, like a silent sculptor, molds the clay of our existence, leaving behind contours that define who we are and how we navigate the world.

I. The Shaping of Personality:

Our early experiences, from the gentle whispers of caregivers to the thundering echoes of childhood adventures, etch patterns onto the canvas of our personality. The encouragement we receive, the challenges we face, and the love we are given contribute to the shaping of traits – kindness, resilience, empathy – that become the cornerstones of our identity

Imagine a young sapling swaying in the wind; each breeze leaves a subtle mark, shaping its eventual form. Similarly, our interactions and experiences, especially in our formative years, influence the way we perceive ourselves and others. Positive affirmations nurture confidence, while negativity can breed self-doubt. The past, in this sense, is a mirror reflecting the essence of our self-worth and esteem.

II. Behaviour as an Echo of History:

Behaviors are the footprints we leave behind, imprinted by the paths we tread in the past. Consider a dancer, her movements a dance of history, each step a reflection of the lessons learned and the experiences lived. Our past encounters and responses to challenges create behavioural patterns – resilience in adversity, kindness in the face of cruelty – that echo through our actions in the present.

The nurturing environment of childhood, or its absence, can influence our ability to trust, empathize, and connect with others. Acts of kindness witnessed during our upbringing can cultivate compassion, just as cruelty endured can sow the seeds of anger or fear. Our behavioural inclinations are like ripples, spreading from the pebble dropped in the pond of our past experiences.

III. Decision-Making: A resultant of Experience:

Our past decisions are the stepping stones upon which we tread toward an uncertain future. Each choice made, every crossroad navigated, is colored by the experiences and lessons of yesteryears. Imagine a sailor, skilfully steering his ship through stormy seas, drawing wisdom from past voyages. Our past decisions, whether triumphs or tribulations, shape our discernment and influence our judgment.

The consequences of past choices, both positive and negative, leave imprints on our psyche. Failures teach resilience; successes foster confidence. Regrets serve as cautionary tales, urging us to tread carefully, while triumphs fuel our ambitions. The past thus becomes a mentor, guiding our hands as we sketch the contours of our future decisions.

IV. The Essence of Self:

Within the intricate labyrinth of our memories and experiences lies the essence of self. Our past joys, sorrows, triumphs, and defeats converge to create a mosaic that is uniquely ours. Picture an ancient library, its shelves laden with volumes of personal history, each chapter contributing to the narrative of who we are.

The tapestry of the self is woven with threads of laughter shared with friends, tears shed in solitude, dreams nurtured in the quiet of night, and fears whispered in the shadows. It is an amalgamation of cultural heritage, familial roots, and individual aspirations. Our past is the loom upon which the fabric of our identity is crafted, imbibing the essence of generations past while leaving room for the brushstrokes of our personal journeys.

In conclusion, the past, with its myriad hues and shades, is the canvas upon which the masterpiece of our lives is painted. It shapes our personality, molds our behaviours, guides our decisions, and weaves the very fabric of our self. Embracing the lessons of our past, both bitter and sweet, empowers us to navigate the present with wisdom and grace, ensuring that our story, like an epic tale, resonates with the echoes of history.

"The present moment is a double-edged sword, cutting through certainty and unveiling the unknown. In its unpredictability lies both the thrill of endless opportunities and the peril of unforeseen consequences."

In the subtle folds of the present, there lies a perilous power, a force that, if mismanaged, can wreak havoc upon our lives and the lives of those around us. The present, with its fleeting moments, harbours the potential for destruction, silently waiting for a lapse in judgment to unleash its wrath.

When we succumb to the illusions of the present, we risk becoming prisoners of instant gratification, blinding ourselves to the consequences of our actions. In the blink of an eye, decisions made in haste can shatter the foundation of our being, leaving us vulnerable and broken. The choices we make, driven by the impulsive urges of the moment, can lead us down a treacherous path, eroding the very essence of our character.

Moreover, the destructive tendrils of the present don't limit their reach to our individual selves; they stretch out, entangling the lives of those we hold dear. Our recklessness, born from the impulsiveness of the moment, can inflict wounds upon the hearts of our loved ones, leaving scars that may never fully heal. The ripples of our actions spread far and wide, affecting the emotional landscape of our relationships, leaving behind a trail of devastation.

In this whirlwind of the present, we must be vigilant, for the decisions we make today cast shadows upon our tomorrow. It is a stern warning, a beacon amidst the darkness, urging us to pause, reflect, and consider the far-reaching implications of our actions. Let us not be seduced by the fleeting pleasures of the moment, but instead, strive for a balance between seizing the day and safeguarding our future.

Let this cautionary tale be a reminder: the present, if mishandled, can morph into a destructive force, leaving in its wake a landscape of ruin. Let us tread carefully, mindful of the fragile equilibrium between the now and the future, for in this delicate balance lies the key to preserving our well-being, our relationships, and ultimately, our happiness.

"The future belongs to those who believe in the beauty of their dreams and have the courage to pursue them, for it is not a destination but a daring journey, shaped by the choices of the present, and illuminated by the unwavering faith in possibilities yet unseen."

The future is a molder of dreams and architect of destinies. It shapes the landscapes of our aspirations and sculpts the contours of our ambitions. It molds the foundation upon which we build our hopes, urging us to cast our visions toward the horizon of what could be.

In the hands of the future, talents are honed into skills, passions are forged into purpose, and potential is transformed into reality. It weaves the threads of innovation, technology, and progress, stitching together the fabric of tomorrow. It is the canvas upon which the artists of change paint their strokes of transformation, ushering in new eras and paradigms.

Moreover, the future molds our character and resilience. It challenges us, tests our mettle, and forges our strength through adversities. It shapes our beliefs, inspiring us to persevere in the face of uncertainty. It is a teacher, imparting lessons from the past, guiding us toward wisdom, and instilling within us the courage to embrace the unknown.

In essence, the future is a powerful sculptor, crafting the legacy of generations yet unborn. It is a mirror reflecting the collective efforts, dreams, and innovations of humanity. It is a realm of endless possibilities, reminding us that our actions today influence the contours of the world that will unfold tomorrow.

In the quiet recesses of our subconscious mind, the future resides as a seed of infinite potential, waiting to sprout and bloom into the reality we shape with our thoughts and beliefs. It is a profound reservoir of energy, a force both tangible and ethereal, capable of molding our destiny in ways we might not fully comprehend.

In the depths of our subconscious, the future whispers its secrets. It is a sacred space where our dreams take flight, where our deepest desires find expression, and where the universe listens intently to the intentions we set forth. Each thought, every aspiration, is a brushstroke on the canvas of our fate, painting the masterpiece of what is yet to come.

The power of the future in our subconscious mind is not just a concept but a spiritual truth. It is a reminder that our thoughts are not mere fleeting notions but potent energies that have the ability to shape the reality we experience. Through introspection and spiritual atonement, we can tap into this reservoir of potential, aligning our consciousness with the divine flow of creation.

In the quietude of meditation and self-reflection, we can sense the pulsating energy of the future, urging us to dream grander dreams and to believe in the limitless possibilities that lie ahead. It is a reminder that the universe is conspiring in our favor, responding to the vibrations of our thoughts and intentions, orchestrating events and opportunities that align with our deepest desires.

Embracing this spiritual truth empowers us to be mindful custodians of our thoughts. It encourages us to cultivate positivity, to nurture hope, and to envision a future that is not bound by the limitations of the past. As we harness the power of the future in our subconscious mind, we embark on a transformative journey, awakening to the immense creative potential that resides within us, and co-creating a reality that mirrors the divinity of our souls.

Let us repeat some affirmations:

- "I honor my past, learning from its lessons, and embracing the strength it bestowed upon me."

- "I am mindful of the present, steering clear of destructive paths, and nurturing my well-being with every choice I make."

- "I envision my future with clarity, shaping it with positivity, determination, and unwavering belief in my potential."

- "My past is a stepping stone, my present is a canvas, and my future is a masterpiece in the making."

- "I release the burdens of the past, I cherish the blessings of the present, and I trust in the possibilities of the future."

- "In the cocoon of my past, I found strength; in the embrace of my present, I find peace; in the hands of my future, I find endless potential."

- "I acknowledge my past as a teacher, my present as a gift, and my future as a canvas of endless opportunities."

- "I am the architect of my destiny, shaping my future with purpose, guided by the wisdom of my past and the clarity of my present."

- "With gratitude for the past, awareness of the present, and vision for the future, I navigate life's journey with grace and resilience."

- "I let go of what no longer serves me from the past, I embrace the blessings of the present, and I step into the future with courage and conviction."

The Extra in the Ordinary Is Mastery

In the intricacy of human existence, extraordinary skills stand as intricate threads woven by the hands of exceptional individuals. These abilities, diverse and captivating, trace their origins to the depths of innate talent, nurtured by relentless passion and unwavering determination. They are the products of countless hours spent honing a craft, the result of minds that dare to explore uncharted territories and hearts that refuse to succumb to mediocrity.

The importance of extraordinary skills resonates far beyond personal achievement; it reverberates through the corridors of economies and societies alike. Economically, these skills are the engines of innovation and progress. They carve pathways to new technologies, usher in groundbreaking discoveries, and foster industries that create jobs and fuel growth. In a world defined by rapid change, these skills are the currency of competitiveness, driving nations forward in the global marketplace.

Socially, extraordinary skills inspire and elevate. They become beacons of aspiration, proving that human potential is boundless. These skills bridge divides, bringing people together through shared appreciation for mastery and creativity. They redefine societal standards, challenging conventions and encouraging others to explore their own unique potentials. Moreover, extraordinary skills often serve as catalysts for social change, breaking barriers of prejudice and opening minds to new possibilities. They become symbols of resilience, reminding us of the human spirit's capacity to overcome challenges and adversities.

In essence, extraordinary skills are the keystones of a thriving society and a prosperous economy. They enrich cultures, fuel imaginations, and create a legacy that echoes across generations. As we celebrate these exceptional talents, we acknowledge not only the individuals who possess them but also the collective capacity of humanity to reach unparalleled heights when nurtured, celebrated, and shared. In their essence, extraordinary skills remind us of the boundless potential that resides within every soul, waiting to be discovered and illuminated for the betterment of the world.

What is mastery?

Raising an ordinary soul to extraordinary heights is akin to nurturing a delicate bud into a resplendent bloom, a metamorphosis that occurs through a symphony of inspiration, perseverance, and unwavering belief. Imagine an unassuming canvas, blank and waiting, where every stroke of encouragement is a vibrant hue that brings it to life.

- The Spark of Recognition: In the heart of every ordinary person lies a dormant spark, a latent brilliance waiting to be ignited. Imagine this spark as a tiny, flickering flame in the darkness. The first step towards transformation is the recognition of this ember, seeing beyond the surface and glimpsing the hidden potential within.

- Belief, the Magic Elixir: Now, picture belief as a potion, shimmering with possibility. Pour it generously, for belief is the foundation upon which extraordinary feats are built. Belief from mentors, from loved ones, and most importantly, self-belief, infuses courage into the timid heart, allowing it to dream audaciously.

- Guidance, the Guiding Constellation: Visualize guidance as a constellation of stars in the night sky, illuminating the path ahead. Wise mentors and teachers are these stars, their wisdom shaping the journey of the ordinary person. With their guidance, the budding talent finds direction, learning the secrets of the craft under their celestial light.

- Endless Curiosity, the Ever flowing River: Imagine curiosity as a river, meandering through the landscape of the mind. The extraordinary soul is insatiably curious, thirsty for knowledge and hungry for experience. Every pebble of information creates ripples, expanding the boundaries of understanding. Curiosity fuels the desire to explore, innovate, and excel.

- Adversity, the Forge of Strength: See adversity as a blacksmith's forge, where ordinary individuals are tempered into extraordinary beings. Challenges and failures, when embraced with resilience, become the hammer and anvil that shape character. Adversity teaches the art of rising after every fall, instilling a tenacious spirit.

- Passion, the Eternal Flame: Passion is the eternal flame that burns within the extraordinary soul. Picture it as a beacon, casting a warm, illuminating glow. Passion drives the individual to invest countless hours, toil endlessly, and overcome insurmountable odds. It transforms the mundane into the extraordinary, infusing life into skills and endeavours.

- Courage, the Wings of Flight: Courage is the ethereal wings that enable the ordinary to soar to unprecedented heights. Visualize it as a pair of majestic wings unfurling, lifting the spirit above self-doubt and societal constraints. With courage, the individual dares to step into the unknown, confront fears, and embrace challenges, transcending the ordinary limitations.

- Legacy, the Echo of Extraordinary Deeds: Envision legacy as an echo, resonating through time. The extraordinary deeds of an individual create ripples that influence generations. Like a stone cast into a tranquil pond, these deeds inspire others to reach for the stars. The legacy becomes a testament to the transformative power of belief, resilience, passion, and courage.

Raising an ordinary person to extraordinary heights is the alchemy of the human spirit, a magical process where belief and perseverance blend seamlessly, sculpting a masterpiece from the clay of potential. It is the celebration of human capacity, a reminder that within every ordinary heart, an extraordinary story awaits, waiting to be written in the ink of determination and colored with the hues of passion.

How to gain extra-ordinary skills?

Attaining extraordinary skills is a multifaceted journey that combines practical dedication with a profound spiritual connection to oneself and the world. Here's a guide that integrates both practical and spiritual approaches:

Practical Embodiment:

- Passion as the Guiding Light: Imagine your passion as a flickering flame within the vast darkness of the unknown. Embrace it; let it guide your steps. Your passion isn't just what you love; it's a magnetic force that pulls you toward mastery.

- The Art of Deliberate Practice: Picture a sculptor meticulously carving a masterpiece from stone. Deliberate practice is your chisel. It's the focused, relentless effort, the refining of your techniques until they gleam like polished gems. Every repetition shapes your skill, molding it into perfection.

- The Wisdom of Mentors: Envision yourself as a sapling, leaning toward the wisdom of ancient trees. Mentors are your sunlight, nurturing your growth. Their experiences are the roots that anchor you, allowing you to withstand storms and reach for the skies. Their guidance is your compass, steering you through uncharted waters.

- Continuous Learning: See yourself as a weaver, entwining threads of knowledge into a vibrant tapestry. Learning is your loom. With every book you read, every lecture you attend, the tapestry grows richer. Each thread represents a lesson, a revelation, interlaced with the others to form a masterpiece of understanding.

- Patience as the Silent River: Imagine your journey as a river carving through mountains. Patience is the water, persistent and unwavering. It smoothens rough edges, creating valleys of experience. It might meander, but every twist and turn teaches. The river knows; it eventually reaches the boundless sea.

Spiritual Essence:

- Mindfulness, the Elixir of Presence: Close your eyes and feel the moment. Mindfulness is a lantern illuminating the darkness within. It's the art of being present, of immersing yourself so deeply in your practice that the world outside dissolves. In this profound presence, your senses sharpen, your intuition awakens.

- Meditation, the Sacred Silence: Envision a serene lake mirroring the heavens above. Meditation is your reflection. In its depths, thoughts settle like ripples fading into calm. The silence is pregnant with creativity; it births ideas, visions, and epiphanies. It's where your inner voice speaks, guiding your hands and thoughts.

- Gratitude, the Fragrance of Humility: Imagine gratitude as a fragrant blossom. Its scent fills the air, reminding you of the countless hands that nurtured you. Gratitude humbles you; it's the recognition that your skill is a gift, a culmination of efforts from teachers, peers, and even the adversities that forged your resilience.

- Purpose, the North Star: Picture yourself sailing under a starlit sky, the North Star guiding your ship. Purpose is your guiding light. When your skill aligns with a purpose greater than yourself, it transcends mere proficiency. It becomes a beacon of change, inspiring others and infusing your journey with meaning.

- Connection with Nature, the Source of Renewal: Visualize yourself in a forest, the air thick with ancient wisdom. Nature is your sanctuary. Its rustling leaves and flowing streams echo the rhythms of your heart. It's where you find solace, where the vibrant energy of the earth seeps into your being, grounding you, revitalizing your spirit.

- Faith, the Wings of Belief: Imagine faith as wings unfurling from your back. It's the audacity to believe in your potential, even when the world doubts. Faith is the wind beneath your wings, lifting you higher. It's the quiet assurance that every stumble is a step toward mastery, every setback a prelude to a greater comeback.

In the bonding of the practical and the spiritual, your pursuit of extraordinary skills transforms into a sacred art. It's not just about what you do; it's about who you become in the process. Each moment of practice, every note played or stroke painted, becomes a prayer, a testament to your devotion to the craft and to the boundless depths of human potential.

What affirmations can you repeat in your journey extraordinaire?

Affirmations can be instrumental in shaping your mindset and supporting your journey toward attaining mastery and extraordinary skills. Here are some affirmations specifically crafted to empower you on this path:

- I am a master in the making; every day I am improving and evolving.

- My dedication to continuous learning fuels my journey to extraordinary skills.

- I am unlocking my limitless potential and tapping into extraordinary abilities within me.

- I embrace challenges as opportunities to sharpen my skills and deepen my expertise.

- I am committed to relentless practice, knowing it is the key to mastering any skill.

- My passion for learning and growing propels me toward mastery in my chosen field.

- I am in tune with my intuition, guiding me toward innovative and creative solutions.

- Every setback is a stepping stone to success; I learn, adapt, and excel.

- I am patient with my progress, understanding that mastery is a journey, not a destination.

- I am disciplined, focused, and dedicated to honing my craft daily.

- My mind is sharp, my abilities are honed, and I am capable of extraordinary achievements.

- I attract mentors, resources, and opportunities that accelerate my path to mastery.

- I believe in my unique talents; I have something special to offer the world.

- I am resilient; I bounce back from challenges stronger and more determined than ever.

- I am a beacon of inspiration, encouraging others to pursue their own path to mastery.

Repeat these affirmations daily, internalize them, and let them instill confidence and determination within you. As you reinforce these positive beliefs, you'll find the strength and motivation to persist in your efforts, leading you closer to the mastery and extraordinary skills you aspire to achieve.

Every teacher was once a student, a truth etched into the foundation of education, reminding us of the perpetual cycle of learning and teaching. A good teacher understands the delicate balance between being a guide and a lifelong learner. They recognize that knowledge is not stagnant but a flowing river, ever-evolving and adapting to the currents of time. In the quiet corridors of classrooms, they inspire young minds to explore, question, and challenge the world around them. Yet, they remain humble, acknowledging that their wisdom is not a final destination but a milestone in their journey of learning. The essence of a great teacher lies not only in the imparting of knowledge but also in their ability to instil the thirst for continuous learning, for it is in the pursuit of knowledge that minds are illuminated and futures are shaped. With each lesson taught, they plant seeds of curiosity, nurturing a forest of lifelong learners, where the distinction between teacher and student blurs, and the quest for knowledge becomes a shared odyssey.

How do we perceive leadership?

In the contemporary world, leadership has transcended traditional hierarchical structures, evolving into a multifaceted concept that embraces diversity, inclusivity, and adaptability. Modern leadership is not confined to commanding from the front but rather a dynamic process of collaboration, inspiration, and empowerment. It is about harnessing the collective wisdom of a diverse group, fostering innovation, and navigating through the complexities of our globalized society. The profound wisdom encapsulated in the quote, "Every leader was once a follower," resonates deeply in the modern context. It underscores the fundamental truth that leadership is a journey, not a destination. Every influential leader, from historical icons to contemporary visionaries, has walked the path of learning, emulation, and growth. They have been shaped by the wisdom of their predecessors and the collective experiences of society.

Accepting and imbibing modern leadership involves recognizing the power of inclusivity. It is about embracing diverse perspectives, acknowledging that every individual, regardless of their position, possesses unique insights and skills. In this framework, leadership becomes a collaborative endeavour, where ideas are shared, and decisions are made collectively. Inclusivity fosters a sense of belonging and encourages active participation, creating a society where every voice is heard and valued. Furthermore, modern leadership thrives on empathy and emotional intelligence. Leaders must understand the aspirations and challenges of their followers deeply. By cultivating empathy, they can inspire trust and build meaningful connections. Emotional intelligence enables leaders to navigate complex interpersonal dynamics, resolve conflicts, and foster a positive work environment.

Additionally, modern leadership demands adaptability in the face of rapid technological advancements and societal changes. Leaders must be agile, open to learning, and willing to embrace innovation. They should encourage a culture of continuous learning and experimentation, empowering individuals to adapt and thrive in an ever-changing world. For society at large to accept and imbibe modern leadership, education plays a pivotal role. Educational institutions should emphasize not only academic excellence but also the development of critical thinking, communication, and interpersonal skills. Moreover, fostering a culture that celebrates diversity, promotes inclusivity, and nurtures creativity is essential.

In conclusion, the evolution of leadership in the modern world calls for a paradigm shift—one that celebrates collaboration, inclusivity, empathy, and adaptability. Embracing the wisdom that every leader was once a follower fosters a society where leadership is not limited to a select few but is a shared responsibility, empowering individuals to contribute meaningfully and shape a future that is inclusive, innovative, and harmonious.

Let's understand leading and following first:

The relationship between leaders and followers emerges as a profound and intricate dance, a symbiotic connection that shapes the course of nations, organizations, and societies. Leaders, the torchbearers of vision and direction, stand at the helm, steering the ship toward uncharted horizons. Yet, they are not solitary entities; they are intricately entwined with their followers, the heartbeat of their aspirations and the embodiment of their dreams.

At its core, leadership is not a solitary ascent but a collective odyssey. Leaders are not elevated above their followers; instead, they walk shoulder to shoulder, their fates interlinked. In the act of leading, a leader pledges not just guidance but understanding, empathy, and unwavering support. Their vision becomes a guiding star, illuminating the path for their followers, instilling hope and purpose in their hearts. In return, followers infuse the leader's vision with life, breathing vitality into the dreams that guide the collective toward a shared destiny. Moreover, the relationship between leaders and followers is built on trust, a delicate yet formidable foundation. Followers bestow their trust upon a leader, believing not just in their competence but also in their integrity, empathy, and sincerity. In return, leaders honor this trust with transparency, accountability, and a deep sense of responsibility. This reciprocal trust forms the bedrock upon which great movements, revolutions, and transformations are built.

Leaders inspire, not through coercion or authority, but through the magnetic pull of their character, the authenticity of their actions, and the wisdom of their decisions. They recognize the potential within each follower, nurturing it like a gardener tending to a delicate bloom, allowing it to flourish and contribute meaningfully to the collective tapestry of goals and aspirations. However, in this intricate relationship, leaders find strength in the diversity of their followers—their varied perspectives, experiences, and talents. They embrace dissent as a catalyst for growth, understanding that it is through dialogue and debate that the most profound solutions emerge. Followers, in turn, find solace in the leader's guidance, a sturdy anchor amidst the storms of uncertainty, propelling them to achieve heights hitherto unimagined.

Together, leaders and followers create a harmonious symphony, each note resonating with purpose and determination. The leader conducts, but it is the collective melody of followers' efforts, aspirations, and dedication that gives the music its soul. In this intricate dance, leaders inspire, guide, and unite, and followers, in their unwavering support and dedication, breathe life into the vision. It is a relationship of mutual respect, shared aspirations, and the collective pursuit of greatness—a testament to the indomitable spirit of humanity working together to shape a better tomorrow.

Leading and following – two sides of the same coin:

The roles of leading and following intertwine, creating a profound duality that shapes our societies, organizations, and personal lives. Much like two sides of the same coin, leading and following are not static positions but fluid, ever-transitioning roles that adapt to the challenges and situations thrown at us. This dynamic interplay between leaders and followers is not merely a reflection of authority but a testament to the transformative power of empathy, understanding, and co-dependence.

Leading, in its essence, is not about wielding power or authority; it's about inspiring, guiding, and facilitating growth. A true leader understands the subtle art of listening, learning, and empathizing with those they lead. They recognize that leadership is not a pedestal to stand upon but a responsibility to shoulder. A leader embraces vulnerability, acknowledging that they, too, have moments of doubt and uncertainty. In these moments, they may find wisdom in following, in learning from the experiences and perspectives of others.

Following, on the other hand, is not synonymous with subservience; it's about trust, collaboration, and active participation. Followers are the pillars upon which great leaders stand. Their insights, dedication, and unique perspectives enrich the leadership landscape. A follower is not passive but engaged, offering their expertise, feedback, and creativity. However, even the most dedicated followers find themselves in moments where they must lead—where their expertise or vision guides others forward.

The beauty of this duality lies in its transformative potential. A leader can emerge from the most unexpected of places, driven by passion and a vision for change. Similarly, a leader must be receptive to the collective wisdom of their team, recognizing that innovation often sprouts from the collaborative minds of both leaders and followers.

In today's rapidly changing world, where challenges are multifaceted and solutions are nuanced, the ability to transition seamlessly between leading and following is a valuable skill. It requires humility, adaptability, and a deep understanding of the interconnectedness of all roles within a team or society. Leaders must be adept followers, learning from the diverse talents they lead, while followers must possess the courage to lead when their expertise is called upon.

This co-dependent relationship between leading and following exemplifies the essence of true collaboration and shared responsibility. It transcends the constraints of hierarchy, fostering an environment where ideas flow freely, and innovation knows no bounds. Embracing the duality of leading and following is not just a pragmatic approach but a transformative mindset—one that nurtures growth, fosters inclusivity, and paves the way for a harmonious coexistence where everyone, regardless of their role, contributes meaningfully to the ever-evolving tapestry of progress.

Let us invite success through leadership by repeating some affirmations:

- "I embrace the duality of leading and following, recognizing that each role contributes to my personal and professional growth."

- "I trust in my ability to lead with wisdom and follow with grace, adapting seamlessly to the demands of every situation."

- "I am a confident leader, drawing inspiration from my experiences as a follower, understanding the value of diverse perspectives."

- "I am open to learning from others, acknowledging that success lies not just in leading but in the willingness to follow and absorb valuable insights."

- "I lead with empathy and follow with humility, creating a harmonious balance that fosters cooperation and innovation."

- "I recognize the power of collaboration, understanding that by leading and following effectively, I contribute to a thriving and interconnected community."

- "I am a successful leader because I know when to guide and when to listen, embracing the wisdom of both roles to achieve meaningful outcomes."

- "I find strength in my ability to adapt, seamlessly transitioning between leading and following, ensuring harmony and progress in every endeavour."

- "I honor the journey of growth, celebrating my experiences as both a leader and a follower, knowing that each role has shaped my unique perspective."

- "I trust my instincts to discern when to take charge and when to support, creating a positive impact on those around me through my balanced approach to leadership and followership."

In the dynamic interplay between leading and following, we find the essence of true leadership. Understanding that every leader was once a follower, and that successful individuals discern when to guide and when to learn, enriches our capacity for collaboration and growth. Embracing both roles allows us to navigate the complexities of life with grace, humility, and adaptability. It is in this balance, this seamless transition between leading and following, that we discover the true art of leadership. By recognizing the inherent wisdom in each position, we not only foster harmonious relationships but also pave the way for innovation and progress. As we integrate the lessons from both roles, we not only become better leaders but also contribute meaningfully to the collective human experience, fostering a world where the coherence between leading and following is a symphony of mutual respect and boundless potential.

If It Is to Be, It Is by Us

The origins of impossibility:

In the shadowy corridors of the human psyche, there exists a mysterious creature named Impossibility. Its origins are shrouded in fear, born from the depths of uncertainty and nurtured by the whispers of doubt. Impossibility, with its invisible shackles, weaves a tangled web around the dreams and aspirations of humanity, constraining the limitless potential that resides within every soul.

Imagine a young child, eyes wide with wonder and dreams boundless as the sky. In this innocence, Impossibility is but a distant echo, drowned out by the laughter of imagination. Yet, as the child ventures into the world, the tendrils of Impossibility creep stealthily, whispering tales of inadequacy and limitation. With each setback, every unkind word, Impossibility tightens its grip, casting a veil of doubt upon once-bold ambitions.

Impossibility thrives on fear - fear of failure, fear of rejection, and fear of the unknown. It lurks in the corners of the mind, distorting dreams into nightmares and turning aspirations into unattainable mirages. It whispers, "You cannot," and we, in our moments of vulnerability, listen. It affects us in subtle ways, sowing seeds of hesitation where there could be courage, nurturing self-doubt where there could be confidence. It convinces us that the extraordinary is beyond our reach, that the stars are meant for others to touch, not us. Impossibility paints the sky with shades of gray, obscuring the vibrant hues of our potential.

Yet, amidst this darkness, there is a glimmer of hope. Impossibility, for all its cunning, is a phantom, a creation of the mind. Its shackles, though invisible, are not unbreakable. With each act of bravery, with every leap of faith, we weaken its hold. Courage, after all, is not the absence of fear, but the triumph over it.

Therefore, in the face of Impossibility, we must become warriors of our own narratives. We must recognize that the chains it wraps around our dreams are illusory, and the key to freedom lies within us. By acknowledging the fear that breeds impossibility, we disarm it. By embracing failure as a teacher and rejection as redirection, we diminish its power.

Let us be architects of possibility, builders of bridges over the chasms of doubt. Let us teach our children that the word 'impossible' is but a challenge, a call to action. Let us redefine the boundaries of our capabilities, for in the realm of the human spirit, there are no limits, only unexplored horizons. Impossibility may have fearful origins, but its defeat lies in the courageous hearts of those who dare to challenge it. Let us be among those brave souls, shattering the invisible shackles, and stepping into the boundless expanse of our own potential. For in the face of Impossibility, we shall write a new story - a story of triumph, of resilience, and of the extraordinary made possible.

The beauty of will power:

In the vast symphony of human capabilities, willpower stands as a resounding crescendo, a testament to the indomitable spirit that resides within us. It is the quiet but formidable force that drives us to overcome challenges, to pursue dreams against all odds, and to transform obstacles into stepping stones. Willpower is not just a trait; it is a superpower, a wellspring of resilience and determination that empowers us to navigate the complexities of life with unwavering resolve.

Consider the story of a marathon runner, the beads of sweat glistening on their brow as they press forward against the pull of exhaustion. Their legs ache, their lungs burn, but it is their willpower that carries them through every grueling mile. It is the same willpower that fuels the artist working tirelessly through the night, the scientist conducting endless experiments in pursuit of a breakthrough, and the student poring over books in the quest for knowledge. Willpower is the unyielding belief that propels ordinary individuals to achieve extraordinary feats.

At its core, willpower is a conscious choice – a decision to persevere, to endure, and to triumph. It is a force that resides within each of us, waiting to be summoned in moments of challenge. With willpower, we can transform self-doubt into self-belief, turn setbacks into setups for comebacks, and convert dreams into tangible realities.

The power of willpower lies not only in its ability to overcome external obstacles but also in its capacity to conquer the inner battles that we wage within ourselves. It empowers us to silence the whispers of self-doubt, to defy the limits imposed by our fears, and to rise above our own expectations. With willpower, we can reshape our habits, conquer addictions, and emerge stronger from the storms that life throws our way. Moreover, willpower is contagious; it inspires others to believe in their own capabilities. When one person demonstrates the strength of willpower, it sends ripples of motivation through the collective consciousness of humanity. It serves as a beacon of hope, reminding us that no challenge is insurmountable, no dream too grand, as long as we have the willpower to pursue it.

In the awesomeness of human achievement, willpower weaves the threads of resilience, determination, and courage. It is the force that propels us toward our goals, fuels our passions, and transforms ordinary individuals into extraordinary trailblazers. So, let us harness the boundless power of willpower within us. Let us believe in our dreams, cultivate our inner strength, and face life's challenges with unyielding resolve. With willpower as our guiding star, there is no limit to what we can achieve, and no obstacle that can deter our relentless pursuit of greatness.

Miracle: When impossible turns possible:

Joe Simpson's real-life story of survival in the Andes is nothing short of a testament to human resilience and determination. In 1985, Simpson and his climbing partner, Simon Yates, set out to conquer the unclimbed west face of Siula Grande in the Peruvian Andes.

In the unforgiving embrace of the Peruvian Andes, where the air is thin and the mountains loom like ancient sentinels, a tale of unimaginable courage and tenacity unfolded—one that would etch itself into the annals of human endurance.

Joe Simpson, a seasoned mountaineer, found himself dangling on the precipice of death after a harrowing fall on Siula Grande's treacherous west face. His leg shattered, his body broken, he lay at the bottom of a seemingly endless crevasse, the darkness swallowing him whole. His mind, clouded with pain and despair, teetered on the edge of sanity.

Alone in the icy abyss, Simpson confronted the dreadful extent of his injuries. His leg, twisted and mangled, throbbed with a pain that eclipsed the biting cold surrounding him. In that desolate crevasse, he battled not only the excruciating physical agony but also the haunting specter of loneliness. Yet, in the face of sheer hopelessness, he refused to succumb.

His mental state teetered on the brink of collapse as he grappled with the reality of his situation. Yet, amidst the darkness, a fierce determination ignited within him. He knew he couldn't die alone in that icy chasm. Defying the throes of despair, he dragged himself inch by agonizing inch, his hands raw and bleeding, his spirit undeterred.

The journey back to the camp was a symphony of agony and willpower. Every movement sent waves of torment through his broken body, but he pressed on. With each painful crawl, he whispered words of encouragement to himself, refusing to surrender to the abyss that threatened to engulf him. In the face of unimaginable odds, Simpson's spirit blazed like a defiant flame. His sheer will to survive turned the impossible into a battle cry. He envisioned the camp, a haven amidst the desolation, and clung to that image like a lifeline. The very thought of reaching it became his driving force, a beacon guiding him through the darkness.

Finally, after what felt like an eternity of suffering, he emerged from the crevasse, battered and broken but miraculously alive. His tale of survival echoed through the mountains, a testament to the strength of the human spirit. Joe Simpson's harrowing journey remains a poignant reminder that even in the direst of circumstances, the sheer determination to live can transform the impossible into a testament of unwavering resolve, a story of enduring against all odds that continues to inspire generations.

What do we learn from him?

From Joe Simpson's incredible tale of survival in the Peruvian Andes, we learn several invaluable lessons that resonate deeply with the human spirit:

Determination in the Face of Despair: Simpson's story teaches us the power of determination even in the direst circumstances. Despite insurmountable odds and excruciating pain, he refused to succumb to despair. His unwavering determination became his lifeline.

The Strength of the Human Spirit: Simpson's resilience showcases the incredible strength inherent in every human being. It reminds us that even in the face of extreme adversity, the human spirit has the capacity to endure, overcome, and emerge stronger.

Courage to Face Fear: Simpson's journey exemplifies the courage to confront fear head-on. He faced the terrifying prospect of death and, instead of succumbing to it, chose to fight. His story inspires us to confront our own fears with bravery and fortitude.

Importance of Perseverance: The arduous journey of crawling back to safety despite severe injuries highlights the significance of perseverance. Simpson's refusal to give up, no matter how difficult the path, teaches us the importance of persistence and resilience in the face of challenges.

The Power of Hope: In the depths of despair, Simpson clung to the hope of survival. His story emphasizes the transformative power of hope, reminding us that even a glimmer of optimism can fuel our determination and guide us through the darkest of times.

Lessons in Resilience: Simpson's ability to bounce back from an almost fatal situation showcases the resilience of the human body and mind. It teaches us that resilience is not just a trait but a skill that can be nurtured and developed, enabling us to navigate life's challenges.

The Value of Human Connection: Simpson's refusal to die alone in the crevasse underlines the importance of human connection. His determination to return to his campmates emphasizes the strength we draw from our relationships and the lengths to which we go for those we care about.

Let us repeat some affirmations:

- "I am the architect of my destiny; what I desire to achieve, I shall create with my actions, determination, and belief in myself."

- "I hold the pen that writes my story, and with each choice I make, I shape the narrative of my life."

- "I am the master of my fate; my dreams are not mere possibilities but promises waiting to be fulfilled by my dedication and effort."

- "I trust in my abilities; I am capable, determined, and deserving of the success and happiness I seek."

- "My actions are the seeds of my future; I sow them with purpose, nurture them with perseverance, and reap the harvest of my aspirations."

- "I acknowledge my power to create change; my thoughts, words, and actions manifest the reality I desire."

- "I am the captain of my ship, steering it towards the shores of my dreams with unwavering resolve and unshakable belief."

- "I embrace the responsibility of shaping my own destiny; I am proactive, decisive, and committed to bringing my dreams to fruition."

- "I recognize the boundless potential within me; I am the driving force behind my ambitions, and I have the strength to turn them into reality."

- "I trust in the divine partnership between my efforts and the universe; together, we co-create a future filled with limitless opportunities and abundant blessings."

Leadership Is the Love for Humanity

At its very core, leadership transcends the mere act of guiding others; it embodies a profound love for humanity. True leadership is not about wielding power for personal gain but about selflessly dedicating oneself to the service of others. It stems from a genuine, deep-rooted affection for humanity—a love that fuels a leader's passion to inspire, uplift, and empower those around them. Leaders, driven by this love, understand the intricacies of human emotions, the diversity of perspectives, and the depth of individual experiences. They empathize with the struggles and celebrate the triumphs of the people they lead. This love for humanity translates into actions that foster inclusivity, equality, and compassion.

A leader who loves humanity is a beacon of hope, a source of inspiration, and a catalyst for positive change. Their actions ripple through communities, breaking down barriers, and nurturing a sense of belonging. They prioritize the well-being of others, valuing every voice, every dream, and every aspiration. In their pursuit of a better world, they champion causes that uplift the marginalized, advocate for justice, and stand against discrimination. Their love for humanity fuels their determination to create environments where individuals can flourish, irrespective of their background or circumstances.

Moreover, a leader's love for humanity manifests in their ability to listen intently, to understand without judgment, and to guide with wisdom. It is a love that drives them to invest in the education, healthcare, and overall well-being of their people, recognizing that nurturing the potential within each person is the key to societal progress.

True leaders are not just administrators of tasks; they are compassionate guides, inspiring and empowering others to reach their full potential. This love for humanity manifests in their unwavering commitment to the well-being of those they lead, nurturing a sense of belonging, purpose, and dignity among their followers. Leaders with a genuine love for humanity recognize the inherent worth of every individual, fostering an environment where diversity is celebrated, and each voice is heard and respected. Their decisions are guided not by selfish ambition but by a deep empathy for the struggles, aspirations, and dreams of the people they serve. In the face of adversity, they stand as beacons of hope, demonstrating resilience, kindness, and understanding. Their love for humanity permeates every action, every policy, and every endeavour, creating a legacy of positive change and transformative impact. In a world often marred by division and discord, leaders who embody love for humanity become catalysts for unity, compassion, and progress. Their leadership becomes a testament to the enduring power of love, reminding us that at the heart of every great leader lies an unwavering commitment to the betterment of humanity, illuminating the path toward a more just, compassionate, and harmonious world.

What does our current society reflect on this thought?

NGOs (Non-Governmental Organizations), self-help groups, donation funds, and various societal leaders embody the essence of leadership as the love for humanity. These entities and individuals operate on the premise of making a positive impact, focusing their efforts on addressing societal issues, providing aid, and fostering development. NGOs, often driven by volunteers and funded by donations, tirelessly work to alleviate poverty, provide healthcare, education, and disaster relief, emphasizing their love for humanity through their actions. Self-help groups empower individuals, especially women, to become financially independent, promoting self-reliance and a sense of dignity. Donation funds, whether for education, healthcare, or disaster recovery, channel resources to where they are needed the most, reflecting a profound love for humanity by improving the quality of life for those less fortunate.

Societal leaders, whether in the form of community organizers, activists, or philanthropists, contribute significantly to societal progress. Their leadership is marked by a deep commitment to social justice, equality, and human rights. They advocate for change, challenge injustices, and amplify the voices of the marginalized. Through their initiatives, they provide resources, mentorship, and opportunities, nurturing a sense of hope and belonging among communities. By addressing societal issues at their roots, these leaders not only enhance the well-being of individuals but also contribute to the overall betterment of society.

The leadership displayed by NGOs, self-help groups, donation funds, and societal leaders is invaluable to society and humanity as a whole. Their selfless efforts reflect a genuine love for humanity by promoting social welfare, fostering inclusivity, and advocating for the rights and dignity of every individual. By addressing pressing challenges and championing noble causes, they inspire others, creating a ripple effect of compassion and kindness. In essence, their work embodies the true spirit of leadership as the love for humanity, showcasing the profound impact that dedicated and compassionate leaders can have on the world.

Tony Robbins – a life coach with unwavering love and devotion for humanity:

The perfect example of a successful leader with love for humanity is Tony Robbins.

Tony Robbins stands as a beacon of inspiration in the realm of life coaching, his impact resonating deeply with countless individuals worldwide. His exemplary work transcends mere motivational speeches; it delves into the very core of human potential, unlocking doors to self-discovery and empowerment. With unwavering passion and profound insights, Robbins has guided people to navigate the complexities of life, transforming challenges into opportunities. His teachings evoke introspection, urging us to confront our fears, embrace change, and sculpt our destinies with purpose and resilience. Through his transformative strategies, he has empowered individuals to break barriers, redefine limits, and live lives of fulfilment. Robbins' legacy lies not only in his remarkable ability to ignite change but also in his genuine dedication to helping others. His work serves as a testament to the transformative power of belief, determination, and the unwavering pursuit of personal growth, inspiring us all to reach for our highest potential and live lives of extraordinary meaning.

In the vast landscape of leadership, where authority often overshadows compassion, the story of Tony Robbins shines as a beacon of hope and inspiration. Robbins, renowned globally as a life coach and motivational speaker, has not merely achieved success; he has redefined it by infusing his leadership with an unparalleled love for humanity.

To start with, Robbins' philanthropic journey is a testament to his deep-seated compassion. Through the Anthony Robbins Foundation, he has orchestrated transformative initiatives that echo across continents. One of the Foundation's remarkable projects, the International Basket Brigade, embodies his commitment. Imagine the holiday season, a time of joy for many but a stark reminder of scarcity for others. Robbins, with his unyielding dedication, mobilizes an army of volunteers worldwide. Together, they assemble baskets brimming not only with food but with hope. These baskets, delivered door to door, transcend material value. They signify humanity's interconnectedness and our shared responsibility to uplift one another.

Yet, Robbins' philanthropy extends far beyond festive seasons. He pioneers programs for the homeless, advocating for shelter, sustenance, and dignity. He champions educational initiatives, recognizing education as the cornerstone of progress. His Foundation's efforts echo in the halls of learning institutions, bringing the gift of knowledge to those hungry for it.

Robbins' love for humanity finds its expression in disaster-stricken regions. Natural calamities may shatter communities, but Robbins' love stitches them back together. His foundation stands as a pillar of support, providing relief and rebuilding shattered lives. His impact reverberates in the smiles of children who, despite adversity, find hope in the midst of despair. What makes Robbins' story truly motivational is not merely the financial assistance he provides but his personal involvement. He doesn't sit on the sidelines; he's there, on the ground, actively participating in projects, interacting with the people he helps. His hands-on approach underscores the importance of empathy and human connection in philanthropy. It's a reminder that leadership, at its core, is not about distance but about closeness, understanding, and shared humanity.

Tony Robbins' philanthropic journey is more than a narrative; it's a call to action. It challenges us to look beyond our own lives and extend our hands to lift others. His story resonates with the potential within each of us to be not just successful but significant, not just accomplished but compassionate. It reminds us that true leadership isn't about standing above others but about standing with them, embracing their struggles, and celebrating their triumphs. Robbins' story ignites a spark within us, urging us to become leaders who not only love humanity but actively work to make a difference—one basket, one smile, one life at a time.

Let us repeat a few affirmations:

- "I lead with love, compassion, and empathy, recognizing that true leadership is rooted in the genuine care and respect I have for every individual."

- "My leadership is a beacon of light, illuminating the path of kindness, understanding, and support for all those I guide and inspire."

- "I embrace the diversity of humanity, fostering an inclusive and harmonious environment where everyone's voice is heard and valued."

- "I am a catalyst for positive change, making decisions that prioritize the well-being, happiness, and growth of the people I lead."

- "My love for humanity fuels my determination to create a world where every person's potential is nurtured, and their dreams are encouraged to flourish."

- "I approach challenges with grace and understanding, knowing that every obstacle is an opportunity to demonstrate my love for humanity through perseverance and resilience."

- "I inspire others to act with kindness and compassion, cultivating a culture of love and unity in every aspect of our shared journey."

- "I lead by example, demonstrating that love for humanity is not just a sentiment but a driving force capable of transforming lives and communities."

- "My leadership is a gift to humanity, a testament to the power of love and the positive impact it can have on the lives of others."

- "I commit to continuous growth, learning, and self-reflection, recognizing that my love for humanity deepens as I strive to become a better leader each day."

- "I lead with a heart full of love, fostering an environment where compassion, understanding, and respect are the guiding principles of every decision and action I take."

- "My leadership is a testament to the beauty of human connection; I believe that every interaction is an opportunity to spread love, inspire hope, and create a positive impact in the lives of others."

- "I recognize the inherent worth and potential in every individual I encounter; my leadership is a journey of empowering others to discover their unique strengths and contributions to the world."

- "I approach challenges with a spirit of collaboration and unity, understanding that together, we can overcome any obstacle and create a world where love and empathy triumph over adversity."

- "My love for humanity drives me to serve selflessly, reminding me that leadership is not about authority but about uplifting others, nurturing their dreams, and helping them flourish in the garden of life."

True leaders recognize that their purpose extends beyond authority; it encompasses a profound care for every individual they guide. In embracing the diversity of humanity and fostering an environment of respect and empathy, they create spaces where dreams flourish, and potential blossoms. Leadership, at its essence, is the art of spreading love, inspiring hope, and nurturing the inherent goodness in people. In every act of kindness, in every decision rooted in empathy, leaders show the world the unparalleled power of love, shaping not just destinies but a brighter, more harmonious future for us all.

The First Step for Attaining Wisdom Is Curiosity

"Curiosity is the wick in the candle of learning."
- William Arthur Ward

The age-old saying, "Curiosity killed the cat," has been used to caution against excessive inquisitiveness. However, let us consider an alternative perspective. Curiosity, when channelled positively, is not a perilous endeavour but a beacon that lights the path of knowledge and understanding. It is the driving force behind exploration, innovation, and the relentless pursuit of discovery. In the grand tapestry of human progress, curiosity has been the catalyst for countless breakthroughs, encouraging us to venture into the unknown and uncover the mysteries of the universe. Rather than being a threat, curiosity is the very essence of human ingenuity, inspiring us to push boundaries, challenge assumptions, and embark on transformative journeys. As we delve into the realms of curiosity, we embrace the opportunity to unravel the complexities of life and enrich our understanding of the world, reminding ourselves that, in the pursuit of knowledge, curiosity is not a liability but an invaluable asset.

At first glance, wisdom and curiosity might seem like distinct traits, each with its unique characteristics. Wisdom is often associated with deep insight, sound judgment, and a profound understanding of life, while curiosity typically embodies a thirst for knowledge, a desire to explore, and a tendency to ask questions. However, delving into the intricacies of these traits reveals a profound and intricate relationship between them.

Curiosity, the innate drive to seek understanding and explore the unknown, is the spark that ignites the journey toward wisdom. It serves as the compass guiding us through the vast landscape of knowledge and experience. Curious minds are naturally drawn to unravel mysteries, challenge assumptions, and probe the depths of existence. It is this curiosity that compels us to ask profound questions about the universe, human nature, and the meaning of life.

In the pursuit of answers, curiosity leads us to exploration and learning. We read, observe, experiment, and engage with the world, absorbing knowledge like a sponge. This continuous process of learning shapes our perspectives, expands our horizons, and deepens our understanding of the complexities of the world. Curiosity, therefore, acts as the catalyst that propels us along the path of intellectual and emotional growth.

As we accumulate knowledge and experiences, our curious nature encourages us to reflect deeply upon them. We contemplate the significance of our discoveries, the intricacies of human behavior, and the interconnectedness of all things. This introspection, fuelled by curiosity, lays the foundation for wisdom. It allows us to discern patterns, recognize universal truths, and appreciate the nuances of life.

Wisdom, then, emerges as the profound synthesis of curiosity, knowledge, and reflection. It is not merely the possession of facts but the ability to apply them judiciously and empathetically in diverse situations. Wise individuals possess a keen awareness of their limitations, understanding that the more they learn, the more they realize the vastness of the unknown. This humility, born out of curiosity, is a hallmark of wisdom.

Furthermore, wisdom nurtures curiosity in a cyclical fashion. Wise individuals are open-minded and receptive to new ideas, always eager to explore uncharted territories of knowledge. Their wisdom allows them to approach novel information with discernment, separating the profound from the trivial. Their curiosity remains insatiable, driving them to continuously seek deeper understanding and broader perspectives.

In essence, curiosity acts as the fertile soil from which the seeds of wisdom grow. It initiates the journey, fuels the quest for knowledge, and sustains the ongoing pursuit of understanding. The relationship between wisdom and curiosity, therefore, is symbiotic and transformative. It reminds us that embracing our innate curiosity is not just a gateway to wisdom; it is an enriching and enlightening voyage that shapes the very essence of our being, making us lifelong learners and seekers of profound truths.

Let us ask a lot of questions!

One historical figure known for asking a lot of questions was Socrates, the ancient Greek philosopher. Socrates is famous for his Socratic method, a form of cooperative argumentative dialogue to stimulate critical thinking and illuminate ideas. Instead of providing answers, Socrates would ask probing questions, encouraging his students and interlocutors to think deeply, question assumptions, and arrive at their own conclusions.

Socrates' method of questioning, known as elenchus, involved a series of open-ended questions that forced people to reevaluate their beliefs and explore the underlying principles of their thoughts. Through this process, he aimed to uncover contradictions, inconsistencies, and gaps in reasoning, leading to a more profound understanding of the topic under discussion. The Socratic method, as we know it today, was driven by a deep sense of curiosity about the fundamental nature of knowledge, virtue, and truth.

Socrates believed that genuine understanding could only be attained through relentless questioning. His curiosity was not satisfied with surface-level answers; he sought to explore the underlying assumptions, beliefs, and reasoning behind people's statements. By asking probing questions, he encouraged others to critically examine their own thoughts and beliefs, fostering a spirit of curiosity within them.

Socratic questioning exemplifies the transformative power of curiosity. Instead of merely accepting information at face value, Socrates encouraged individuals to delve deeper, question their assumptions, and engage in thoughtful reflection. This method of inquiry stimulated intellectual curiosity, prompting people to explore different perspectives, consider alternative viewpoints, and expand their understanding of complex issues.

Moreover, Socrates' approach highlights the connection between curiosity and critical thinking. Curiosity serves as the catalyst for questioning, enabling individuals to challenge established norms, explore diverse ideas, and arrive at well-informed conclusions. By embracing curiosity, individuals can cultivate a deeper understanding of the world, encouraging continuous learning and personal growth. In essence, the Socratic method exemplifies how curiosity can be a guiding force in intellectual exploration. It encourages a mindset of inquiry, where questions become pathways to knowledge and understanding. By nurturing curiosity and embracing the spirit of inquiry, individuals can navigate the complexities of life, uncover profound truths, and embark on a journey of continuous curiosity-driven learning, just as Socrates did in his philosophical pursuits.

Socrates' emphasis on questioning and dialogue has laid the foundation for Western philosophy and influenced countless philosophers and thinkers throughout history. His approach highlighted the importance of curiosity, critical inquiry, and self-examination in the pursuit of knowledge and wisdom.

Unleashing Curiosity: A Skill to Cultivate, Not a Gift to Await:

Curiosity, often hailed as the spark of innovation and the gateway to knowledge, is a trait many admire but few believe they possess inherently. The common misconception that curiosity is a divine gift bestowed upon a select few is a myth that deserves to be shattered. In reality, curiosity is a skill, a mindset, and an attitude that can be consciously nurtured and developed. Here's how to initiate and cultivate curiosity within oneself, dispelling the notion that it is an exclusive talent:

- **Cultivate a Growth Mindset:** Embrace the belief that abilities and intelligence can be developed through dedication and hard work. A growth mindset encourages you to see challenges as opportunities to learn, fostering curiosity about new solutions and perspectives.

- **Embrace the Unknown:** Curiosity thrives in unexplored territories. Be willing to step outside your comfort zone, engage with unfamiliar subjects, and ask questions about the world around you. Embracing the unknown with an open mind sparks curiosity and encourages exploration.

- **Ask Questions Liberally:** Cultivate the habit of asking questions. Curiosity flourishes when you inquire about the hows, whys, and what-ifs. Ask questions not only to others but also to yourself. Challenge assumptions and seek deeper understanding.

- **Follow Your Interests:** Curiosity often starts with genuine interest. Follow your passions and hobbies. Dive deep into topics that fascinate you, whether it's art, science, history, or technology. The more passionate you are, the more questions you'll naturally ask.

- **Practice Active Listening:** Actively engage in conversations. Listen to others with genuine interest, and ask follow-up questions. Curiosity is not just about the world but also about people. Everyone's story can teach you something new.

- **Read Widely:** Reading exposes you to a plethora of ideas, cultures, and perspectives. Explore diverse genres and authors. A well-read mind is a curious mind, constantly seeking new knowledge and experiences.

- **Embrace Failure:** Fear of failure can stifle curiosity. Embrace mistakes as learning opportunities. Curiosity flourishes when you are unafraid to explore, even if it means making errors along the way.

- **Practice Mindfulness:** Being present in the moment enhances your ability to observe and wonder. Mindfulness cultivates curiosity about the world as it is, allowing you to appreciate the intricate details often overlooked.

- **Encourage Childlike Wonder:** Children are naturally curious, exploring the world with wide-eyed wonder. Rekindle your inner child; view the world with fresh eyes, appreciating its beauty and complexity.

- **Be Patient:** Cultivating curiosity is a process. It takes time and effort. Be patient with yourself as you develop this skill. Celebrate your moments of curiosity and use them as stepping stones for further exploration.

In essence, curiosity is not an elusive talent reserved for a select few; it is a skill that can be acquired and honed by anyone willing to embrace the wonders of the world. By adopting a curious mindset, asking questions, and being open to new experiences, you unlock the door to a lifetime of learning, growth, and endless possibilities. Curiosity, far from being a gift, is a treasure waiting to be discovered within every individual.

Spirituality Is the Only Answer to the Unanswered

"Spirituality is the art of finding peace in the midst of chaos, light in the darkest corners, and love when the heart feels empty."

In the ancient tapestry of existence, where the threads of the cosmos weave tales of profound wisdom, Sanatan Dharma stands as a luminous constellation, illuminating the path to spiritual enlightenment. Within the sacred embrace of this timeless tradition, spirituality transcends the mundane and becomes a vivid, introspective odyssey, inviting the seeker to delve deep into the realms of the self and the universe.

Self-Realization: The Awakening Within In the whispers of the soul, Sanatan Dharma reveals the secret of self-realization, an exquisite dance between the individual and the divine. It beckons the seeker to explore the boundless landscapes of their own being, to recognize the eternal flame within — the Atman. This journey is not a mere discovery; it is a homecoming, a reunion with the divine essence that unites all living things.

Dharma: Harmonious Existence Amidst the tapestry of moral and ethical threads, Dharma emerges as a radiant jewel. It is not a rigid set of rules but a harmonious melody that resonates with the universe. Each soul is entrusted with a unique dharma, a purpose that intertwines with the cosmic symphony. Living in alignment with one's dharma is a spiritual art, painting life's canvas with shades of compassion, honesty, and selflessness.

Karma: The Cosmic Ledger In the cosmic dance of cause and effect, Karma weaves its intricate patterns. It is the silent architect of destiny, inscribing every action, every thought upon the scroll of existence. Sanatan Dharma teaches that understanding the intricate dance of karma is the key to spiritual growth. By cultivating positive actions and purifying the heart, one ascends the ladder of spiritual evolution.

Yoga and Meditation: Union with the Divine In the sanctuary of breath and body, yoga becomes a sacred communion with the divine. Asanas become graceful hymns, sung by the body to the universe, while pranayama becomes the rhythm of life itself. Meditation, the art of silencing the mind, transforms into a bridge connecting the seeker with the boundless realms of consciousness. It is here, in the quietude of the soul, that one finds communion with the divine.

Bhakti and Jnana: The Language of the Heart and Mind Bhakti, the language of the heart, sings hymns of devotion and love for the divine. It is a sacred river flowing from the depths of the soul, nourishing the spirit with the elixir of love. Jnana, the language of the mind, embarks on a quest for knowledge, unraveling the mysteries of existence through contemplation and wisdom. Together, they form a harmonious symphony, guiding the seeker toward spiritual enlightenment.

Moksha: Liberation's Embrace Beyond the veils of illusion lies Moksha, the ultimate destination of the spiritual odyssey. It is not a destination reached but a state of being, where the soul is liberated from the cycle of birth and death. Moksha is the union of the individual soul with the cosmic consciousness, a transcendent ecstasy that dissolves the boundaries of the self, merging it with the infinite.

In the heart of Sanatan Dharma, spirituality is not a rigid doctrine but a vibrant, living tapestry woven with threads of introspection, devotion, and wisdom. It is an exploration of the self, a communion with the universe, and a journey toward the sublime. This spiritual odyssey, filled with the fragrance of incense and the echoes of ancient mantras, invites every seeker to embark, to discover the profound mysteries within and without, and to find the divine in the very core of their being.

Guardian of Ayodhya: The Divine Intervention:

In the heart of Ramnagri Ayodhya, where ancient temples whispered tales of divine guardianship and the winds carried echoes of prayers, there existed a spiritual aura that transcended the realms of the ordinary. It was in this sacred land, where the legacy of Lord Ram and his devoted disciple Hanuman was revered, that a remarkable incident unfolded in the fateful year of 1998.

As the sun dipped below the horizon, casting a warm glow upon the town, a nefarious plot was hatched by forces seeking to disrupt the peace of Ayodhya. Unbeknownst to the residents, hidden beneath the cover of darkness, a sinister group planted explosives in a strategic location, intending to shatter the tranquillity that enveloped the town.

However, divine forces often work in mysterious ways. That night, a humble troop of monkeys, descendants of Hanuman's lineage, roamed the ancient streets. One particular monkey, bearing an uncanny resemblance to the revered deity himself, was drawn towards the concealed danger. Guided by an unseen hand, the monkey sensed the malevolence that lurked beneath the soil. With instinctual wisdom, the monkey began to investigate the area, guided by an inexplicable sense of purpose. In a dramatic twist of fate, it discovered the hidden explosives and the wires that connected them. Undeterred by the perilous task, the monkey, embodying the spirit of Hanuman, chewed through the wires with a divine determination that seemed to defy the very laws of nature.

As the first light of dawn broke, the town of Ayodhya woke to a scene of astonishment. The explosives, rendered harmless by the courageous act of the monkey, lay defused, their nefarious purpose thwarted. News of the miraculous event spread like wildfire, reaching the ears of the town's residents.

In the days that followed, the story of the divine intervention echoed through the streets of Ayodhya. Many believed that it was not just an ordinary monkey but a manifestation of Hanuman himself, guarding his beloved land from the clutches of destruction. The incident served as a powerful reminder of the spiritual guardianship that enveloped Ayodhya, where divine forces stood sentinel, protecting the town and its people.

The event left an indelible mark on the hearts of the residents, fostering a profound sense of faith and gratitude. The once-sceptical were now devout believers, acknowledging the inexplicable intervention that had saved their town. In the face of adversity, the divine presence of Hanuman had shone brightly, demonstrating that even in the darkest of nights, the light of spirituality could guide and protect, ensuring that Ayodhya remained the sacred haven it was destined to be.

And so, the tale of the monkey that chewed through bomb wires became a legend, a dramatic narrative with a spiritual angle that reinforced the belief that in the town of Ayodhya, where the echoes of ancient chants resonated, divine intervention was not merely a myth but a tangible reality, proving once again that faith and spirituality were powerful forces that could overcome even the most sinister of plots.

Spirituality: The Answer to the Unanswered:

In the quiet corners of our existence, where the noise of the world fades into a hushed whisper, there exists a profound question that echoes through the chambers of the soul — the question of meaning. In the tapestry of our lives, woven with threads of joy and sorrow, triumphs and defeats, there are moments when we find ourselves standing at the precipice of the unknown, gazing into the abyss of existential uncertainty. It is in these moments of profound introspection that we realize we are seekers, forever in pursuit of answers to questions that seem to elude the grasp of our intellect.

In the obscureness of existence, spirituality emerges as the guiding star, illuminating the path to the answers we seek. It is not a mere collection of rituals or dogmas but a profound journey inward, an exploration of the infinite landscapes of the self and the cosmos. Spirituality invites us to embark on a quest that transcends the boundaries of the tangible, urging us to delve into the mysteries of existence with the eyes of the heart and the wisdom of the soul.

At its core, spirituality is the sanctuary where our deepest questions find resonance. It is the mirror that reflects the unspoken inquiries of our spirit, offering profound insights into the nature of reality and the purpose of our existence. In the depths of meditation, in the serenity of prayer, and in the whispers of the wind, we find the subtle hints of the answers we seek. Spirituality is the silent language through which the universe communicates with us, unveiling the secrets of the cosmos one revelation at a time.

In the embrace of spirituality, we find solace in the face of life's uncertainties. It is the balm that soothes the wounds of doubt and fear, reassuring us that there is a divine order in the midst of chaos. When the storms of life threaten to engulf us, spirituality becomes the anchor, grounding us in the unwavering faith that there is a purpose to every experience, even the most bewildering ones. Moreover, spirituality is the bridge that connects us to the collective wisdom of humanity. It is the timeless thread that weaves through the tapestries of various religions, philosophies, and mystical traditions, reminding us that we are part of a grand narrative, a cosmic story that transcends the limitations of time and space. Through the teachings of ancient sages, the scriptures of diverse cultures, and the shared experiences of spiritual seekers, we find echoes of our own questions and the profound answers that have guided humanity through the ages.

In the quest for meaning, spirituality becomes the lantern that illuminates the unexplored corridors of our consciousness. It is the alchemical process through which our doubts, fears, and uncertainties transform into wisdom, love, and inner peace. It is the answer to the unanswered, the key that unlocks the mysteries of existence, and the whispered secret that resonates in the depths of our being.

As we navigate the enigmas of life, let us embark on this introspective odyssey into spirituality, embracing the unanswered questions as invitations to delve deeper into the essence of our existence. In the silence of our contemplation, in the depths of our prayers, and in the vastness of our spiritual journeys, let us discover that the answers we seek are not separate from us but are woven into the very fabric of our souls. Spirituality, indeed, is the answer to the unanswered, inviting us to explore, to wonder, and to awaken to the profound truths that have the power to transform our lives and illuminate our paths with the brilliance of divine wisdom.

Let us repeat some affirmations:

Here are some affirmations to help nurture spiritual growth and mindfulness:

- "I am connected to the divine source, and I trust the journey of my life."

- "Every challenge is an opportunity for spiritual growth, and I embrace them with grace."

- "I radiate love and compassion to all beings, understanding that we are all interconnected."

- "My thoughts are positive, my actions are kind, and my heart is open to the beauty of the universe."

- "I am grateful for the abundance of the present moment and trust in the abundance of the future."

- "I release all worries and doubts, knowing that I am guided and supported by the universe."

- "I am a vessel of peace, and I share this peace with the world."

- "I forgive myself and others, releasing all negativity and embracing the freedom of a light heart."

- "I am mindful of my thoughts, words, and actions, aligning them with my spiritual values."

- "I trust the process of life, and I am patient in my spiritual journey."

Remember, affirmations are most effective when spoken with conviction and repeated regularly. They can help create a positive mindset, enhance self-awareness, and deepen your spiritual connection.

Knowledge, Talent and Potential Is of No Use, If It Is Unused

In the universal quest of glory, few threads are as precious and transformative as knowledge, talent, and potential. These intrinsic qualities are the building blocks of innovation, the seeds of progress, and the foundation upon which extraordinary achievements are crafted. Yet, their mere existence is not enough; they are akin to uncut diamonds waiting to sparkle, dormant until ignited by the flames of purpose and application.

Knowledge, the cornerstone of wisdom, is a beacon illuminating the path of understanding. It encompasses the collective insights of generations, offering a map to navigate the complexities of our world. Talent, the unique flair embedded within each individual, paints the world with vibrant hues of creativity and brilliance. Potential, the latent energy residing within us, is the raw clay from which greatness can be sculpted. However, these invaluable gifts, akin to a treasure trove, remain idle and ineffective when left untapped. Like a library collecting dust, or an artist's palette untouched, their true worth lies in their utilization. Knowledge, talent, and potential find their purpose when they are applied, shared, and cultivated.

It is in the fusion of these elements with action that revolutions are sparked, innovations are born, and societies are transformed. History bears witness to the extraordinary feats accomplished by those who dared to venture beyond the realms of the known, who harnessed their knowledge to challenge the status quo, who nurtured their talents into skills that inspired generations, and who unlocked their potential to leave an indelible mark on the sands of time.

In this age of limitless possibilities, the emphasis lies not only on the possession of knowledge, talent, and potential but also on their active deployment. It is a call to action, a reminder that the dormant can be awakened, the silent can find voice, and the ordinary can achieve the extraordinary. Each untapped idea, unspoken word, and unrealized dream represents a missed opportunity to contribute to the collective growth of humanity.

So, let us embark on a journey of exploration and application. Let us recognize that the true measure of these gifts is not in their mere existence but in the impact they make when unleashed upon the world. By honoring our knowledge, nurturing our talents, and realizing our potential, we not only enrich our own lives but also inspire others to do the same. Together, let us turn the pages of possibility, paint the canvas of innovation, and sculpt the future with the tools bestowed upon us, for knowledge, talent, and potential are not just gifts; they are catalysts for change, awaiting the hands that will shape the world. Let us understand it in a deeper context!

Scenario 1: The Forgotten Library of Rare Books:

In the heart of the town, the library stands as a majestic testament to human knowledge and creativity. Its architecture is grand, and inside, the shelves are adorned with rare, impactful books, representing the collective wisdom of generations. There are volumes on science, philosophy, art, history, and technology, each holding the keys to profound discoveries and insights. The air is heavy with the scent of aging paper, and the silence is broken only by the occasional whisper of pages turning in the wind. Despite its magnificence, the library remains largely deserted. Its doors creak open, but few venture inside. The knowledge within, although vast and transformative, lies dormant, much like untapped talent and potential in individuals.

The books contain blueprints for innovation, solutions to pressing global issues, and the inspiration needed to fuel creative minds. However, without curious readers to explore their contents, these books might as well be blank pages. The library represents the untapped knowledge waiting to be applied. The potential for enlightenment, discovery, and progress is immense, but it remains locked away, a wasted resource that could have otherwise sparked revolutions and catalyzed societal advancements.

Scenario 2: The Unfarmed Fertile Land:

Amidst the picturesque countryside, there stretches a vast expanse of fertile land. The soil is rich, dark, and teeming with nutrients. The sun casts its warm glow upon the land, and the gentle breeze carries the promise of a fruitful harvest. The landowner, however, fails to recognize the potential beneath his feet. Despite possessing this prime agricultural space, he neglects it, leaving the soil untouched by the plow and the seeds dormant in their packets. The land, which could be a source of sustenance and prosperity, remains barren, mirroring the untapped potential within individuals.

The unfarmed land represents the vast, latent potential residing within people. Just as the land has the capability to yield abundant crops and support livelihoods, individuals harbor talents, skills, and ideas that, when nurtured and cultivated, can contribute significantly to society. The failure to farm the land robs the community of a vital food source and economic growth. Similarly, neglecting personal development and allowing talents and potential to lie fallow means missing out on opportunities for self-growth, innovation, and positive contributions to the community and the world at large.

In both scenarios, the tragedy lies not in the absence of resources but in their unused state. The library remains silent, and the land lies idle, emblematic of the unrealized possibilities that exist in the world and within each person. The key to progress and fulfillment lies in recognizing, nurturing, and actively utilizing these resources, whether they are knowledge and talent or fertile land, to create a better, more prosperous future for all.

Let us compare ourselves in this scenario.

A brain full of knowledge and potential is akin to a library of rare books and a fertile land, both scenarios representing vast resources waiting to be unlocked. In this context, the quote "Knowledge, talent, and potential are of no use if unused" emphasizes the critical importance of active application and realization of one's capabilities.

The Brain as a Library of Rare Books:

Imagine the brain as a vast library filled with knowledge, ideas, and potential. Every experience, every piece of information, and every skill acquired is like a precious book in this mental library. However, if this knowledge remains unapplied, it's comparable to the scenario of the forgotten library of rare books. The information, no matter how profound, loses its significance if it's not utilized. Much like untouched books gathering dust, knowledge in the brain loses its transformative power if it's not put into action. Ideas remain unexplored, solutions to problems remain undiscovered, and innovations never come to fruition. The brilliance of the mind, when left idle, becomes a wasted resource, symbolizing the quote's message: knowledge, regardless of its depth, holds no value if it remains unused.

The Brain as Unfarmed Fertile Land:

The brain's potential can also be likened to a piece of fertile land. Just as a farmer must till the soil, plant seeds, and nurture the crops to reap a harvest, individuals must actively engage their potential to yield meaningful results. If the brain's potential remains untapped, it's similar to the scenario of the unfarmed fertile land. Despite its inherent richness, the land fails to produce crops that could nourish the community. Similarly, the untapped potential within the human mind results in a lack of personal growth, missed opportunities, and unfulfilled ambitions. Ideas that could change the world, talents that could inspire others, and skills that could solve complex problems remain dormant, highlighting the profound truth of the quote: talent and potential are worthless if left unexplored.

In summary, the quote underscores the vital importance of action and application in the realm of knowledge, talent, and potential. These inherent qualities, like a library of rare books or a fertile land, hold immense value when utilized. However, if they remain unused, they represent lost opportunities and untapped reservoirs of growth and innovation. The true power of knowledge, talent, and potential lies not in their existence but in their activation, making a difference in both individual lives and the broader world.

How to achieve optimum use of knowledge, talent and potential?

Putting knowledge, talent, and potential to optimum use requires a deliberate and focused approach:

- **Continuous Learning**: Cultivate a thirst for knowledge by embracing lifelong learning. Stay curious, read widely, attend workshops, and explore diverse subjects to expand your understanding.

- **Skill Development**: Identify your talents and skills, then actively work on honing them. Practice regularly, seek mentorship, and invest time in developing expertise in your areas of interest.

- **Setting Goals**: Define clear, realistic, and achievable goals that align with your talents and potential. Break down these goals into actionable steps and create a roadmap to guide your efforts.

- **Embrace Challenges**: Don't shy away from challenges; they are opportunities to grow. Step out of your comfort zone, take on new projects, and be open to learning from failures.

- **Networking:** Surround yourself with supportive and knowledgeable individuals. Engage in meaningful conversations, collaborate on projects, and learn from the experiences of others.

- **Practice Perseverance**: Success often comes to those who persevere. Keep pushing forward, even in the face of setbacks. Learn from failures, adapt, and keep refining your approach.

- **Apply Creativity**: Think innovatively. Find unique ways to apply your knowledge and skills. Creativity can transform ordinary ideas into extraordinary achievements.

- **Contribute to Others**: Share your knowledge and skills with others. Mentorship, teaching, and collaboration not only help others but also reinforce your own understanding and expertise.

- **Stay Adaptable**: The world is constantly evolving. Stay updated with current trends, technologies, and methodologies. Adaptability ensures your knowledge and skills remain relevant.

- **Mindful Reflection**: Regularly reflect on your progress. Assess what works and what doesn't. Adjust your strategies and goals accordingly, ensuring a continuous cycle of improvement.

By integrating these principles into your life, you can harness your knowledge, talent, and potential to their fullest, making a meaningful impact on your personal and professional journey.

Let us repeat a few affirmations:

- "I am a constant learner, and my knowledge grows with every experience. I utilize this knowledge to create meaningful solutions and contribute positively to the world."

- "My talents are unique and valuable. I embrace my strengths and use them creatively to achieve my goals, inspiring others along the way."

- "I recognize my untapped potential and I am committed to unlocking it. I approach challenges with confidence, knowing they are opportunities for growth and innovation."

- "I am the master of my abilities. I use my talents and skills to their fullest extent, bringing passion and dedication to everything I do, and achieving excellence in the process."

- "Every day, I strive to reach new heights. My potential is limitless, and I tap into it fully, creating a positive impact on my life and the lives of those around me."

The world is brimming with untapped creativity, undiscovered talents, and vast knowledge waiting to be utilized. Inaction renders these invaluable gifts dormant, akin to a locked treasure chest. It is not enough to possess knowledge, talent, or potential; their transformative power lies in their active engagement. As we embark on the journey of self-discovery, let us remember that these gifts are not meant to be mere ornaments, but catalysts for change and innovation. Only when we unlock, nurture, and channel them towards meaningful endeavours can we truly harness their limitless potential and make a lasting impact on the world.

Making a Contribution in Anything You Do, Is the Biggest Devotion

In the intricacies of human existence, every action, every effort, and every intention we invest can be seen as threads that weave together the fabric of our existence. Among these threads, the one that stands out in its significance is the act of making a contribution. It is a gesture that transcends the ordinary, a commitment that goes beyond the self, and a devotion that speaks volumes about the depth of one's character and purpose.

At its core, making a contribution is not merely a social obligation; it is a profound testament to our humanity. It is the acknowledgment that our lives are intertwined with others, that our actions ripple through the lives of those around us. Whether in the realm of work, relationships, education, or society, making a contribution means adding value, inspiring change, and fostering growth. It embodies the spirit of selflessness, empathy, and generosity, reflecting the best of what it means to be human.

The act of contributing is transformative, both for the giver and the recipient. It has the power to create connections, bridge gaps, and build bridges of understanding. When we contribute, we invest in the collective progress, fostering an environment where collaboration and cooperation thrive. Moreover, making a contribution instils a sense of purpose, infusing our actions with meaning and fulfilment. It ignites a chain reaction, inspiring others to follow suit, creating a positive cycle of impact and change.

Devotion lies not in the grand gestures, but in the everyday acts of kindness, compassion, and support. It is found in the teacher who imparts knowledge, the friend who lends a listening ear, the volunteer who extends a helping hand, and the professional who dedicates expertise to a cause larger than oneself. It is in the small choices we make, the words we speak, and the actions we take that reflect our devotion to making a difference. Moreover, making a contribution is a journey that requires mindfulness, awareness, and a genuine desire to serve. It calls for empathy, understanding, and the willingness to step into the shoes of others. It is a journey that invites us to explore the limitless ways in which we can give back to the world, leaving it better than we found it.

Therefore, making a contribution is not just a noble act; it is the biggest devotion one can offer to the world. It is a testament to our shared humanity, a celebration of our interconnectedness, and a beacon of hope in a world that often yearns for positive change. So, let us embark on this journey of contribution with open hearts and willing hands, for in our collective efforts, we can truly make a difference that echoes through generations, defining our legacy as individuals and as a society.

The Spiritual Essence of Contribution: A Divine Pathway:

In the quest towards spiritual awakening, the path of contribution stands as a radiant thread, woven with the golden light of selflessness and love. In the realm of the spirit, making a contribution is not just an act; it is a profound expression of our divine nature. It is a sacred act of giving, where the ego dissolves, and the soul finds its true purpose.

The Divine Flow: Spirituality teaches us that we are not isolated beings but interconnected souls, part of a cosmic tapestry woven by the same universal thread. Making a contribution is aligning ourselves with this cosmic rhythm, where we become channels of the divine flow. When we contribute, we open our hearts to the boundless love of the universe, allowing it to flow through us and touch the lives of others. In this divine exchange, we experience the oneness of all creation.

Karma Yoga – The Yoga of Selfless Action: In the ancient teachings of yoga, there exists a path called Karma Yoga, the yoga of selfless action. It emphasizes the importance of performing one's duties and actions without attachment to the results. When we make a contribution with a pure heart, without expecting recognition or reward, we are practicing Karma Yoga. Through this practice, we purify our minds and hearts, aligning ourselves with the divine will.

The Ripple Effect of Love: Every act of contribution, no matter how small, sends ripples of love and kindness into the universe. These ripples touch not only the immediate recipients but reverberate across the cosmos, creating waves of positive energy. Just as a pebble creates expanding circles when dropped into a still pond, our contributions create waves of love that uplift the collective consciousness of humanity.

A Pathway to Spiritual Evolution: Making a contribution is a transformative journey on the spiritual path. It is a way to transcend the limitations of the ego and realize the interconnectedness of all life. When we contribute selflessly, we cultivate virtues such as humility, compassion, and gratitude. These virtues are stepping stones on the path to spiritual evolution, leading us closer to the divine source from which we all emanate.

In the realm of the spirit, making a contribution is not just a noble endeavour; it is a sacred duty. It is an expression of our divine essence and a pathway to spiritual illumination. As we tread this path with reverence and love, we not only uplift others but also elevate our own souls. Let us, therefore, embrace the spiritual essence of contribution, recognizing it as a divine blessing bestowed upon us, and in turn, share this blessing generously with the world.

Making Contributions Count: A Practical Guide to Meaningful Impact:

The significance of our existence lies not just in the breaths we take, but in the contributions we make. However, merely contributing is not enough; it's the intention, depth, and impact of our actions that truly matter. Here's a guide to ensuring your contributions are not just gestures, but impactful and worthwhile endeavours.

Identify Your Passion and Strengths: Understand what ignites your spirit. Your passion fuels your commitment and sustains your efforts. Identify your strengths—what you're good at. Your contributions will be most impactful when they align with your passion and capitalize on your skills.

Educate Yourself: Knowledge empowers meaningful action. Stay informed about the issues you care about. Understand the root causes, historical context, and current challenges. Education sharpens your perspective, enabling you to make well-informed and effective contributions.

Collaborate and Network: No significant change is achieved in isolation. Collaborate with like-minded individuals and organizations. Share ideas, pool resources, and create synergies. Networking expands your reach, allowing your contributions to have a broader and more profound impact.

Be Consistent and Reliable: Reliable contributions build trust. Whether it's volunteering, financial aid, or expertise, consistency is key. Regular, dependable contributions create a stable foundation upon which positive change can be built.

Think Beyond Monetary Contributions: Contributions are not solely measured in monetary terms. Your time, skills, mentorship, and emotional support are invaluable. Sometimes, a kind word or a listening ear can make a significant difference. Assess the various ways you can contribute meaningfully.

Empower Others: The most enduring contributions empower others. Share your knowledge, teach skills, and inspire confidence. Empowered individuals become agents of change, perpetuating the positive impact of your contributions.

Measure Impact, Learn, and Adapt: Establish metrics to measure the impact of your contributions. Reflect on what worked and what didn't. Be willing to adapt your strategies based on the outcomes. Continuous learning ensures your contributions evolve and remain effective.

Practice Gratitude and Humility: Gratitude reminds you of the privilege of being able to contribute. Stay humble; remember that you are part of a collective effort. Acknowledging the contributions of others fosters a culture of mutual respect and strengthens the impact of the entire community.

Inspire and Encourage Others: Your actions serve as a beacon. Share your experiences, challenges, and successes. Inspire others to contribute meaningfully. Encouragement creates a ripple effect, amplifying the positive impact across communities.

Nurture Self-Care: To make sustained, worthwhile contributions, take care of yourself. Nurture your physical, mental, and emotional well-being. Self-care rejuvenates your spirit, ensuring that your contributions continue to be vibrant, compassionate, and impactful.

In making your contributions count, remember that it's not about the scale of your actions but the depth of your commitment and the authenticity of your intention. By approaching your contributions with purpose, knowledge, humility, and empathy, you can truly make a difference that resonates far beyond the immediate moment, shaping a better world for generations to come.

Let us repeat some affirmations together:

Affirmations are powerful tools to reinforce positive beliefs and intentions. Here are affirmations to inspire meaningful contributions with devotion:

- I contribute to the world with love and devotion, knowing that my actions create ripples of positive change.

- Every day, I am guided by the spirit of service and compassion, making a difference in the lives of others.

- My contributions are a reflection of my inner light; I give with sincerity and receive with gratitude.

- I am a channel of divine love and kindness, embracing every opportunity to make a meaningful impact.

- With each act of kindness, I inspire others to contribute meaningfully, creating a chain of goodness in the world.

- I trust in the wisdom of my heart; it leads me to the places and causes where my contributions are needed the most.

- My devotion infuses my contributions with purpose and significance; I am devoted to making the world a better place.

- I am a beacon of hope and positivity, illuminating the lives of those I touch with my heartfelt contributions.

- My efforts, no matter how small, are significant. I contribute with humility, knowing that every contribution counts.

- I am open to receiving guidance and opportunities to contribute; the universe aligns circumstances for me to make a meaningful difference.

- My devotion is unwavering, my actions purposeful; I am dedicated to leaving a lasting legacy of love and service.

- I radiate love, kindness, and generosity; my contributions are a testament to the goodness within me.

- My devotion fuels my determination; I persist in my efforts to contribute meaningfully, even in the face of challenges.

- I am an instrument of positive change, and my contributions create a world filled with love, compassion, and understanding.

- With each contribution, I grow spiritually, aligning myself further with the divine purpose of making the world a more beautiful place.

Repeat these affirmations daily, internalizing their meaning and letting them guide your actions. With devotion and a sincere heart, you will undoubtedly make meaningful contributions that create a profound impact on the world around you.

Leading Life Both Queen Size and King Size Is the Ultimate Inclusion

"Leading life both queen size and king size" encapsulates the essence of gender equality in a profound way, emphasizing the importance of empowering individuals, regardless of gender, to live their lives to the fullest. Traditionally, society has been structured around gender roles, where men and women were assigned specific roles and expectations. However, the modern perspective advocates for a world where individuals, irrespective of their gender, have equal opportunities, rights, and responsibilities.

Equal Opportunities and Choices: Gender equality ensures that both men and women have access to the same opportunities in education, careers, and personal pursuits. It allows individuals to choose their paths based on their interests, skills, and passions, rather than being confined by societal expectations associated with their gender. Whether it's pursuing a career in engineering or becoming a homemaker, both choices are respected and supported.

Economic Empowerment: Gender equality is instrumental in bridging the wage gap and ensuring that women have equal opportunities in the workforce. When women are empowered economically, it not only benefits them but also contributes to the overall economic growth of a nation. Women entrepreneurs, leaders, and professionals bring diverse perspectives, enriching workplaces and fostering innovation.

Shared Responsibilities: In a truly gender-equal society, household and caregiving responsibilities are shared equitably between partners. Both men and women are encouraged to participate in parenting, household chores, and other caregiving tasks. This sharing of responsibilities not only promotes a harmonious family life but also allows individuals to pursue their interests and careers without being burdened by traditional gender roles.

Challenging Stereotypes and Norms: Gender equality challenges harmful stereotypes and norms associated with masculinity and femininity. It promotes the idea that traits such as empathy, strength, ambition, and nurturing qualities are not confined to any specific gender. Breaking these stereotypes creates a more inclusive society where individuals are accepted for who they are, allowing them to express themselves authentically.

Empowering Future Generations: By embracing gender equality, we set an example for future generations. Children raised in an environment where gender equality is the norm grow up with a mindset that values diversity and inclusion. They learn to respect and appreciate the unique qualities and strengths of individuals, irrespective of their gender, paving the way for a more egalitarian society in the future.

Therefore, "leading life both queen size and king size" signifies a world where individuals, regardless of gender, are empowered to lead their lives with dignity, respect, and equal opportunities. Embracing gender equality is not just a societal need but a fundamental human right, fostering a world where everyone can live up to their fullest potential, contributing meaningfully to society, and achieving personal fulfilment.

Spirituality: The balance between divine feminine and the divine masculine:

The interplay between the divine masculine and the divine feminine is fundamental, akin to the yin and yang, the balance of light and dark, and the harmony of creation itself. The universe, in its magnificent orchestration, thrives on this delicate equilibrium, where the masculine and feminine energies coalesce in a dance of cosmic proportions.

The divine masculine embodies qualities of strength, assertiveness, logic, and order. It is the driving force behind creation, the foundation upon which the universe is built. Yet, without the gentle caress of the divine feminine, these raw energies would lack direction and purpose. The divine feminine represents intuition, compassion, nurturing, and creativity. It weaves the threads of life into a meaningful tapestry, infusing existence with beauty and empathy. When these energies are in balance, there is harmony in the cosmos. It is the union of these polarities that brings forth the cycles of life, the birth and decay of stars, the changing seasons, and the very essence of existence. In humans, finding this balance within oneself is a spiritual journey, a quest for inner peace and enlightenment.

Embracing the divine masculine and feminine within us enables a holistic approach to life. It fosters understanding, cooperation, and a deep sense of connection with the universe. Just as day turns into night and summer yields to winter, the interplay of these energies reminds us of the cyclical nature of life. In this harmonious union, we discover our true essence and align ourselves with the universal flow.

To acknowledge and honour both the divine masculine and feminine is not just a spiritual practice but a way of life. It is a recognition of the interconnectedness of all things and an affirmation of the sacred balance that sustains the very fabric of existence. As we integrate these energies within ourselves, we contribute to the equilibrium of the universe, fostering a world of love, compassion, and understanding, where the divine dance of creation continues in all its magnificent glory.

How to strike a balance?

Every human possesses both spiritual masculine and feminine energies within them, regardless of their gender. These energies represent universal qualities such as strength, compassion, creativity, and intuition. Embracing both aspects fosters a balanced, holistic understanding of the self, allowing individuals to access a fuller range of human experiences and emotions, promoting harmony and self-realization.

Embracing the divine feminine in you:

Embracing the divine feminine within yourself is a profound and empowering journey that involves connecting with the nurturing, intuitive, creative, and compassionate aspects of your being. Here are some ways to embrace the divine feminine within you:

- **Self-Acceptance:** Embrace all facets of yourself, including your emotions and vulnerabilities. Allow yourself to feel deeply without judgment. Accept and love yourself just as you are.

- **Connect with Nature:** Spend time in nature to reconnect with the natural cycles of life. Nature embodies the divine feminine energy, and being in nature can help you attune yourself to its rhythms.

- **Cultivate Creativity:** Engage in creative activities that allow your imagination to flow freely. Whether it's painting, writing, dancing, or any other form of creative expression, creativity is a powerful way to channel the divine feminine energy.

- **Practice Intuition**: Trust your intuition and inner wisdom. Learn to listen to your inner voice and follow your instincts. Meditation and mindfulness practices can help you enhance your intuitive abilities.

- **Nurture Others**: Practice acts of kindness and compassion. Nurturing others, whether it's your family, friends, or community, allows you to express the caring and empathetic qualities of the divine feminine.

- **Honoring Your Body:** Treat your body with respect and love. Engage in self-care practices that honor your body, mind, and spirit. This could include yoga, meditation, healthy eating, and adequate rest.

- **Explore Goddess Archetypes**: Study different goddess archetypes from various cultures. Each goddess embodies different aspects of the divine feminine. Learning about these archetypes can help you understand and embrace different facets of your own feminine energy.

- **Embrace Sensuality**: Embrace your sensuality and the physical sensations of being in a body. Sensuality is a natural and beautiful aspect of the feminine energy. Engage in activities that make you feel sensual and alive, whether it's through dance, touch, or other sensual experiences.

- **Create Sacred Space**: Create a sacred space in your home where you can connect with your inner self. This could be a corner for meditation, prayer, or simply a place where you feel safe and connected to your spiritual essence.

- **Celebrate Sisterhood**: Connect with other women who are on a similar spiritual journey. Celebrate the divine feminine together, share experiences, and support each other's growth.

- **Embrace Emotional Intelligence:** Cultivate emotional intelligence by acknowledging, understanding, and expressing your emotions authentically. The divine feminine energy values emotional depth and empathy, allowing for genuine connections with others and a profound understanding of the human experience.

- **Practice Forgiveness and Compassion:** Develop the capacity to forgive, both yourself and others. Embracing the divine feminine involves letting go of grudges and practicing compassion. Forgiveness liberates the soul and opens the heart, allowing love and understanding to flourish in your life.

Remember that embracing the divine feminine is a personal and individual journey. Be patient and gentle with yourself as you explore and integrate these aspects of your being. It's about embracing the wholeness of who you are and honoring the divine feminine within you.

Embracing the divine masculine in you:

Embracing the divine masculine within yourself involves connecting with qualities such as strength, assertiveness, logic, and action. Here are some ways to embrace the divine masculine within you:

- **Self-Reflection**: Take time to reflect on your goals, values, and priorities. Understand your strengths and weaknesses. Self-awareness is a cornerstone of the divine masculine energy.

- **Set Boundaries:** Learn to set healthy boundaries in your personal and professional life. Assertiveness and the ability to say no when necessary are qualities associated with the divine masculine.

- **Physical Fitness:** Engage in physical activities that challenge and strengthen your body. Regular exercise, weight training, or martial arts can help you connect with your physical strength and vitality.

- **Mindfulness and Focus:** Cultivate the ability to be present in the moment. Practice mindfulness meditation to enhance your focus and concentration. The divine masculine is about directed, purposeful action.

- **Leadership and Responsibility:** Take on leadership roles in your personal and professional life. Being responsible for your actions and decisions is a key aspect of the divine masculine energy.

- **Courage:** Embrace challenges and face your fears with courage. The divine masculine is about confronting obstacles and moving forward despite adversity.

- **Logical Thinking:** Develop your logical and analytical thinking abilities. Solve problems, engage in critical thinking, and seek to understand complex issues. The divine masculine energy appreciates logic and rationality.

- **Honoring Traditions:** Respect and honor the traditions and wisdom of the past. Learn from the teachings of ancestors and incorporate valuable traditions into your life.

- **Protector and Provider:** Embrace the roles of protector and provider, not just in a material sense but also emotionally and spiritually. Support and nurture those around you.

- **Express Yourself:** Find healthy ways to express your emotions and passions. Engage in creative pursuits, write, draw, or play music. Expressing your feelings in constructive ways is a manifestation of the divine masculine energy.

- **Mind-Body Balance:** Foster a balance between your physical and mental well-being. Engage in practices like yoga or tai chi that integrate both physical and mental discipline.

- **Connect with Male Role Models:** Seek inspiration from positive male role models who embody qualities of the divine masculine. Learn from their experiences and emulate their positive traits.

Remember that embracing the divine masculine within you does not mean suppressing your emotions or rejecting the divine feminine aspects of your being. It's about finding a balance between these energies, honoring both the strength and gentleness within you, and integrating them harmoniously into your life.

Let us repeat some affirmations:

Affirmations can be powerful tools to connect with both the divine feminine and divine masculine energies within yourself. Here are some affirmations tailored for this purpose:

For Connecting with Divine Feminine:

- "I embrace the nurturing power of the divine feminine within me, allowing compassion and love to flow freely."

- "I trust my intuition and honor my emotions, tapping into the wisdom of the divine feminine energy within my soul."

- "I celebrate the creative force within me, expressing my unique talents and ideas with grace and confidence."

- "I am in harmony with the cycles of nature, recognizing the divine feminine in the ebb and flow of life."

- "My heart is open, and I receive and give love freely, embodying the divine feminine essence of love and empathy."

For Connecting with Divine Masculine:

- "I embrace the strength and determination of the divine masculine within me, empowering me to overcome challenges with resilience."

- "I trust my logic and intuition in perfect balance, making decisions that align with my highest purpose."

- "I take bold and decisive action in pursuit of my goals, embodying the divine masculine energy of assertiveness and courage."

- "I am a provider and protector, nurturing my loved ones and creating a safe space for growth and love."

- "I honor the divine masculine within me, recognizing that my power is a force for positive change in the world."

Repeat these affirmations regularly, with conviction and belief, to reinforce your connection with both the divine feminine and divine masculine energies within yourself. Over time, these positive statements can help you align with these energies, fostering a sense of balance and harmony in your life.

There Is So Less We Know About Ourselves. Self-Realization Leads to True Glory

Self-realization, the profound journey of understanding oneself at the deepest level, is not just a personal endeavor but a transformative odyssey that leads to true glory. In a world often marred by superficial achievements and external validations, the essence of self-realization is a beacon of authentic living and profound wisdom.

At its core, self-realization involves peeling away the layers of societal conditioning, ego, and material attachments to discover the pure essence of one's being. It is a process of introspection, self-exploration, and spiritual awakening. Through self-realization, individuals gain a heightened awareness of their thoughts, emotions, and actions, leading to a profound understanding of their purpose in life. The journey towards self-realization is not an easy one. It demands courage to confront one's fears, honesty to face one's flaws, and resilience to navigate the complexities of the inner self. Yet, in this arduous expedition, one finds the truest form of freedom. Liberation from self-imposed limitations and societal expectations paves the way for the emergence of the authentic self, unburdened by illusions and falsehoods.

Self-realization is not about egoic pursuits or selfish desires. Instead, it fosters empathy, compassion, and a genuine connection with others. When individuals realize their interconnectedness with the universe, they naturally extend their understanding and kindness to all living beings. This interconnectedness fuels a sense of responsibility towards the world, inspiring actions that promote harmony, equality, and environmental stewardship.

Furthermore, self-realization is the cornerstone of enduring happiness. In a world where external circumstances are constantly in flux, the internal peace derived from self-awareness remains unwavering. Material possessions and external achievements might bring temporary pleasure, but the profound contentment arising from self-realization transcends fleeting moments of happiness. It is a state of being that remains undisturbed by external chaos, a sanctuary of tranquillity amidst life's storms. Moreover, self-realization is the key to unlocking one's full potential. When individuals understand their innate talents, passions, and purpose, they are better equipped to contribute meaningfully to society. It ignites creativity, innovation, and a sense of purpose that propels individuals towards their goals. By aligning their actions with their authentic selves, they become catalysts for positive change, inspiring others to embark on their own journeys of self-discovery.

In the pomp and grandeur of life, self-realization is the golden thread that weaves through the fabric of existence. It is the essence of true glory, the radiance that emanates from individuals who have delved deep within themselves and emerged with profound wisdom and self-awareness. Those who embark on this transformative odyssey not only illuminate their own lives but also light the path for others, guiding humanity towards a future where self-realization is revered as the ultimate achievement, and true glory is synonymous with inner enlightenment.

Self-enlightenment or self-realisation?

The spiritual journey of Gautama Buddha, one of the most revered figures in the history of spirituality, is a profound tale of self-realization that unfolded through deep introspection, meditation, and enlightenment. His story is woven with spiritual details and insightful dialogues that have inspired seekers for centuries.

In the opulent palace of Kapilavastu, Prince Siddhartha, destined for kingship, was shielded from the harsh realities of life. However, his spiritual journey began with a stirring discontentment within him. One night, he ventured out of the palace and encountered the elderly, the sick, and the deceased. Stricken by the inevitability of suffering, he embarked on a quest for understanding the nature of existence.

Siddhartha, witnessing suffering for the first time, exclaimed, "Why is there pain? Why is there sorrow?"

A wise sage passing by responded, "Suffering is inherent in the cycle of life, yet there is a path to transcend it. It begins with understanding the self."

Renouncing his princely life, Siddhartha embraced asceticism. For years, he lived in the forests, practicing extreme austerities and engaging in profound meditative practices. Yet, enlightenment eluded him.

Siddhartha, emaciated and weary, asked a group of ascetics, "How can one attain liberation from suffering?"

An elder ascetic replied, "True liberation comes not through self-mortification but through understanding the middle path - the balance between indulgence and austerity."

Siddhartha, realizing the futility of extreme practices, decided to meditate under the Bodhi tree. There, he delved deep into his consciousness, battling the illusions of the mind and the temptations of Mara, the embodiment of desire.

Mara, tempting Siddhartha, sneered, "Who do you think you are to attain enlightenment?"

With unwavering determination, Siddhartha replied, "I am the universe; I am boundless. The illusions that bind me are but creations of the mind. I conquer them with self-realization."

Under the Bodhi tree, Siddhartha attained enlightenment. He saw the interconnectedness of all beings, the impermanence of existence, and the path to liberation from suffering - the Four Noble Truths and the Eightfold Path.

Siddhartha, now the Buddha, declared to his disciples, "The truth of suffering is universal. It arises from attachment and ignorance. But there is a path - a path of righteousness, mindfulness, and compassion. Follow it, and you shall find liberation."

The Buddha spent the rest of his life teaching the Dharma, guiding countless souls toward self-realization and enlightenment. His dialogues and sermons echoed the essence of his own journey, inspiring generations to seek truth within themselves.

In the journey of spiritual evolution, the journey of Gautama Buddha stands as a testament to the power of self-realization. Through his wisdom and compassion, he illuminated the path for humanity, emphasizing that the ultimate truth and glory lie within, awaiting discovery through the profound journey of self-awareness and enlightenment.

From Self-reflecting to self-realisation:

Once, in the dense forests of ancient India, there lived a ruthless robber named Ratnakar. He was feared by all, his name whispered in dread around campfires at night. One day, as he prepared to loot a group of travellers, he encountered the sage Narada, known for his wisdom and compassion.

Narada, aware of Ratnakar's sinister intentions, calmly approached him. "Why do you commit such heinous acts?" Narada asked, his voice gentle yet firm.

Ratnakar scoffed, "Why should I care? My family approves of my ways; they depend on the riches I bring home."

Narada, with a wisdom that penetrated the soul, challenged him, "Go and ask your family if they would share the burden of your sins."

Intrigued, Ratnakar returned home and posed the question. To his shock, his family vehemently disowned him, refusing to be associated with his crimes.

Feeling a pang of remorse he had never felt before, Ratnakar returned to Narada, his eyes clouded with guilt and confusion. "I am lost," he confessed. "How can I atone for my sins?"

Narada, recognizing the sincerity in Ratnakar's voice, smiled gently. "Repentance and penance are the first steps toward redemption," he said. "Meditate on the divine, let your heart and soul seek forgiveness."

Driven by newfound purpose, Ratnakar retreated into the depths of the forest, determined to cleanse his soul. He sat in deep meditation, his chants filling the air as he sought redemption. Such was his dedication that anthills grew around him, hiding his body from the world.

As Ratnakar immersed himself in his penance, the divine, moved by his sincerity, decided to test his resolve. One day, the divine voice echoed around him, "Ratnakar, you have transformed yourself. You shall now be known as Valmiki, 'the one born out of ant-hills.' Your story will inspire generations."

With these words, Valmiki was chosen to be the vessel through which the epic tale of Lord Rama, the embodiment of righteousness and virtue, would be narrated to the world. Valmiki's penance had purified his heart, and his transformation from a ruthless robber to a sage was complete.

Valmiki embraced his newfound purpose with humility and dedication. He composed the Ramayana, a timeless epic that echoed the principles of dharma, love, and sacrifice. His story became an inspiration, illustrating that the path from self-reflection to self-realization was open to all, regardless of their past.

Generations later, people would sit around campfires, not whispering his name in dread, but chanting it with reverence, honoring the journey of a man who had once been lost in darkness but had found his way to the light through repentance, reflection, and divine grace.

Valmiki's transformation from a ruthless robber to a revered sage signifies the immense power of self-realization, repentance, and divine grace. His life story teaches that no one is beyond redemption, and the path to righteousness is always open to those who genuinely seek it. Valmiki's journey stands as a beacon of hope, inspiring souls to embark on their own transformative paths, no matter how dark their past may be. Furthermore, Valmiki's tale served as a beacon of hope, reminding humanity that redemption was always attainable for those who earnestly sought it.

What do we learn from this?

In the vast realm of self-discovery, we often stand on the precipice of our own depths, realizing that there is so much more to fathom about who we truly are. Despite our continuous introspection and self-exploration, the intricacies of our minds, emotions, and spirits remain enigmatic. The more we learn, the more we comprehend the boundless complexity of our being. This realization, though humbling, is also profoundly liberating.

Accepting the notion that there is so less we know about ourselves opens the door to endless possibilities. It encourages us to approach life with curiosity and humility, ready to learn from every experience, every person, and every emotion. It invites us to embark on a perpetual journey of self-discovery, embracing the mysteries within us with wonder and reverence.

In this ongoing quest for self-knowledge, we find the beauty of human existence. It is the exploration of the unknown within ourselves that fuels our growth, compassion, and empathy. As we peel back the layers of our identity, we unearth hidden strengths, untapped talents, and unexplored passions, illuminating the path to self-realization.

So, let us embrace the enigma of our existence with open hearts and open minds. Let us celebrate the endless possibilities that come with the realization that there is so less we know about ourselves. In this acknowledgment, we find the freedom to evolve, to transform, and to become the fullest expression of our authentic selves.

Here are a few affirmations to help you with self-realisation:

- "I am on a journey of self-discovery, and I embrace every aspect of who I am, knowing that self-realization leads to true freedom."

- "I trust the wisdom of my inner self. Through self-reflection and awareness, I unlock the doors to my true potential."

- "Every experience in my life is a stepping stone to self-realization. I learn and grow from each moment, gaining deeper insights into my authentic self."

- "I release all self-doubt and embrace my worthiness. I am deserving of self-realization, and I trust in my ability to achieve it."

- "I am a unique and valuable individual. I honor my journey, and I am open to the profound transformations that come with self-realization."

- "I am connected to the divine wisdom of the universe. Through self-reflection and spiritual practices, I awaken my inner knowing and achieve self-realization."

- "I release fear and embrace love. Love for myself and for others guides me on my path to self-realization, illuminating the way to a fulfilling life."

- "I am in tune with my intuition. I trust the whispers of my heart and soul, leading me towards self-realization and profound spiritual awakening."

- "I forgive myself for past mistakes and let go of guilt. Through self-realization, I embrace my imperfections, learning and growing from every experience."

- "I am a being of immense potential. Self-realization is my birthright, and I commit to exploring the depths of my soul to achieve true enlightenment."

Me and We Are Incomplete Without Each Other. It Is Always You and Around You

The adage "darkness under the lamp" carries profound wisdom about self-awareness and the nature of existence. It suggests that sometimes, what we seek is right in front of us, yet we fail to recognize it due to our limited perspective or lack of self-awareness. This concept resonates deeply with the idea that "Me and we are incomplete without each other. It is always you and around you."

In the vastness of universal experiences, our individuality (represented by "Me") and our interconnectedness with others (symbolized by "we") are inseparable threads. Our personal growth and self-realization often stem from interactions with the world around us, with "we" representing the collective experiences, relationships, and wisdom we gather. Likewise, our individuality influences and enriches the collective consciousness of the communities we are part of.

The phrase "It is always you and around you" emphasizes the constant interplay between the self and the external world. Our perceptions, beliefs, and actions not only shape our own reality ("you") but also influence the environment and people ("around you") we encounter. This mutual influence creates a dynamic relationship, highlighting the intricate balance between personal identity and social interconnectedness.

When we fail to recognize the wisdom and opportunities within ourselves and the immediate surroundings ("darkness under the lamp"), it signifies a lack of self-awareness or mindfulness. Often, the answers to our questions, the solutions to our problems, and the fulfillment of our desires are within our reach, but they elude us due to our preconceptions or distracted minds.

Embracing the adage and the insight that "Me and we are incomplete without each other. It is always you and around you" encourages us to cultivate self-awareness, mindfulness, and a deeper connection with our surroundings. By acknowledging the intricate relationship between self and others, we open ourselves to the richness of human experience, realizing that the light of understanding and fulfillment is ever-present, waiting to be discovered in the most familiar places and within ourselves.

The Me and the WE!

Let's consider a real-life scenario in a community garden to further illustrate the concept:

In a bustling urban neighborhood, a community garden becomes the heart of the community. Residents from diverse backgrounds (representing the "we") come together to grow fresh produce, herbs, and flowers collectively. Among them is Sarah, a retired botanist with a wealth of knowledge about plant species and soil health (the "Me").

One day, the community faces a challenge: a mysterious disease starts affecting the tomato plants. Sarah, with her expertise, recognizes the symptoms and identifies the issue as a soil-borne disease. She knows the solution lies in planting marigold flowers, which naturally repel the disease-causing organisms.

However, some gardeners are unaware of this solution, representing the "darkness under the lamp." Sarah, understanding the importance of sharing her knowledge, organizes a workshop. During the workshop, she educates the community about companion planting and the benefits of marigold flowers. The gardeners, now enlightened, enthusiastically plant marigolds alongside the tomatoes.

As a result of this collective effort ("Me" sharing knowledge with "we"), the tomatoes thrive. The garden not only produces a bountiful harvest but also becomes a hub of learning and collaboration. The gardeners realize that the solution to their problem was within their reach, in the form of Sarah's expertise and the simple marigold flowers ("you and around you").

This real-life scenario showcases how individual expertise and communal collaboration are essential in addressing challenges. It emphasizes that the brilliance of the solution was right there, within the community, waiting to be illuminated through shared knowledge and teamwork. In this way, the community garden becomes not just a source of fresh produce but also a symbol of the collective wisdom and completeness that arises when "Me and we" work hand in hand.

The farmer's lesson:

Although we all have heard this story numerous times, yet let us repeat it once again and revisit our childhood.

Setting: A sprawling estate with rolling fields, an opulent farmhouse, and a sense of wealth and grandeur. The wealthy farmer, Mr. Thompson, faces a dilemma as his four sons - Robert, William, James, and Edward - quarrel over their inheritance.

The grand dining hall echoes with heated arguments as the four sons confront their father.

Robert: "Father, I deserve the largest portion of the land. I have worked the hardest!"

William: "No, it should be divided equally among us. We are all your sons, after all!"

James: "This estate is my birthright! I won't settle for less!"

Edward: "I just want my fair share, Father. Is that too much to ask?"

Mr. Thompson, deeply troubled, decides to teach them a lesson.

Each son is sent away with a portion of the estate. Alone, they face unexpected challenges.

Robert: Struggles to manage his land and resources, facing drought and crop failure.

William: Encounters financial trouble, unable to maintain the estate's grandeur.

James: Deals with a pest infestation, threatening his agricultural yield.

Edward: Faces social isolation, lacking the support and community of his family.

Each son faces their difficulties, realizing the weight of their individual burdens.

The sons, weary and disheartened, return home. Mr. Thompson gathers them in the grand hall, presenting a bundle of sticks.

Mr. Thompson, the wise farmer, observes his sons' struggles and decides to impart a crucial lesson. He presents each son with a single stick, symbolizing their individuality and self-reliance.

Mr. Thompson (to Robert): "Try to break this stick, Robert."

Robert, determined, tries to snap the stick in half, but it breaks easily.

Mr. Thompson (to William): "Your turn, William."

William attempts to break his stick, encountering little resistance, and it breaks without much effort.

Mr. Thompson (to James): "Now, James, your turn."

James, with confidence, tries to break his stick, but it too breaks effortlessly.

Mr. Thompson (to Edward): "And you, Edward."

Edward, the youngest son, also breaks his stick without much difficulty.

The room is filled with a momentary silence as the sons look puzzled, wondering what their father's point might be. Mr. Thompson then reaches for the bundle of sticks, tightly bound together.

Mr. Thompson: "Now, I want each of you to try and break this bundle of sticks."

One by one, the sons attempt to break the bundle, but despite their combined efforts, they fail. The bundle remains intact, unyielding to their strength.

Robert: "Father, it's impossible. These sticks won't break."

Mr. Thompson (smiling): "Exactly. Individually, like these single sticks, you are vulnerable and easily overcome. But together, like this bundle, you create a formidable force. 'Me and we' are incomplete without each other. It is always 'you and around you.' Your strength lies in unity and collaboration."

Mr. Thompson: "Each of you tried to face your challenges alone, like these single sticks. Look at what happens when I bind them together."

He proceeds to bundle the sticks together, forming a strong unit.

Mr. Thompson: "Individually, you are vulnerable, like these sticks. But together, you create an unbreakable bond. 'Me and we' are incomplete without each other. It is always 'you and around you.'"

The realization dawns upon the sons as they grasp the profound truth their father has just revealed. They begin to understand the power of working together, appreciating that their collective strength far surpasses their individual efforts.

The sons, humbled by their experiences and their father's wisdom, come to understand the importance of unity.

Robert: "I see now. We are stronger together."

William: "We need to work as a team, not against each other."

James: "Father, we were blinded by our desires. Thank you for showing us the way."

Edward: "Let us embrace the 'we,' Father. Together, we can overcome any challenge."

The family embraces each other, realizing that their true wealth lies not in the land, but in their unity.

In this tale, the wealthy farmer's wisdom and the symbolism of the sticks illustrate the profound truth that unity and collaboration are essential, especially in the face of challenges. The story serves as a reminder that the power of 'we' is far greater than the sum of its individual parts, emphasizing the importance of togetherness and cooperation in overcoming adversity and achieving shared success.

In this moment, the symbolism of the sticks becomes a powerful metaphor, illustrating the importance of togetherness, teamwork, and the interdependence of individual and collective strength. The sons recognize that embracing the "we" concept is not just a lesson in family unity but a guiding principle for life, reminding them that their true power lies in their ability to collaborate and support each other, no matter the challenges they face.

Let us repeat some affirmations:

- "I honor my individuality (Me) and cherish the power of unity (We). Together, we create a harmonious balance, reminding me that 'Me and we' are incomplete without each other."

- "I recognize that my strength (Me) is amplified when I collaborate and support others (We). In this unity, I find resilience, compassion, and boundless potential."

- "I embrace the interconnectedness of life, understanding that my actions affect not just myself (Me) but also the world around me (You and Around You). With awareness, I contribute positively to the collective tapestry of existence."

- "I celebrate my uniqueness (Me) while appreciating the diversity and richness of the communities I am a part of (We). It is in this diversity that I find inspiration, learning, and growth."

- "I acknowledge that my dreams and aspirations (Me) are woven into the dreams of those around me (We).

Together, we create a shared vision, reminding me that 'Me and we' are incomplete without each other."

- "I find strength in my solitude (Me) and solace in my connections with others (We). In this delicate dance, I recognize the constant interplay of 'you and around you,' reminding me of the beauty of human connection."

- "I respect the value of collaboration and cooperation (We), understanding that my individual efforts (Me) are enhanced when harmonized with the collective wisdom and support of those around me."

- "I acknowledge the impact of my thoughts and actions on the world (Me), fostering empathy and understanding (We) in my interactions. In this awareness, I realize the perpetual dance of 'you and around you.'"

- "I cultivate self-love and acceptance (Me), recognizing that these qualities empower me to love and appreciate others (We). Together, we create a circle of love that expands endlessly, embodying the essence of 'Me and we.'"

- "I find fulfillment in serving others (We), understanding that my purpose (Me) is intricately connected to the well-being of the community around me. In this symbiotic relationship, I find purpose and meaning."

Embracing Your Ignorance Is the First Step Towards Wisdom

In the vast expanse of existence, ignorance and wisdom, like two cosmic dancers, twirl around the essence of human understanding. They are not adversaries but companions, intricately linked, shaping the narrative of our lives. Imagine them as two sides of an ancient, weathered coin, each side bearing the weight of its unique significance.

Ignorance is akin to a mysterious veil, shrouding our minds in a haze of the unknown. It is not a void but a canvas waiting to be painted. In ignorance, there is curiosity, a fertile ground where questions sprout like delicate buds, seeking the nourishment of knowledge. It is the first chapter of every story, the initial stroke on the canvas of learning. Ignorance is the hum of anticipation before the melody of wisdom begins, the fertile soil from which the tree of knowledge grows.

Wisdom, on the other hand, is the illuminating light that pierces through the darkness of ignorance. It is the product of curiosity nurtured, questions answered, and experiences assimilated. Wisdom is not static; it is a river that flows, shaping the landscape of our thoughts and actions. It transforms ignorance into understanding, fear into courage, and confusion into clarity. Wisdom is the culmination of countless stories, the masterpiece painted with the hues of experience and reflection.

Picture a dance, slow and rhythmic, where ignorance and wisdom move in harmony. Ignorance takes the lead, guiding us into the realms of curiosity. It is the dancer's whisper, sparking the desire to explore, to question, to seek. Wisdom follows, gracefully stepping in, weaving intricate patterns of comprehension through the threads of ignorance. It is the dancer's eloquence, translating the language of the unknown into the poetry of understanding.

The coin of life, embossed with ignorance on one side and wisdom on the other, is constantly flipping, marking the cyclical nature of human knowledge. As we journey through life, we flip this coin with every experience, every lesson learned, and every challenge overcome. Sometimes it lands on ignorance, reminding us of the vast mysteries yet to unravel. At other times, it lands on wisdom, showcasing the brilliance of human intellect and the power of comprehension.

In acknowledging that ignorance and wisdom are intertwined, we embrace the duality of our existence. We recognize that every moment of ignorance is an opportunity for wisdom to emerge. We understand that the dance of light and shadow is essential, for it is within this dance that the most beautiful stories are written. Ignorance and wisdom, two sides of the same coin, remind us that life's journey is not about reaching a destination but about savoring the dance, finding joy in every twirl, and marveling at the ever-changing patterns they create.

The Importance of Ignorance: A Gateway to Knowledge:

In the pursuit of wisdom, it is paradoxically the acceptance of ignorance that becomes the foundation upon which knowledge is built. Ignorance, often viewed as a lack, is, in fact, the canvas upon which curiosity paints its first strokes. It is the fertile soil in which the seeds of inquiry are sown.

Embracing our ignorance is an acknowledgment of our limitless capacity to learn. It is the realization that there is always more to discover, encouraging us to ask questions, explore the unknown, and seek understanding. In the face of ignorance, curiosity becomes our guiding star, leading us toward enlightenment. Moreover, ignorance fosters humility. It humbles us, reminding us that no matter how much we know, the universe is infinitely vast, with mysteries that continue to elude even the brightest minds. This humility breeds empathy and openness, encouraging us to listen to diverse perspectives and learn from others.

Ignorance also fuels innovation. The gaps in our knowledge inspire researchers, scientists, and thinkers to delve deeper, to push the boundaries of what is known. Every scientific breakthrough, artistic masterpiece, and philosophical revelation starts with a question born out of ignorance. In essence, ignorance is not a state of darkness, but a doorway to the light of knowledge. It is the first step on the journey to wisdom, prompting us to explore, question, and grow. So, let us embrace our ignorance, for within its depths lies the spark that ignites the flames of curiosity and drives us toward the boundless horizons of understanding.

The Ignorance of Socrates:

The wisest man alive on earth, was ignorant. Let us know how.

the story of Socrates' encounter with the Oracle at Delphi and his realization of his own ignorance, as recounted in Plato's "Apology," with additional dialogues and details:

Socrates, the renowned philosopher of ancient Greece, was troubled by a statement made by the Oracle at Delphi, the prophetic priestess of the Temple of Apollo. The Oracle had declared that no one was wiser than Socrates. Perplexed by this pronouncement, Socrates decided to unravel the meaning behind these words.

Socrates (to himself): "How can I be the wisest man alive? I must investigate this further."

Socrates embarked on a journey, questioning the intellectuals and craftsmen of Athens, seeking someone wiser than himself.

Socrates approached a prominent politician, known for his eloquence and influence.

Socrates: "Tell me, wise statesman, what do you know that I do not?"

Politician: "I know the art of governance, of leading the city to prosperity."

Socrates: "But do you truly understand the nature of justice and virtue, or are you merely skilled in persuasion?"

The politician was left silent, realizing he lacked a deep understanding of fundamental truths.

Next, Socrates turned to a renowned poet, celebrated for his verses and creativity.

Socrates: "Dear poet, enlighten me with your wisdom. What profound knowledge do you possess?"

Poet: "I can weave words into beauty, capturing the essence of life's emotions."

Socrates: "Yet, can you explain the deeper meaning of your poetry, the truths that lie beneath the surface?"

The poet faltered, realizing his poetic brilliance did not necessarily translate into profound understanding.

Finally, Socrates approached a skilled craftsman, known for his meticulous workmanship.

Socrates: "Master craftsman, surely your expertise grants you great wisdom. What can you teach me?"

Craftsman: "I can mold materials into intricate shapes, creating artistry from raw elements."

Socrates: "But do you comprehend the essence of existence, the purpose of life that transcends the physical realm?"

The craftsman paused, realizing his expertise was limited to his craft.

Socrates, after his encounters, reflected deeply on his conversations and the Oracle's words. He realized that while others claimed knowledge, they were ignorant of their own ignorance. In contrast, Socrates was aware of his lack of knowledge, a realization that made him wiser.

Socrates (to himself): "I am the wisest man alive, for I know one thing, and that is that I know nothing."

This profound insight became the cornerstone of Socratic wisdom, emphasizing the importance of acknowledging one's ignorance as the first step toward true enlightenment.

In this story, the dialogues highlight Socrates' humble quest for wisdom and his realization that true wisdom begins with the acceptance of one's ignorance. It illustrates the transformative power of self-awareness and the willingness to question, a fundamental principle that continues to inspire seekers of knowledge and truth to this day.

Embracing Your Ignorance: The Gateway to Wisdom:

In the vast tapestry of human eperiences, there is an intrinsic desire to unravel the mysteries of the universe, to understand the complexities of life, and to gain wisdom that illuminates our path. Paradoxically, the first step toward true wisdom lies not in the acquisition of knowledge but in embracing one's ignorance.

The Humility of Ignorance: Acknowledging what we do not know requires profound humility. It is a brave admission that there are vast realms of understanding, unexplored and undiscovered. This humility forms the bedrock upon which the foundation of wisdom can be built. When we embrace our ignorance, we open ourselves to learning with an uncluttered mind, ready to absorb knowledge like a sponge, unburdened by preconceived notions.

The Curiosity of the Childlike Mind: Children, with their unbridled curiosity, exhibit a remarkable acceptance of their ignorance. They ask questions incessantly, unafraid to admit they do not know. This childlike wonder, coupled with the acceptance of not knowing, is the essence of lifelong learning. Embracing ignorance is akin to nurturing the curiosity of a child within ourselves, encouraging a continuous thirst for knowledge and understanding.

The Journey of Exploration: Embracing ignorance propels us on a journey of exploration. It kindles the spirit of inquiry, leading us to question, analyze, and seek answers. This journey, often challenging and uncertain, transforms ignorance into a powerful driving force for discovery. It urges us to venture into the unknown, where we confront our limitations and expand the boundaries of our understanding.

The Evolution of Perspective: Wisdom, born from the acceptance of ignorance, shapes our perspective. It enables us to perceive the world with open-mindedness, empathy, and tolerance. When we realize the vastness of our ignorance, we become more receptive to diverse viewpoints and ideas. Our judgments soften, and we embrace the rich tapestry of human experiences, acknowledging that every person we meet can teach us something valuable.

The Humble Student of Life: Embracing ignorance transforms us into humble students of life. We become receptive to the teachings of nature, the wisdom of cultures, and the experiences of others. Every failure becomes a lesson, every mistake a stepping stone, guiding us toward greater understanding. We learn to appreciate the subtleties of life, finding wisdom not only in books but also in the rustle of leaves, the laughter of children, and the stories etched on wrinkled faces.

The Liberating Power of Not Knowing: Paradoxically, the acceptance of not knowing liberates us from the constraints of arrogance and ego. It frees us from the pressure of pretending to have all the answers. In this liberation, we find the courage to ask questions, to admit mistakes, and to seek guidance. It fosters a culture of continuous improvement and self-reflection, paving the way for personal and societal growth.

In essence, embracing your ignorance is not a declaration of incompetence but a celebration of potential. It is the recognition that the journey toward wisdom is endless and that every step taken in ignorance is a step toward enlightenment. So, let us embrace our ignorance with open hearts, for in doing so, we embark on a transformative voyage toward profound wisdom, understanding, and a richer, more enlightened existence.

Let us repeat some affirmations:

- "I embrace my ignorance as a gateway to wisdom, understanding that every question I ask leads me toward greater knowledge and insight."

- "I acknowledge my limitations, knowing that in my ignorance lies the potential for profound learning and enlightenment."

- "I celebrate my curiosity, for in the pursuit of answers to my questions, I discover the path to wisdom and understanding."

- "I welcome the unknown, recognizing that within my ignorance lies the opportunity to expand my horizons and deepen my understanding of the world."

- "I am open to learning from every mistake, understanding that each error is a valuable lesson that propels me toward greater wisdom."

- "I approach the vast sea of knowledge with humility, appreciating that the more I learn, the more I realize how much there is to discover."

- "I embrace the process of learning, knowing that every moment of confusion or uncertainty is a stepping stone on my journey toward wisdom."

- "I trust in my ability to transform my ignorance into wisdom, understanding that every challenge I face is an opportunity for personal and intellectual growth."

- "I release the fear of not knowing, embracing my ignorance as a canvas upon which I paint the colors of understanding and enlightenment."

- "I am a lifelong learner, and I welcome the unknown with open arms, knowing that within it lies the key to my continuous evolution and wisdom."

The Rich Always Go the Wise. Being Wise Is the Greatest Richness

"True richness isn't counted in coins, but in the wisdom that enlightens, the talents that inspire, and the compassion that connects us all. In the currency of the soul, the truly wealthy are those adorned with wisdom, talent, and boundless compassion."

In the tapestry of existence, true wealth transcends material boundaries. Beyond the glitter of gold and the rustle of banknotes, lies a profound richness that defines the essence of our being. It is a spiritual wealth, woven from threads of wisdom, talent, and compassion. This form of richness delves into the depths of our souls, encompassing the boundless wisdom that guides our actions, the innate talents that paint our purpose, and the compassionate hearts that unite us in the shared journey of life.

In this spiritual paradigm, being rich is not about what we possess, but about what we offer to the world. It's a sacred balance between understanding the profound truths of existence, honing our unique abilities to inspire others, and extending boundless compassion to every being we encounter. This holistic richness illuminates our path, not only enriching our lives but also leaving a luminous trail for others to follow. In the realms of wisdom, talent, and compassion, true wealth is discovered, transforming the ordinary into the extraordinary and the mundane into the divine.

The endless treasure – love and wisdom:

In the bustling city lived a young couple, Jim and Della, deeply in love but struggling to make ends meet. Christmas was fast approaching, and both were eager to surprise each other with the perfect gift. Della had long, flowing hair, her most prized possession, while Jim owned a treasured pocket watch, passed down from his grandfather.

Despite their financial constraints, Della decided to buy a chain for Jim's pocket watch, while Jim planned to purchase combs for Della's beautiful hair. Little did they know, their love for each other would lead to a poignant lesson about true wealth.

On Christmas Eve, Della sold her hair to a wig-maker, and with the money earned, she bought the chain for Jim's watch. Meanwhile, Jim sold his watch to a jeweler and used the funds to purchase the finest set of combs for Della's hair. Unbeknownst to each other, they exchanged their most precious possessions to buy gifts for the other.

When they exchanged their gifts that evening, their initial joy turned into bittersweet realization. Despite the sacrifices they had made, their love remained unshaken. In their humble home, surrounded by love and the remnants of their sacrifices, they discovered the true meaning of richness and wisdom.

Jim (smiling warmly): "Della, my love, we may not have our prized possessions anymore, but we have each other. Our sacrifices show the depth of our love."

Della (teary-eyed): "Jim, you're right. We may not have material wealth, but our love, sacrifice, and wisdom have made us the richest people in the world."

Their story spread throughout the city, capturing the hearts of everyone who heard it. The rich and powerful, moved by their wisdom, sought to learn from their example. The quote, "The rich always go to the wise. Being wise is the greatest richness," echoed in the city's corridors, reminding everyone that material possessions fade, but the wisdom to love and sacrifice for others is the true measure of wealth.

And so, Jim and Della's story became a timeless tale, reminding the world that in the grand tapestry of life, love, wisdom, and the capacity for selfless sacrifice are the true treasures, making one richer than the wealthiest kings.

The Wise Owl and the Greedy Squirrel: A Fable:

In a dense forest, there lived a wise old owl named Ophelia and a greedy squirrel named Squeaky. Ophelia was respected by all the animals for her wisdom, while Squeaky was known far and wide for his insatiable greed.

One day, a rumor spread through the forest about a hidden treasure buried near the ancient oak tree. Excited by the news, Squeaky decided to find the treasure and claim it all for himself. He approached Ophelia for advice.

Squeaky (eagerly): "O Wise Owl, tell me how to find the treasure quickly, so I can be the richest squirrel in the forest!"

Ophelia (calmly): "Patience, young one. Greed often blinds us to the wisdom of waiting. To find the treasure, you must first understand the value of true wealth."

Ophelia then shared a fable with Squeaky:

The Fable of the Golden Acorn:

Once, in the heart of the forest, there grew a tree that bore a single golden acorn every hundred years. The animals, enchanted by its brilliance, desired to possess it. The rabbit, the deer, and even the bear tried to take it by force, but the golden acorn was always out of reach.

One day, a wise old tortoise named Terrance approached the tree. Instead of reaching for the golden acorn, he sat down in its shade and began to share stories with the other animals. Over time, friendships blossomed, kindness was exchanged, and the forest flourished with harmony.

On the hundredth year, the golden acorn fell. Terrance, now surrounded by friends, offered it to the forest as a symbol of unity. The animals realized that the true treasure was not the acorn itself, but the friendships they had formed and the love they had shared.

Ophelia (reflectively): "Squeaky, the fable teaches us that true wealth is not found in material possessions alone. It resides in the bonds we forge, the wisdom we share, and the kindness we offer. The rich, indeed, go to the wise, for wisdom is the greatest richness of all."

Squeaky, touched by the wisdom of Ophelia's words, abandoned his quest for the hidden treasure. Instead, he spent his days learning from Ophelia, sharing acorns with his fellow squirrels, and fostering friendships in the forest. In time, he discovered a richness that no amount of gold could ever match—the wealth of a heart enlightened by wisdom and compassion. And so, the forest thrived, echoing the wisdom of the old owl, reminding all who lived there that true riches are found in the virtues of the heart.

The Tale of King Midas and the Golden Touch: A Lesson in Wisdom:

In ancient Greece, there lived a wealthy king named Midas. He was known for his immense wealth and love for gold. One day, Dionysus, the god of wine and revelry, was pleased with Midas's hospitality and offered him a reward. Midas, being a lover of gold, wished that everything he touched would turn into gold.

At first, Midas was delighted with his newfound power. He touched ordinary objects, turning them into gold and reveling in his wealth. However, his joy soon turned into despair when he realized that even his food and drink turned to gold upon touch, rendering him unable to eat or drink.

Realizing the consequences of his greed, Midas prayed to Dionysus, begging him to take back the golden touch. Dionysus, in his wisdom, granted Midas's request, instructing him to bathe in the River Pactolus to cleanse himself of the golden curse.

Upon being freed from the golden touch, Midas learned a valuable lesson. He realized that true wealth was not in material possessions but in wisdom and contentment. He abandoned his obsession with gold and embraced a simpler, wiser way of life, valuing his family, his people, and the wisdom gained from his experience.

This tale illustrates that wisdom and contentment are far greater treasures than material wealth. It echoes the sentiment of the quote, emphasizing the value of being wise over being rich and highlighting the importance of understanding the true worth of one's desires and actions.

What do we learn from this?

Wealth often signifies opulence and material abundance. Yet, beneath the surface, the true essence of affluence lies in wisdom. The adage "The rich always go to the wise. Being wise is the greatest richness" encapsulates profound insights about the nature of true wealth.

Wisdom, unlike material possessions, is eternal and transcends the boundaries of time and circumstance. It is the beacon that illuminates the path of discernment, enabling one to navigate life's challenges with grace and understanding. A wise person possesses the ability to make sound decisions, foster meaningful relationships, and find contentment in simplicity.

When the rich seek the counsel of the wise, they acknowledge the immeasurable value of knowledge and insight. In the realm of wisdom, the pursuit of understanding becomes a treasure trove, enriching the soul and fostering empathy and compassion. It transforms material wealth into a tool for positive change, enabling the privileged to uplift others and contribute meaningfully to society.

Furthermore, being wise fosters humility and gratitude. It teaches one to appreciate the richness of experiences, the depth of human emotions, and the interconnectedness of all life. In the presence of wisdom, arrogance and materialism fade, making room for a profound sense of fulfillment derived from understanding the intricacies of existence.

In essence, the adage underscores that while material riches can be fleeting, the wealth of wisdom endures. It is a legacy that shapes not only individual lives but also entire communities and societies. Embracing wisdom allows one to live a life of purpose, leaving a lasting impact and creating a legacy far more enduring than any material possession. Thus, in the pursuit of wealth, the wisest investment one can make is in the acquisition of knowledge, empathy, and the deep understanding of the human experience.

Let us repeat some affirmations:

- "I embrace the wisdom within me, knowing it is the true source of my richness and abundance."

- "My wisdom grows with each experience, enriching my soul and enhancing my understanding of life."

- "I value the lessons learned from both triumphs and challenges, for they contribute to my profound wisdom."

- "Every day, I am becoming wiser and more enlightened, aligning myself with the greatest richness of all."

- "My decisions are guided by wisdom; I trust my intuition and inner knowledge to lead me to the right path."

- "I seek wisdom in every encounter, finding valuable lessons that enrich my spirit and expand my understanding."

- "I am a beacon of wisdom, illuminating my own life and inspiring others to embrace the richness of wisdom."

- "My mind is open to new perspectives and ideas, allowing wisdom to flow freely into my life."

- "I honor the wisdom of the past, learn from the present, and prepare for a future guided by profound understanding."

- "I am grateful for the wisdom I possess, recognizing it as the greatest richness that shapes my purpose and fulfillment in life."

The Journey Towards Spirituality Is Through Simplicity

In the hustle and bustle of the modern world, spirituality serves as a sanctuary for the soul, offering solace and profound insights that navigate the complexities of life. It is not merely a set of rituals or esoteric beliefs; spirituality is a practical guide, a compass that directs us toward a meaningful, harmonious existence.

Firstly, spirituality encourages us to embark on a journey of self-discovery. Through meditation, mindfulness, or contemplation, we delve deep within, unraveling the layers of our consciousness. This self-awareness is the cornerstone of emotional intelligence, empowering us to understand our feelings, reactions, and motivations, thereby fostering better relationships and emotional resilience. Secondly, spirituality teaches us to be present in the moment, appreciating the beauty of life's simple pleasures. By practicing gratitude, we shift our focus from what we lack to what we have, fostering contentment and reducing stress. Mindfulness, rooted in spiritual principles, helps us respond thoughtfully to life's challenges, promoting mental clarity and inner peace.

Thirdly, at the heart of spirituality lies compassion. It inspires us to empathize with others, recognizing the shared human experience. Acts of kindness and selfless service become a natural extension of our spiritual practice, fostering a sense of interconnectedness and community. Through helping others, we find fulfillment and purpose, transcending the limitations of the ego.

However, most importantly, spirituality equips us with the tools to navigate life's storms. It teaches us that challenges are opportunities for growth and transformation. With spiritual resilience, we face adversity with grace, learning valuable lessons amidst difficulties. This resilience stems from the understanding that life's ups and downs are part of a larger, divine plan, instilling hope even in the face of despair. Additionally, in the pursuit of spiritual balance, we learn to harmonize various aspects of our lives. Balancing material pursuits with spiritual growth, work with rest, and ambition with contentment becomes second nature. This equilibrium fosters a sense of wholeness, where the physical, mental, and spiritual dimensions align, creating a fulfilling life.

Spirituality reminds us of our connection with the natural world. Spending time in nature becomes a spiritual practice, grounding us in the present moment and reminding us of the intricate web of life in which we are a part. This connection fosters reverence for all living beings and deepens our appreciation for the Earth's beauty and abundance.

The Essence of Sanatan Dharma: Simplicity in Spirituality:

At the heart of Sanatan Dharma, the ancient and revered tradition of Hinduism, lies a profound truth: simplicity is the essence of spiritual connection. In contrast to opulent rituals, Sanatan Dharma emphasizes a spirituality that transcends ostentation and grandeur, focusing instead on the purity of the heart and the simplicity of devotion.

Sanatan Dharma teaches that the divine is not confined within ornate temples or extravagant ceremonies but resides in the quiet moments of introspection, the sincerity of prayers, and the humility of the soul. It values the serenity found in a silent meditation, the profoundness of a compassionate gesture, and the depth of understanding in spiritual teachings.

This emphasis on simplicity is a reminder that spirituality is not a spectacle for the eyes but a journey of the soul. It is in the simplicity of a heartfelt prayer, the unadorned devotion of a devotee, and the genuine acts of kindness that the true essence of Sanatan Dharma shines through. By embracing simplicity, one discovers the boundless depth of spiritual wisdom and the timeless connection with the divine, making the spiritual journey a deeply personal and transformative experience.

In essence, spirituality, when practiced with sincerity and mindfulness, becomes a practical guide for living authentically. It offers us not just a set of beliefs, but a way of being—a transformative journey that enhances our daily lives, enriches our relationships, and brings profound meaning to our existence. As we embrace the practical wisdom of spirituality, we find ourselves not only traversing the path of enlightenment but also illuminating the world around us with the light of compassion, wisdom, and love.

Sanatan Dharma, commonly known as Hinduism, is one of the world's oldest and most diverse religions. In the context of Sanatan Dharma, spirituality is a deeply ingrained aspect of life, intertwined with religious beliefs, philosophical concepts, and cultural practices. Here's an overview of spirituality in Sanatan Dharma:

Universal Spirituality: In Sanatan Dharma, spirituality is not limited to rituals or dogmas; it is seen as a universal concept. It acknowledges the divinity in all living beings, emphasizing interconnectedness and the oneness of the universe.

Pursuit of Moksha (Liberation): Central to Hindu spirituality is the concept of Moksha, the liberation from the cycle of birth, death, and rebirth (samsara). Achieving Moksha is considered the ultimate spiritual goal, leading the soul to eternal union with the divine (Brahman).

Dharma (Righteousness): Dharma is the moral and ethical code that governs an individual's conduct. It is a key aspect of spiritual practice, emphasizing righteousness, duty, and moral responsibilities. Following one's dharma is believed to purify the soul.

Yoga and Meditation: Sanatan Dharma offers various paths to spiritual realization, including Jnana Yoga (the path of knowledge), Bhakti Yoga (the path of devotion), Karma Yoga (the path of selfless action), and Raja Yoga (the path of meditation and control of the mind). Yoga and meditation are essential practices to achieve spiritual growth and self-realization.

Reincarnation and Karma: Hindus believe in the cycle of reincarnation, where the soul is reborn into different bodies based on its karma (actions) from previous lives. Spiritual progress is made by accumulating good karma through righteous actions and selfless deeds.

Bhakti (Devotion) and Seva (Service): Bhakti, or devotion to a personal deity, is a fundamental aspect of Hindu spirituality. Devotees express their love and surrender to the divine through prayers, rituals, and devotional practices. Seva, or selfless service, is another essential component, emphasizing helping others and serving humanity as a way to connect with the divine.

Scriptures and Philosophy: Hindu spirituality is deeply rooted in ancient texts such as the Vedas, Upanishads, Bhagavad Gita, and Puranas. These scriptures provide philosophical insights, ethical guidelines, and spiritual knowledge, guiding individuals on their spiritual journey.

In summary, spirituality in Sanatan Dharma encompasses a holistic approach to life, emphasizing the pursuit of self-realization, moral conduct, devotion, and service. It recognizes the divinity within all beings and encourages individuals to live a life of righteousness, wisdom, and compassion.

The Humble Sage and the Cosmic Serpent: A Vedic Tale of Simplicity in Spirituality:

In the ancient Vedic era, there lived a humble sage named Siddharth in a small village nestled at the foot of the majestic Himalayas. Siddharth was known not for his opulent rituals or elaborate ceremonies, but for his unwavering simplicity and profound spirituality.

One day, as Siddharth was meditating by the sacred river, a magnificent cosmic serpent named Ananta approached him. Ananta was adorned with jewels and had a resplendent aura that dazzled like a thousand suns. Intrigued by Siddharth's simplicity, Ananta inquired, "Wise Sage, you possess no material wealth, no grand offerings. Yet, your aura glows with an extraordinary light. How is this possible?"

Smiling gently, Siddharth replied, "Dear Ananta, true spirituality lies not in external grandeur but in the simplicity of the heart. In the quiet depths of meditation and the sincerity of devotion, one finds the path to the divine. Material wealth fades, but the purity of the soul endures."

Intrigued by Siddharth's wisdom, Ananta decided to stay and learn from him. For years, they meditated together on the banks of the river. Ananta, the cosmic serpent, realized that spirituality was not about the magnificence of form but the depth of substance. Through Siddharth's teachings, Ananta shed his external grandeur and embraced simplicity.

In time, Ananta's aura, once blindingly bright, became a gentle glow that illuminated the entire village. People, animals, and even plants felt a newfound sense of peace and tranquility in his presence. Ananta, now humble and serene, became a symbol of spiritual depth.

This ancient tale from the Vedas teaches that the journey towards spirituality is indeed through simplicity. It emphasizes that in the quiet corners of our hearts, devoid of worldly complexities, we find the true essence of spiritual enlightenment. Just as the cosmic serpent learned from the humble sage, we too can discover the profound beauty of spirituality when we embrace simplicity, sincerity, and the purity of intention on our spiritual paths.

Let us repeat some affirmations:

- "I embrace the simplicity of my spiritual journey, finding profound meaning in the quiet moments of reflection and sincerity."

- "My spirituality deepens as I simplify my life, focusing on the purity of my intentions and the authenticity of my actions."

- "I release the need for complexity, understanding that the true essence of spirituality lies in the simplicity of my heart and the clarity of my soul."

- "In simplicity, I find the profound wisdom of the universe. My spiritual path is clear, uncomplicated, and filled with serenity."

- "I let go of material attachments, embracing the simplicity of being. In this simplicity, I discover the richness of my spiritual essence."

- "Each day, I simplify my thoughts and actions, allowing the beauty of spirituality to shine through in every aspect of my life."

- "I find peace in the uncomplicated nature of my spiritual practices. My heart is open, my mind is clear, and my soul is free."

- "My spiritual journey is a path of simplicity, humility, and authenticity. I am grounded in the pure essence of my being."

- "Simplicity is the key to my spiritual growth. I release the unnecessary and embrace the essential, finding enlightenment in the simplicity of existence."

- "I am at peace with the simplicity of my spiritual evolution. Each step I take brings me closer to the profound truths of the universe."

The Profound Wisdom of Simplicity in Spiritual Journey:

Amidst the cacophony of the world, there exists a path to profound spiritual enlightenment, and it is paved with the bricks of simplicity. The quote, "The journey towards spirituality is through simplicity," echoes with timeless wisdom, guiding us toward the essence of our being and the core of universal truth.

Simplicity is not a mere absence of complexity; it's a conscious choice to strip away the layers of superficiality that shroud our lives. It is in this bare authenticity that spirituality finds its truest expression. When we simplify our desires, thoughts, and actions, we create space for the sacred to enter. The clutter of materialism dissipates, making room for the profound insights that lie within.

In the simplicity of a heartfelt prayer, the quietude of meditation, and the genuine warmth of a smile, we find the language of the soul. It is not in grand temples adorned with gold but in the humblest of hearts that the divine truly resides. In simplicity, we embrace the now, appreciating life's subtleties and finding divinity in the ordinary.

Simplicity invites us to shed the weight of unnecessary burdens, freeing us to experience life's beauty fully. The minimalist approach to spirituality teaches us that richness isn't measured by possessions but by the depth of our connections—with ourselves, with others, and with the universe. In simplicity, there is a profound sense of unity, an understanding that we are all threads woven into the same cosmic tapestry.

As we tread this path, we discover that spirituality isn't a complex puzzle to solve but a gentle unveiling of our true nature. It's the unearthing of compassion, the acknowledgment of our interconnectedness, and the acceptance of the present moment as a sacred gift.

In conclusion, the journey towards spirituality is a return to the basics, a rediscovery of the uncomplicated truths that have always existed within us. It's an invitation to embrace the elegance of simplicity, for within its folds, we find the boundless wisdom of the universe and the eternal peace that every soul seeks. So, let us embark on this journey, guided by the profound insight that simplicity is not just a choice; it is the very essence of our spiritual evolution.

The Best Possible Gift to Your Child as a Parent Is Not to Interfere Much

"Finding Balance: A Journey Beyond Helicopter Parenting"

In a bustling city, Sarah, a caring mother, and Michael, a doting father, lived with their only child, Emily. From the moment Emily was born, they enveloped her in love, attention, and a strong sense of protection. They were determined to provide her with the best of everything, but their good intentions took a turn down the path of helicopter parenting.

As Emily grew older, Sarah and Michael's overprotective instincts intensified. They meticulously planned every aspect of her life, from playdates to school projects. They monitored her friendships, her extracurricular activities, and even her online interactions. While their intentions were rooted in love, Emily began to feel suffocated.

The social suffocation:

Emily, once a vibrant and confident young girl, started to face humiliation as a result of her parents' helicopter parenting. Their constant intrusion into her life, decisions, and relationships began to erode her self-esteem and social standing.

In social situations, Emily found herself unable to make decisions without seeking her parents' approval, even for simple matters like choosing clothes or participating in activities. Her friends noticed this dependency, and whispers of her parents' overbearing nature began to circulate. Classmates, once her friends, started excluding her from gatherings, sensing her lack of independence and individuality. They assumed she was incapable of forming opinions or making choices, which led to mockery and exclusion.

Additionally, Emily's academic life was affected. While her parents meant well, their constant involvement created a crutch she couldn't escape. When she faced challenges at school, she lacked the problem-solving skills and resilience that come from making mistakes and learning from them. Her peers, who had developed these skills through trial and error, excelled in problem-solving tasks, while Emily struggled, further fueling her embarrassment.

Even in online spaces, Emily faced humiliation. Her parents, concerned about her safety, monitored her every online interaction. This led to social isolation, as her peers perceived her as different and unapproachable due to the lack of freedom in her digital life.

As a result, Emily became a target for ridicule and teasing. She felt humiliated and isolated, her self-confidence eroded by the constant scrutiny. The humiliation she experienced was a painful consequence of her parents' well-intentioned but overprotective approach, highlighting the importance of finding a balance between protection and independence in parenting.

The pitfall:

Sarah and Mark, well-meaning but overly protective, believed they were shielding Emily from harm. However, their constant monitoring created a sense of dependency that Emily struggled to escape.

One day, Emily's school announced a field trip to a nearby nature reserve. Excited yet nervous, Emily hesitated to ask her parents for permission. Accustomed to their involvement, she hesitantly approached them.

Emily (nervously): "Mom, Dad, there's a school trip to the nature reserve. Can I go?"

Sarah (worried): "What if something happens? We can't risk your safety."

Mark (firmly): "You should focus on your studies, not these distractions."

Feeling dejected, Emily decided to go without their consent, hoping to prove her independence. During the trip, she got separated from the group while exploring a trail. Panicked, she realized her phone, a lifeline to her parents, had no signal.

Meanwhile, her parents, growing concerned about Emily's absence, contacted the school. The ensuing search and rescue operation turned the day into a nightmare. Emily was eventually found, safe but shaken.

Upon her return, her parents, torn between relief and anger, scolded her for her disobedience. However, this incident served as a wake-up call for Sarah and Mark. They realized their well-intentioned protection had inadvertently put Emily in more danger by stunting her ability to make decisions.

The confrontation:

One day, Emily approached her parents, her voice laced with a mix of frustration and determination.

Emily (resolute): "Mom, Dad, I appreciate your concern, but I need space to learn and grow. I want to make my own decisions and face the consequences, good or bad."

Sarah and Michael, taken aback by Emily's assertiveness, realized that their well-intentioned protection had inadvertently hindered her independence and self-confidence.

Recognizing their mistake, Sarah and Mark decided to change their approach. . Emily, too, learned to communicate her desires and concerns openly.

Sarah, a wise woman, decided to attend parenting workshops focused on fostering independence. Michael, too, joined support groups where parents shared their experiences and learned healthier ways of guiding their children.

With newfound knowledge and self-reflection, Sarah and Michael began to loosen their grip. They allowed Emily to make decisions, encouraging her to voice her thoughts and learn from her mistakes. It wasn't easy for them; the urge to protect their daughter was deeply ingrained. Yet, they persisted, finding strength in their love for Emily and their desire to see her thrive independently.

Over time, Emily blossomed. She faced challenges head-on, learning resilience and problem-solving skills. With her parents' support, rather than constant supervision, she became confident in her abilities. As she ventured into the world, she knew she could rely on her parents' guidance without feeling stifled.

Emily's story became an inspiration, teaching her family and the community the importance of striking the right balance between sheltering and empowering their children.

This real-life story serves as a reminder that while parental protection is crucial, it must be balanced with the space necessary for children to explore, learn, and grow. Sarah and Michael's journey showcased the transformative power of self-awareness and the enduring love that, when channeled correctly, allows children to soar while knowing that a safety net of support is always there beneath them.

The Best Possible Gift: Allowing Wings to Grow:

In the responsibility of parenthood, woven with love, care, and aspirations, one thread stands out above all — the art of letting go. As parents, our instinct to protect and nurture often leads us to hover over our children, like diligent guardians of their every step. However, in the process of shielding them, we might unintentionally clip their wings, hindering the very growth we seek to encourage. The best possible gift we can offer our children is the freedom to explore, to stumble, and to rise on their own, with minimal interference.

- Fostering Independence: Allowing children the space to make their own decisions fosters independence. When they face challenges without constant intervention, they develop problem-solving skills and resilience. These traits, forged in the crucible of self-reliance, are invaluable life tools.

- Building Confidence: The sense of accomplishment derived from overcoming obstacles independently builds confidence. When children learn to trust their judgment, they grow into adults unafraid to navigate life's complexities. Confidence in their abilities becomes the cornerstone of their self-esteem.

- Encouraging Responsibility: Freedom to make choices brings the responsibility that accompanies those choices. By allowing children to experience the consequences of their actions, they learn accountability. This awareness forms the basis of ethical decision-making, instilling a sense of responsibility towards themselves and others.

- Nurturing Creativity and Curiosity: Unrestricted exploration fuels creativity and curiosity. When children are encouraged to pursue their interests, unrestricted by parental expectations, they discover their passions. Creative thinking and innovation flourish in an environment free from unnecessary constraints.

- Strengthening Parent-Child Bond: Ironically, stepping back strengthens the bond between parents and children. Trusting their abilities communicates faith in their character. When they encounter setbacks, the knowledge that parents are there, not as controllers but as supporters, fortifies the parent-child relationship.

- Developing Emotional Intelligence: Allowing children to navigate emotional experiences independently enhances emotional intelligence. Understanding and managing emotions become more profound when they learn to cope with feelings, positive or negative, without constant parental intervention.

- Fostering Lifelong Learners: A culture of self-driven learning evolves when children are allowed to explore based on their interests. They develop a love for learning, becoming lifelong learners who pursue knowledge not out of obligation but genuine curiosity.

- Embracing Imperfection: Perfection in parenting is a myth, just as it is in life. Acknowledging our imperfections and allowing our children to witness our mistakes, learn from them, and grow together creates an atmosphere of acceptance. This acceptance forms the foundation of a healthy parent-child relationship.

In conclusion, the best possible gift we can offer our children is the gift of freedom – freedom to discover their identity, to pursue their dreams, and to become resilient individuals capable of facing life's challenges. The art of parenting lies not in control but in guidance, in providing a strong foundation while allowing the spirit to soar. By offering this gift of minimal interference, we nurture not just independent individuals but empowered, compassionate, and confident human beings ready to embrace the world with open hearts and unshackled wings.

Let us repeat some affirmations together:

- "I trust in my child's abilities to navigate challenges, allowing them the freedom to learn and grow independently."

- "I empower my child by offering guidance, not control, nurturing their independence and self-confidence."

- "I celebrate my child's unique journey, embracing their choices and supporting them with unwavering trust."

- "I recognize that allowing my child to make mistakes fosters resilience and builds valuable life skills."

- "I am a guiding light, offering support when needed, and encouraging my child to explore the world with curiosity and courage."

- "I believe in my child's potential, knowing that their experiences, both triumphs and setbacks, shape their character."

- "I practice patience, allowing my child the space to express themselves, fostering a strong sense of identity and self-worth."

- "I honor my child's autonomy, respecting their decisions and nurturing their ability to make choices independently."

- "I provide a nurturing environment where my child feels safe to explore, learn, and become the best version of themselves."

- "I am a source of unconditional love and support, allowing my child the freedom to flourish and discover their own path in life.

Youth Should Get a Degree in Life Management Before They Get Any Other Management Degree

In the ever-changing landscape of the 21st century, our education system stands as the cornerstone of societal progress. It equips students with knowledge, skills, and values vital for their future endeavors. However, amid the academic rigor, a significant lacuna exists – the absence of essential life skills. The curriculum often overlooks fundamental aspects such as financial literacy, time management, emotional intelligence, budgeting, and life management. This gap poses a considerable challenge, hindering the holistic development of individuals.

- Financial Literacy: Understanding money matters is integral to navigating the complexities of adulthood. Financial literacy empowers individuals to make informed decisions about savings, investments, debt management, and retirement planning. Without this knowledge, individuals are left vulnerable to financial pitfalls that can have long-lasting repercussions.

- Time Management: Time, a finite and invaluable resource, is often underappreciated in formal education. Effective time management skills are essential for productivity, goal achievement, and maintaining a healthy work-life balance. Mastering time management not only enhances academic performance but also prepares students for the demands of the professional world.

- Emotional Intelligence: Emotional intelligence, encompassing self-awareness, empathy, and interpersonal skills, is crucial for personal and professional success. It enables individuals to navigate social complexities, manage conflicts, and cultivate meaningful relationships. Emotionally intelligent individuals exhibit resilience, adaptability, and a profound understanding of human interactions.

- Budgeting and Financial Planning: Budgeting skills are the foundation of financial stability. Knowing how to create a budget, manage expenses, and save responsibly are essential life skills. Without these skills, individuals are prone to overspending, debt accumulation, and financial stress. Proper financial planning is the key to a secure future and economic well-being.

- Life Management and Coping Strategies: Life management skills encompass a broad spectrum, including stress management, decision-making, problem-solving, and conflict resolution. These skills equip individuals with the ability to navigate life's challenges effectively. Without adequate coping strategies, individuals may succumb to stress, anxiety, and a sense of helplessness.

- Critical Thinking and Problem-Solving: While critical thinking is often emphasized, its practical application is sometimes overlooked. Teaching students to apply critical thinking skills in real-life scenarios fosters problem-solving abilities. These skills are invaluable for addressing challenges, making strategic decisions, and contributing meaningfully to society.

Addressing this educational lacuna requires a paradigm shift in the way we perceive education. Integrating practical life skills into the curriculum, offering workshops and seminars, and encouraging experiential learning can bridge this gap effectively. Parents, educators, and policymakers must collaborate to ensure that students graduate not only academically proficient but also equipped with the life skills necessary to thrive in an ever-evolving world.

In nurturing well-rounded individuals, the education system must recognize the importance of financial knowledge, time management, emotional intelligence, budgeting, and life management. By doing so, it empowers students to not only excel academically but also lead fulfilling lives, armed with the skills needed to navigate the complexities of the modern world.

Need of the hour – Life Management skills:

In the contemporary world, possessing life management skills is not merely an advantage but a necessity. These skills are the bedrock upon which personal and professional success is built. They encompass a range of abilities, including effective communication, adaptability, stress management, emotional intelligence, decision-making, problem-solving, financial literacy, time management, and leadership.

The rapid pace of change in technology, societal norms, and economic landscapes demands adaptability. Individuals equipped with life management skills can navigate these changes with resilience and grace. Effective communication, a vital life skill, enhances relationships, resolves conflicts, and fosters understanding in both personal and professional spheres.

Stress is an inevitable part of life. Life management skills empower individuals to handle stress by teaching them how to prioritize tasks, manage time efficiently, and strike a balance between work and personal life. Emotional intelligence, involving self-awareness and empathy, equips individuals with the ability to navigate complex social situations, fostering healthier relationships and stronger emotional connections.

Decisions and problems are constants in life. Life management skills enable individuals to make sound decisions and solve problems effectively. This ability is invaluable, aiding in personal choices, professional settings, and community engagements. Financial literacy ensures individuals understand concepts like budgeting, investing, and debt management, allowing them to make informed financial decisions.

Time is a precious resource. Life management skills include effective time management, enabling individuals to set goals, prioritize tasks, and meet deadlines. This skill is essential in juggling various responsibilities and pursuing personal aspirations. Additionally, leadership and teamwork skills are cultivated, enabling individuals to inspire and collaborate, not only in the workplace but also in community initiatives.

In essence, life management skills are indispensable tools for leading a fulfilling life. They empower individuals to handle challenges, maintain harmonious relationships, achieve personal and professional goals, and contribute positively to society. As the world continues to evolve, these skills serve as the foundation for personal growth, resilience, and societal progress.

Reviving Wisdom: The Gurukul System and its Modern Relevance:

In the wake of the digital age, where information flows freely and traditional education systems grapple to keep pace, there's a growing realization of the lacunae in our current educational models. The Gurukul system, an ancient Indian method of education, offers a holistic approach that could bridge the gaps in contemporary learning. By understanding its core principles, we can explore how this age-old system can rejuvenate education in the 21st century.

In the ancient Gurukul learning system, education was not limited to textbooks and theoretical knowledge; it encompassed a holistic approach that prepared students for life beyond the classroom. One of the pivotal components of this system was the emphasis on life management skills.

Life management skills, encompassing a wide array of abilities such as time management, emotional intelligence, decision-making, problem-solving, and financial literacy, were regarded as essential for leading a balanced and fulfilling life. In Gurukuls, students were not only taught how to excel academically but also how to navigate the complexities of the real world.

Time management, a cornerstone of life management, was instilled through structured daily routines, teaching students the value of time and how to allocate it effectively. Emotional intelligence was nurtured through interactions with peers and teachers, fostering empathy, communication skills, and conflict resolution abilities. Decision-making and problem-solving were honed through discussions and real-life scenarios, empowering students to make thoughtful choices and tackle challenges confidently.

Moreover, financial literacy and budgeting skills were imparted, ensuring that students understood the importance of financial planning and responsibility from a young age. These life skills were not considered supplementary but integral to the overall development of an individual.

Incorporating these life management skills into modern education is essential. Gurukul learning serves as a timeless reminder that education should not merely prepare individuals for careers but for life itself. By integrating life management skills into the curriculum, we equip students with the tools they need to thrive in various aspects of life, fostering resilience, adaptability, and a well-rounded perspective. In doing so, we prepare them not just for academic success, but for a future where they can lead meaningful, balanced, and successful lives.

- Holistic Learning: One of the Gurukul system's fundamental principles was its emphasis on holistic learning. It didn't merely focus on academics but also nurtured emotional, social, and practical intelligence. Modern education, by integrating life skills, arts, physical education, and spirituality, could create well-rounded individuals capable of navigating life's complexities.

- Teacher-Student Relationship: In Gurukuls, the teacher-student relationship was deeply personal and rooted in mutual respect. Teachers served not just as instructors but as mentors, guiding students through various aspects of life. Re-establishing this bond in modern education could foster trust, empathy, and effective communication, creating a conducive environment for learning and personal growth.

- Experiential Learning: Gurukuls emphasized experiential learning, where students learned by doing. Practical knowledge and life skills were imparted through real-life experiences, ensuring a deep understanding of concepts. Modern education can incorporate hands-on learning, internships, and interactive projects, providing students with practical skills and problem-solving abilities.

- Customized Curriculum: Unlike rigid syllabi, Gurukuls tailored education to individual students, recognizing their unique strengths and interests. Adopting personalized learning approaches in mainstream education can cater to diverse learning styles, allowing students to explore subjects they are passionate about, enhancing their creativity and critical thinking.

- Community and Environment: Gurukuls were often situated in serene natural environments, fostering a connection with nature. Modern education can benefit from eco-friendly campuses and a focus on environmental education, instilling a sense of responsibility towards the planet. Additionally, involving the community in the learning process can enhance social awareness and empathy.

- Character Development: Gurukuls emphasized character development and moral values. Integrating ethics, empathy, and emotional intelligence into the curriculum can mold students into compassionate and responsible global citizens. Teaching mindfulness, resilience, and conflict resolution equips them with essential life skills.

- Life-Long Learning: Gurukuls instilled a love for learning and encouraged students to be curious throughout their lives. In the digital age, fostering a culture of continuous learning, where students are encouraged to explore diverse fields, adapt to new technologies, and engage in lifelong education, ensures they remain intellectually vibrant and adaptable in an ever-changing world.

In conclusion, the Gurukul system offers a timeless blueprint for holistic education, addressing the missing pieces in our current educational framework. By integrating its principles of holistic learning, personalized education, experiential learning, character development, and community engagement, we can create a transformative educational experience. Embracing the essence of Gurukul education in the modern context can nurture individuals not only academically proficient but also emotionally intelligent, socially responsible, and spiritually aware, ensuring they are well-prepared to face the challenges of the future.

Let us repeat some affirmations:

- "I believe in the power of life management skills, essential for personal success and well-being."

- "I prioritize acquiring life management skills as the foundation of my education and personal growth."

- "I recognize that understanding life management is vital before delving into other fields of study."

- "I am committed to developing strong life management skills to navigate life's challenges with grace and resilience."

- "I embrace the idea that a degree in life management is the cornerstone of a successful and fulfilling future."

- "I value life skills as the key to a balanced and harmonious life, enhancing my personal and professional endeavors."

- "I affirm that mastering life management equips me with the tools to lead a purposeful and meaningful existence."

- "I am dedicated to investing in my personal development, starting with acquiring essential life management skills."

- "I understand that a degree in life management empowers me to make informed decisions and achieve my aspirations."

- "I commit to lifelong learning, focusing on developing life management skills that will shape my future endeavors."

You Can Rewrite the Script of Your Life Through Dedication, Determination and Devotion (3D)

"Every great journey begins with a single step, even if that step is taken on a rocky path. A bad start is just a moment in time, not a final destination. With determination and resilience, you can turn any setback into a setup for a comeback."

A very engaging tale from the bible comes to mind when we talk about this topic.

In a distant land, nestled between rolling hills and lush green valleys, there lived a prosperous farmer. He had two sons, each as different from the other as day and night. The elder son, Ethan, was diligent and responsible, always toiling in the fields, tending to the crops and livestock. The younger son, Leo, was restless and adventurous, his eyes constantly filled with dreams of a life beyond the farm.

One day, with a glint of rebellion in his eyes, Leo approached his father. "Father," he said, "I want to explore the world, to see what lies beyond these fields. Please give me my share of the inheritance."

The father, his heart heavy with worry, divided his wealth between his sons. Leo, now with a pocket full of coins, set off on a journey to a distant city. In the city, he embraced the allure of excitement, reveling in the vibrant nightlife, the exotic foods, and the company of newfound friends. His pockets overflowed with gold, and for a while, he lived a life of extravagance.

But as the days turned into nights and the nights into weeks, Leo's wealth dwindled. The friends he had made disappeared, leaving him penniless and alone. Hunger gnawed at his stomach, and he found himself feeding the pigs in exchange for a meager meal. In that moment of despair, he realized the depth of his folly.

Back at the farm, Ethan worked tirelessly, his eyes scanning the horizon every day, waiting for his brother's return. He missed Leo deeply and often wondered where his adventurous spirit had taken him.

One day, a weary and ragged figure appeared on the horizon. It was Leo, his clothes tattered, his face gaunt with hunger. Ethan's heart swelled with mixed emotions – joy for his brother's return and sadness for the state he was in.

Their father, alerted by Ethan's excited shouts, rushed outside. Seeing Leo, he ran towards him, embracing him with open arms. "Welcome home, my son!" he exclaimed, tears of happiness streaming down his weathered face.

Leo, overwhelmed with emotion and shame, said, "Father, I have sinned against heaven and against you. I am no longer worthy to be called your son."

But the father, filled with boundless love, ignored his words. He called for a grand feast, a celebration of his lost son's return.

The story of the prodigal son doesn't really end here:

After his humbling experiences in the distant city, Leo returned to the family farm with a heart burdened by remorse but also filled with newfound determination. He knew that he needed to redeem himself and prove his worth to his family. Fueled by his dedication to change, he immersed himself in the farm work, his hands calloused from hours of hard labor, and his back bent under the weight of responsibility.

Initially, the challenges seemed insurmountable. The farm was in a state of disarray, facing financial strain and struggling to produce enough to sustain the family. Leo's past mistakes haunted him, and the villagers were skeptical of his transformation. However, he persevered, waking up at the crack of dawn and toiling until the last light of day. He poured his sweat and soul into the farm, planting crops, tending to the animals, and fixing the broken fences.

The mental agony was perhaps the toughest battle for Leo. The guilt from his past decisions gnawed at his conscience, making every step forward a painful reminder of his past recklessness. There were nights when he lay awake, haunted by regrets, questioning if he truly deserved redemption.

But Leo's dedication and devotion began to yield results. With his tireless efforts, the farm started to flourish. He collaborated with Ethan, learning from his brother's wisdom and experience. Together, they introduced innovative farming techniques, diversified their crops, and cared for the land like never before. Leo's determination was evident in every furrow he plowed and every seed he planted.

As the farm's produce increased, so did their sales. The once-skeptical villagers witnessed the transformation firsthand. Slowly, they began to recognize Leo's sincerity and hard work. With time, the mental agony began to subside, replaced by a growing sense of accomplishment and self-worth.

Through his dedication to the farm and his devotion to supporting his family, Leo not only found redemption but also became an integral part of the community. His story became an inspiration, a testament to the power of determination and the ability to rise above past mistakes. Leo's journey, marked by physical and mental agony, ultimately led him to a place of peace and acceptance, proving that with unwavering commitment, even the most broken souls can mend and rewrite the story of their lives.

The story of the prodigal son serves as a timeless tale of redemption and forgiveness. It reminds us of the unconditional love that exists within families and the power of second chances. And on that farm, beneath the starlit sky, the prodigal son found not just forgiveness, but a renewed sense of purpose and a deeper understanding of the meaning of family.

Why is it necessary to have dedication, determination and devotion?

In the magnificent constituency of life, dedication, determination, and devotion stand as unwavering pillars, capable of transforming the bleakest moments of despair into triumphs of unparalleled magnitude. In the face of adversity, it is dedication that ignites the spark, the unwavering commitment to a cause or a goal, a promise to oneself to endure despite the challenges. Determination, with its resolute spirit, lends strength to persevere through the darkest nights, steering the ship through stormy seas with an unyielding resolve. And then there is devotion, a deep-seated passion that infuses every action with purpose and meaning, turning mundane tasks into acts of profound significance. Together, these qualities form a formidable arsenal, empowering individuals to rise above circumstances that threaten to shatter the very core of their being.

When despair casts its suffocating shadow, dedication becomes the guiding light, illuminating a path forward. It is the unwavering focus on a goal, the relentless pursuit of improvement, even in the face of setbacks, that paves the way for transformation. Determination, akin to a mighty river carving its course through rugged terrain, pushes against the currents of despair. It fuels the indomitable spirit, urging one to keep going, reminding them that every obstacle is but a stepping stone towards triumph. With determination, challenges become opportunities for growth, failures become valuable lessons, and despair transforms into a mere pit stop on the road to success.

Yet, it is devotion that imparts a profound sense of purpose, infusing life with meaning even in the direst of circumstances. Devotion is the heart's unwavering allegiance to a cause, a dream, or a belief, transcending the boundaries of logic and reason. It lends color to the mundane, turning everyday actions into rituals of significance. With devotion, one finds the strength to endure the unbearable, the courage to face the unknown, and the wisdom to discern the silver lining amidst the darkest clouds of despair.

In the pomp and grandeur of earthly fallacies, the importance of dedication, determination, and devotion cannot be overstated. They are the threads that weave tales of resilience, stories of triumph against all odds. They empower individuals to transform their lives, turning despair into hope, weakness into strength, and dreams into reality. Through unwavering dedication, unyielding determination, and boundless devotion, one can navigate the most treacherous of waters, emerging not only unscathed but also enriched by the journey, a testament to the extraordinary power of the human spirit.

Let us repeat some affirmations:

- I am dedicated to creating a positive change in my life.

- My determination empowers me to overcome any obstacle in my path.

- I am devoted to my goals, and my commitment is unwavering.

- I have the power to rewrite my life story with dedication and hard work.

- I believe in my abilities and stay determined in the face of challenges.

- With dedication, determination, and devotion, I can achieve anything I set my mind to.

- My unwavering commitment shapes my destiny and transforms my life.

- I am resilient, and my determination helps me bounce back from setbacks.

- Every day, I am devoted to becoming the best version of myself.

- My dedication fuels my passion, and my passion fuels my success.

- I am determined to create a life filled with purpose and fulfillment.

- I approach challenges with determination, knowing they are stepping stones to my success.

- My devotion to my dreams guides me toward a future of abundance and joy.

- I am dedicated to my personal growth and continuous improvement.

- My determination strengthens my resolve to achieve my goals, no matter how big they are.

- I am devoted to living a life that is authentic, meaningful, and true to my values.

- With dedication, determination, and devotion, I rewrite my life story with purpose and passion.

- I believe in my dreams, and my determination turns them into achievable goals.

- I am devoted to embracing challenges as opportunities for growth and learning.

- My dedication, determination, and devotion create a life of endless possibilities and fulfillment.

The Biggest Failure in Life Is to Succeed at Things Which Don't Really Matter to You

In the intricate obscureness of human perceptiveness, success and failure are enigmatic constellations - their meanings ever-shifting, elusive as the ephemeral hues of a twilight sky. What constitutes triumph for one may be mere stepping stones for another; what feels like defeat to some could be the genesis of a triumphant saga to others. In the mosaic of human experiences, the definitions of success and failure are as diverse and intricate as the countless cultures that adorn our world.

Picture success as a chameleon, seamlessly blending into the colors of individual aspirations and dreams. For an artist, it might be the stroke of a brush creating a masterpiece that resonates with souls; for a scientist, it could be unraveling the mysteries of the universe, one hypothesis at a time. In the bustling streets of a city, success might manifest as the echo of laughter from a happy family, while in the tranquil embrace of nature, it could be the melody of birdsong harmonizing with the rustle of leaves.

Conversely, failure is a cryptic riddle, inviting interpretations as diverse as the stars in the night sky. A rejected manuscript may be seen as failure by an aspiring writer, yet to an editor, it could signify room for growth. A lost match might devastate a sports enthusiast, but to a seasoned athlete, it's a catalyst for practice, resilience, and eventual victory. The tapestry of failure is woven with threads of disappointment, but it's also embroidered with lessons, each knot representing a chance to evolve.

Cultures, too, cast their own unique shadows upon the definitions of success and failure. In some, success may be synonymous with material wealth and social status, while in others, it's measured by the richness of relationships and the depth of spirituality. Similarly, the concept of failure varies across cultures; in one, it might carry the weight of shame, while in another, it's viewed as a natural part of the learning journey, celebrated for the strength and wisdom it imparts.

In the realm of thought, success and failure become kaleidoscopic, each turn revealing a new perspective. To some, success is a destination, a pinnacle to be reached; to others, it's a continuous, ever-evolving journey. Failure, for one mind, might be a dead end, while for another, it's a crossroads leading to unexplored paths of innovation and self-discovery.

So, as we navigate the enigmatic labyrinth of life, let us embrace the obscurity of success and failure, recognizing that their meanings are as fluid as the river of time. Let us celebrate the diversity of definitions, for within this kaleidoscope lies the essence of our shared humanity—a tapestry woven with the threads of countless dreams, cultures, and thoughts, where success and failure dance together, shaping the intricate story of our existence.

Mournful victory vs rejoicing failure - an enigma:

In the fast-paced and competitive world we live in, the pursuit of financial stability often takes precedence over personal passions and mental well-being. Many individuals globally find themselves battling depression and other mental disorders because they are compelled to choose a career or job solely based on financial prospects, rather than pursuing something they are truly passionate about. This struggle is closely intertwined with the profound wisdom embedded in the quote, "The biggest failure in life is to succeed at things which don't really matter to you."

In the pursuit of financial success, people may find themselves trapped in jobs that don't align with their true interests or talents. The pressure to conform to societal expectations, meet financial obligations, or support their families often leads them down a path where they sacrifice their dreams and aspirations. Consequently, a sense of fulfillment and purpose is lost, giving rise to feelings of emptiness, frustration, and despair.

The impact of this mismatch between personal passion and professional pursuit on mental health cannot be underestimated. When individuals are unable to engage in activities that genuinely resonate with their interests and bring them joy, they may experience symptoms of depression, anxiety, and chronic stress. The constant suppression of one's true calling can lead to a deep sense of dissatisfaction, eroding self-esteem and overall life satisfaction.

To address this issue, it is crucial to encourage a shift in societal values and attitudes. Cultivating an environment where individuals are supported in pursuing their passions, even if they don't align with traditional or lucrative career paths, can significantly alleviate the burden of mental health issues. Education and awareness campaigns can promote the understanding that success should be measured not just in monetary terms but also in personal fulfillment and happiness.

Moreover, individuals should be encouraged to explore their interests and hobbies, even if they don't immediately translate into financial gains. Pursuing creative outlets, hobbies, or entrepreneurial ventures aligned with one's passions can provide a sense of purpose, improve mental well-being, and even lead to unexpected career opportunities. Additionally, seeking therapy and counseling can be immensely beneficial for those struggling with the emotional toll of compromising their dreams for financial stability.

In essence, the battle against depression and other mental disorders stemming from the inability to pursue one's true passions is a profound challenge faced by many globally. By acknowledging the importance of personal fulfillment and aligning one's life choices with genuine interests, society can pave the way for a healthier, more contented populace. Embracing the idea that true success lies in pursuing what truly matters to an individual can lead to a more fulfilling and mentally resilient society, where everyone is empowered to chase their dreams and find genuine happiness.

What do we conclude from this?

The enigma of mournful victory and rejoicing failure weaves a profound narrative of human resilience and introspection. A mournful victory, though seemingly triumphant, often carries the weight of sacrifice and loss. It stands as a poignant reminder of the human cost incurred in the pursuit of triumph, urging us to reflect on the profound sacrifices made in the wake of success. The echoes of battles won, yet at a staggering price, resonate through history, leaving behind a somber legacy that challenges our perceptions of victory.

On the contrary, rejoicing failure embodies the essence of the indomitable human spirit. It is a testament to the ability to find solace in setbacks, to draw wisdom from mistakes, and to emerge stronger after each fall. Rejoicing failure transforms adversity into a stepping stone, a catalyst for growth and innovation. It teaches us that resilience is born not from the absence of failure, but from the courage to embrace it, to learn from it, and to celebrate it as a beacon lighting the way toward progress.

In this enigma, we find the delicate balance of the human experience. Mournful victory teaches us humility amidst our accomplishments, urging us to acknowledge the price paid for our successes. Rejoicing failure, on the other hand, nurtures a mindset of continuous improvement, where setbacks are not roadblocks but rather opportunities for introspection and evolution.

Ultimately, the enigma of mournful victory and rejoicing failure reminds us of the intricate interplay between success and adversity. It challenges us to reevaluate our definitions of triumph and defeat, guiding us to appreciate the depth of human endeavor and the boundless capacity of the human spirit to transcend the most challenging circumstances. It is within this enigma that we discover the profound wisdom that accompanies the journey of both victory and failure, shaping us into resilient, compassionate beings capable of embracing the complexities of life with grace and understanding.

King Ashoka's victory:

In the hushed aftermath of the merciless battle, where the stench of death hung thick in the air like an oppressive fog, King Ashoka stood alone on the blood-soaked battlefield. His once-gleaming armor was tarnished with the evidence of the day's brutality, and his eyes, which had witnessed countless victories, now reflected the weight of an unexpected revelation.

The sun dipped low on the horizon, casting long shadows over the field of carnage. It was a scene of unparalleled horror—the ground littered with the fallen, a symphony of moans and groans echoing through the desolation. The crimson hue of the dying day seemed to intensify the brutality that had transpired.

As Ashoka surveyed the aftermath, a gnawing feeling began to claw at the recesses of his conscience. The victory he had achieved felt hollow, and an unsettling realization unfolded within him like a dark lotus. He had won the battle, but at what cost? The once mighty conqueror now stood amidst the ruins of not just his enemies but his own humanity. His eyes, which had glinted with determination earlier, now mirrored the anguish that gripped his soul. The earth beneath his feet seemed to soak up not only the blood of the fallen warriors but the essence of his own moral decay. The weight of the crown on his head felt heavier than ever before.

The cries of agony that surrounded him began to take on distinct voices—a chorus of suffering that cut through the cold silence. Ashoka's gaze shifted to the fringes of the battlefield, where the forgotten victims of war lay scattered and broken. Old men, once fathers and protectors, now lay discarded like discarded pawns. Women, once the heartbeats of families, lay lifeless and forsaken. However, it was the sight of the orphaned children that tore at the fabric of Ashoka's hardened heart. Their eyes, wide with terror, pleaded for a mercy that the battlefield had long forgotten. Small hands reached out, not for weapons, but for water and a kindness that had evaporated with the last breaths of their guardians.

The king, once consumed by the intoxicating allure of conquest, now faced an adversary more formidable than any he had encountered on the battlefield—the stark reality of his own conscience. The spoils of victory, stained with the blood of the innocent, became a bitter pill to swallow. A single tear traced a path down Ashoka's battle-worn cheek as the full weight of his actions bore down upon him. The once indomitable ruler now stood humbled, his heart cracked open by the undeniable truth that he had become the very monster he had sought to conquer.

In that moment of profound revelation, King Ashoka pledged to mend the tapestry of his legacy. The battlefield, once a canvas for his ruthless ambition, became the backdrop for a transformative journey. The conqueror, now burdened with the realization of his biggest failure as a human being, vowed to reshape his destiny and that of his empire, steering it towards a path of compassion, enlightenment, and redemption.

Let us repeat some affirmations to align with our values, and celebrate victories that matter to us:

- I celebrate victories that align with my values and aspirations.

- My success is defined by my own standards, not external expectations.

- I choose goals that resonate with my passions and bring me true fulfillment.

- I am the architect of my own success, building a path that reflects my authentic self.

- I find joy in the journey, recognizing that each step forward is a personal victory.

- My worth is not determined by societal benchmarks; I am enough as I am.

- I pursue victories that contribute positively to my well-being and the well-being of others.

- I embrace challenges as opportunities for growth, not as measures of external validation.

- I trust my instincts and follow my heart in the pursuit of meaningful victories.

- The pressure of others does not define my success; I define my own path.

- I prioritize balance in my life, recognizing that sustainable victories come from a holistic approach.

- I am proud of my achievements, knowing they are a reflection of my authentic self.

- Success is not a race; I choose to move at a pace that nourishes my well-being.

- I release the need for perfection and embrace the beauty of my unique journey.

- I am resilient, and setbacks are opportunities to learn and grow on my terms.

- I celebrate the victories that matter to me, regardless of others' opinions.

- I am motivated by passion, purpose, and the genuine desire to make a positive impact.

- My victories contribute to a fulfilling and meaningful life, not just a checklist of accomplishments.

- I am free from the expectations of others; my success is a reflection of my authenticity.

- I find joy in the pursuit of goals that align with my true self, creating a life of purpose and fulfillment.

Where There Is Life, There Is Light

In the hushed confines of the laboratory, Dr. Richard Thornton, a seasoned scientist with silver-streaked hair and a meticulous demeanor, peered intently through the eyepiece of the high-powered microscope. His laboratory coat, a canvas of past experiments, bore witness to the countless hours spent unraveling the mysteries of life. Today, however, promised a revelation that transcended the routine of the scientific realm.

Before him lay the delicate canvas of life—a single human ovum delicately cradled on the slide. Dr. Thornton's hands moved with the precision of a maestro, manipulating the micromanipulator to guide the sperm toward its destination. The microscope, a portal to the microscopic world, rendered the dance of life in vivid detail.

As the sperm, a minuscule entity with a singular purpose, approached the awaiting ovum, anticipation hung in the air like an unspoken promise. Dr. Thornton's eyes, usually fixed in unwavering concentration, betrayed a subtle excitement. He had witnessed fertilization countless times, yet this moment held the potential for something extraordinary.

The room, bathed in the sterile glow of fluorescent lights, became a silent theater for the unfolding spectacle. The scientist's breath seemed to synchronize with the rhythmic pulsing of the laboratory equipment. The whir of machinery and the hum of ventilation faded into the background as the drama of creation played out on the microscopic stage.

And then, in a blink that defied the microscopic pace of life, it happened. The sperm pierced the ovum's protective veil, and an ethereal burst of light erupted within the confines of the microscopic realm. Dr. Thornton, his eyes widening in disbelief, leaned in closer, as if trying to fathom the surreal brilliance that now emanated from the microscopic union. The burst of light, a kaleidoscope of hues unseen by the naked eye, painted the laboratory in a transient glow. It was as if the very fabric of existence had momentarily revealed itself, and Dr. Thornton found himself suspended in a moment beyond the constraints of scientific understanding.

For an infinitesimal moment, the scientist was transported from the realm of logic and reason to a place where the mystical dance of life unfolded in radiant splendor. The burst of light, a testament to the profound beauty hidden within the cellular tapestry, left Dr. Thornton momentarily breathless.

As the brilliance faded, leaving only the tracings of the miraculous event, Dr. Thornton sat back in his chair. His scientific composure momentarily shattered, replaced by an awe that transcended the boundaries of the laboratory. In that fleeting burst of light, he had glimpsed the poetry of creation, a reminder that even the most rigorous scientific endeavors held moments of profound wonder.

Later it would be discovered that; the idea of a burst of light during fertilization is often associated with the release of zinc ions. While it's not a visible burst of light in the way it was described in the imaginative narrative, there is indeed a release of zinc ions during the process of fertilization which glows under the microscope due to presence of fluorescent substances, used for research observatory procedures.

What does it signify?

In the silent realm of the microscopic, where life emerges in a delicate dance of cellular intricacies, there exists a profound truth that transcends the boundaries of mere biology—a truth encapsulated in the ethereal glow that accompanies the core of creation. As the scientist, Dr. Richard Thornton, peered through the lens of the high-powered microscope, the laboratory transformed into a theater of creation. The human ovum, a vessel of potential, lay like a cosmic canvas awaiting the touch of life. Dr. Thornton's hands moved with a seasoned precision, orchestrating the delicate choreography of fertilization. In the microscopic theater, the sperm, a minuscule voyager, navigated the labyrinthine journey toward the awaiting ovum. The anticipation hung in the air, a silent crescendo of significance. As the sperm breached the protective fortress of the egg's outer membrane, a cascade of events unfolded at the cellular level. It was not a burst of visible light that graced the scene, but a release of zinc ions, an alchemical dance at the crossroads of creation. Yet, in the scientist's eyes, a burst of wonder illuminated the laboratory. The metaphorical glow, a poetic manifestation of life's essence, shimmered with the brilliance of revelation. In this intimate dance of biology, the spirit of creation whispered through the lens, and the scientist, momentarily liberated from the shackles of empirical rigor, found himself caught in a moment beyond the confines of the tangible. The laboratory, usually sterile and clinical, became a sanctuary of awe, where the convergence of sperm and egg echoed a cosmic truth—a truth encapsulated in the spiritual resonance of the quote, "Where there is life, there is light." The narrative unfolded as a luminous testament to the interconnected dance of life and light, where the act of creation held the ineffable beauty of a celestial symphony, painting the microscopic canvas with strokes of spiritual wonder and scientific revelation.

The quote "Where there is life, there is light" can be interpreted spiritually in the context of the imaginative narrative about fertilization. From a spiritual perspective, light is often associated with illumination, enlightenment, and the essence of life itself.

Symbolism of Light: Light is often used metaphorically to represent knowledge, wisdom, and spiritual insight. In the context of fertilization, the burst of light could symbolize the moment of profound realization or enlightenment that comes with the creation of new life. It's a transformative event that brings clarity and understanding. Light is also associated with the life force or vital energy. In spiritual traditions, the concept of life often goes hand in hand with the idea of light as a symbol of the divine spark or consciousness. The emergence of light in the narrative could signify the infusion of life force into the newly formed entity.

Connection to Creation: Divine Creation: The quote suggests a deep connection between life and light, implying that where there is life, there is a divine spark or creative force. In the context of fertilization, the narrative paints a vivid picture of the creation of life, and the burst of light becomes a symbolic representation of this divine act of creation. The moment of fertilization, when genetic material merges and a new life begins, can be seen as a spiritual birth. The quote underscores the idea that life and light are inseparable, emphasizing the spiritual significance of the creation and continuation of life.

Harmony with Existence: Spiritually, the quote may also point to the interconnectedness of all living things. Life and light are intertwined in a harmonious dance, suggesting that the essence of life itself is a luminous and interconnected force that permeates all aspects of existence. The spiritual interpretation of the quote may encompass the idea that life is cyclical, with each new beginning marked by a burst of light. This cyclical nature could be reflective of the broader spiritual concept of reincarnation or the eternal nature of the soul's journey.

In essence, the quote "Where there is life, there is light" invites contemplation on the spiritual dimensions of existence, emphasizing the profound connection between the vitality of life and the illuminating force of light. In the context of the imaginative narrative, it resonates with the awe and wonder associated with the creation of life during the process of fertilization.

In the adversities and joys of life, where shadows of disappointment may cast an oppressive veil, the profound wisdom encapsulated in the quote "Where there is life, there is light" serves as an illuminating beacon for those traversing through the murkiness of despair. Life, akin to an intricate tapestry, is woven with threads of both joy and sorrow, triumphs and tribulations. It is a testament to resilience, an unfolding narrative where each chapter, no matter how challenging, contributes to the rich tapestry of personal growth. In the face of disappointment, it's essential to recognize that the very essence of life carries an innate luminosity—an indomitable spark that persists even in the darkest of moments. This radiant core within every individual has the power to illuminate the path forward. Life, with its unpredictable twists and turns, invites us to embrace its complexities and find solace in the belief that adversity is often the fertile ground from which the seeds of strength and wisdom emerge. The quote beckons those disheartened by life's trials to remember that each breath, each heartbeat, is a testament to the reservoir of inner light that resides within. Embracing life, with all its imperfections, becomes a transformative act—a conscious choice to seek and cultivate the luminosity within. Just as dawn follows the darkest hour, the challenges of life are temporary shadows that eventually succumb to the inexorable march of time. The promise embedded in "Where there is life, there is light" is a call to rediscover resilience, to recognize that every setback is a prelude to a comeback, and that the human spirit, like a radiant flame, can never be extinguished by the gusts of disappointment. So, let the quote be a rallying cry, echoing in the corridors of the disheartened soul, reminding them that within the canvas of their existence, they carry a light that can pierce through the darkest clouds, guiding them towards a renewed sense of purpose, hope, and the brilliance that awaits on the other side of life's challenges.

Let us repeat some affirmations together:

- I embrace each day with gratitude, focusing on the blessings that surround me.

- My thoughts create my reality, and I choose to cultivate positivity and optimism.

- I am a beacon of positivity, radiating joy and kindness to those around me.

- Challenges are opportunities for growth, and I welcome them with an open heart.

- I trust that everything is unfolding for my highest good, even in moments of uncertainty.

- I release the need for perfection and accept myself with love and compassion.

- Every setback is a setup for a comeback; I am resilient and capable of overcoming any obstacle.

- I choose to see the beauty in every moment and find joy in the simple pleasures of life.

- My past does not define me; I focus on the present moment and create a positive future.

- I attract positivity into my life by radiating positive energy and thoughts.

- I am worthy of success, love, and happiness, and I allow these blessings to flow into my life.

- I let go of what I cannot control and focus on what I can influence positively.

- My mindset shapes my reality, and I choose thoughts that align with a positive and abundant life.

- I am a magnet for positive experiences, and I attract goodness into my life effortlessly.

- I am surrounded by love and support, and I choose to see the good in others.

- Each day is a new opportunity to create a life filled with joy, purpose, and fulfilment.

- I am in charge of my happiness, and I choose to be happy regardless of external circumstances.

- I radiate positivity, and my optimism inspires those around me to see the bright side of life.

- I celebrate my achievements, no matter how small, and acknowledge my growth along the journey.

- I am the architect of my reality, and I design it with positivity, hope, and a grateful heart.

Resisting Change Is like Resisting a Better Version of Yourself

The oak and the reed:

In a tranquil meadow, bathed in the gentle hues of a setting sun, an ancient oak and a slender reed stood side by side. The oak, with its towering presence and gnarled branches, bore the weight of centuries in its dignified stature. On the contrary, the reed, delicate and unassuming, swayed gracefully in the evening breeze.

As the breeze transformed into a whispering wind, the oak spoke boastfully of its unwavering strength and rooted stability. Its branches reached confidently toward the sky, an imposing silhouette against the painted canvas of the twilight. The reed, however, listened with a quiet resilience, acknowledging the oak's grandeur with a humble nod.

Suddenly, the gentle breeze transformed into a tempest, and the once calm meadow became a battleground between the elements. The mighty wind, a force to be reckoned with, swept across the landscape, tearing through the air like an untamed stallion. The oak, with its rigid limbs, stood stoically against the gale, its leaves rustling defiantly.

In contrast, the reed bent and danced with the wind's whims, its supple form bowing gracefully to the invisible forces. As the tempest roared, the oak, once proud and unyielding, began to creak and strain under the pressure. Its branches, like once-mighty warriors, succumbed to the relentless assault.

The reed, however, continued its rhythmic dance, each sway a testament to its flexibility.

In the aftermath of the storm, the meadow stood transformed. The once-majestic oak lay defeated, its branches broken and scattered like fallen soldiers. The reed, however, stood tall and triumphant, its slender form untouched by the chaos. The oak, humbled by the very forces it had defied, realized the futility of its unwavering pride.

The moral of this tale, painted with the brushstrokes of nature, echoed through the winds that whispered across the meadow. The strength of the oak lay in its resilience to endure, but the wisdom of the reed lay in its ability to adapt. In the dance between the two, the meadow became a living canvas, illustrating the timeless truth that in the face of change, flexibility often triumphs over unyielding resistance.

From Saul to Paul:

Along the sun-drenched road to Damascus, dust danced in the golden rays of the Middle Eastern sun, casting a warm glow over the landscape. Saul of Tarsus, a formidable figure with an air of unwavering conviction, traversed this path with a determined stride. His garments billowed in the gentle breeze, a testament to the fervor that propelled him forward.

Suddenly, the azure sky fractured by a blinding light, radiating an ethereal brilliance that eclipsed the sun itself. Saul, once shrouded in the shadows of certainty, found himself bathed in the celestial glow. His journey halted abruptly as he shielded his eyes against the divine radiance, and a voice, resonant and commanding, echoed through the air. "Saul, Saul, why do you persecute me?" The words reverberated like a cosmic symphony, shaking the very foundations of his beliefs.

In this transformative moment, the heavens seemed to part, revealing a vision that transcended the earthly realm. The once unyielding Saul, now humbled and trembling, recognized the voice as that of Jesus Christ. The encounter sparked a metamorphosis—a rebirth that echoed through the ages.

As the celestial radiance subsided, Saul opened his eyes to a world forever changed. The scales that had veiled his vision fell away, revealing not only the physical world but also the profound truth that had eluded him. His once rigid heart, now softened by the divine revelation, embraced a new understanding of grace and redemption.

The road to Damascus, once trodden with zealous conviction, became a metaphorical bridge between the old Saul and the emerging Paul. The transformative journey unfolded in hues of spiritual awakening, with each step resonating like the strokes of an artist's brush on the canvas of his destiny.

From that celestial encounter emerged Paul, a beacon of light amidst the shadows of his past. The epistles he would later scribe, inspired by the divine revelation on that dusty road, would shape the foundations of Christian theology. The once-persecutor became the fervent advocate, and the metamorphosis painted a vivid tableau of redemption and renewal.

In the aftermath of this celestial encounter, the landscape of Saul's existence shifted. The road to Damascus, once a mere physical passage, became a transcendent pilgrimage—an allegory of personal transformation and the infinite possibilities that unfold when one is willing to let go of the familiar and embrace the divine winds of change.

Why do people fear change?

The fear of change is a complex and pervasive aspect of the human experience, often rooted in various psychological, emotional, and social factors. It stems from the inherent discomfort with the unknown, as change brings unpredictability and a sense of uncharted territory. The fear is compounded by a perceived loss of control, disrupting established routines and patterns that offer a sense of stability and security. Familiarity provides a comfort zone, and the prospect of leaving it can evoke anxiety. Additionally, the fear of failure, past negative experiences, social influence, and the potential for loss and grief contribute to the resistance. Humans naturally seek consistency in their beliefs and behaviors, and change may introduce cognitive dissonance, causing internal discomfort. Overwhelm, lack of confidence in adaptation, and the fear of being judged further compound the reluctance to embrace change. Recognizing and addressing these underlying fears can be crucial in fostering a more positive approach to navigating and adapting to change.

However, behind the seemingly serene facade of comfort lies a subtle illusion that can inadvertently become a gilded cage for the unsuspecting soul. Comfort, with its gentle embrace and familiar routines, often disguises itself as a haven, shielding individuals from the unpredictable winds of change. Yet, within this apparent refuge lies the paradox: the illusion that comfort equates to stagnation. The comfort zone, while offering a temporary respite, can subtly morph into a barrier that hinders personal growth and stifles the pursuit of new possibilities. The illusion lies in the false sense of security that comfort provides, lulling individuals into a complacency that discourages them from venturing beyond the boundaries of the known. The very essence of comfort, synonymous with stability, can inadvertently breed a resistance to change, creating an illusionary cocoon that shields individuals from the transformative potential inherent in embracing the unfamiliar. In reality, the illusion behind comfort is the trade-off between the safety of the known and the undiscovered treasures that lie just beyond the edges of familiarity. It is an invitation to question whether the comfort we seek is a genuine refuge or a deceptive illusion that limits our capacity to evolve and thrive in the ever-changing journey of life.

The illusion behind comfort extends beyond its tranquil surface, revealing a more profound paradox that can impede the pursuit of one's fullest potential. It thrives on the idea that the absence of discomfort equates to a life well-lived, yet beneath this façade lies the risk of becoming entrapped in the cocoon of predictability. The illusion is a subtle whisper that suggests that security resides solely within the confines of what is already known. In reality, true growth often demands a departure from the familiar, a willingness to step into the uncharted territories of uncertainty. Comfort, when misconstrued as the absence of challenges, becomes a mirage that obscures the inherent dynamism of life. The illusion is not merely the physical or material aspects of comfort; it is the mental construct that convinces individuals that the avoidance of discomfort is the ultimate pursuit. The paradox lies in realizing that, at times, true fulfillment and self-discovery emerge not within the boundaries of comfort but in the daring exploration of discomfort and the embrace of change. Thus, the illusion behind comfort beckons individuals to question whether the sanctuary they seek is a genuine refuge or a deceptive barrier that conceals the vast landscapes of personal transformation and the untapped reservoirs of resilience within.

Embracing change:

Preparing oneself to embrace change involves a combination of psychological, emotional, and practical strategies. Here are some suggestions to help you navigate and welcome change:

- **Develop a Growth Mindset:** Cultivate a mindset that sees challenges as opportunities for growth rather than threats. Embrace the belief that your abilities and intelligence can be developed over time.

- **Acknowledge and Understand Your Fears:** Take the time to reflect on your fears and concerns about the impending change. Understanding the root causes of your apprehension can help you address and overcome them more effectively.

- **Focus on the Positive Aspects:** Identify the potential benefits and positive aspects that the change may bring. Whether it's personal growth, new opportunities, or enhanced experiences, keeping a positive outlook can make the transition smoother.

- **Break Down the Change:** Instead of viewing the change as one overwhelming entity, break it down into smaller, manageable steps. This approach allows you to tackle the transition incrementally, making it less daunting.

- **Prepare and Plan:** Gather information about the upcoming change and create a plan. Having a clear understanding of what to expect and how you can navigate the change can provide a sense of control.

- **Build a Support System:** Surround yourself with supportive individuals who can offer encouragement, advice, or simply a listening ear. Sharing your feelings and experiences with others can make the process less isolating.

- **Develop Adaptability:** Enhance your adaptability by exposing yourself to new experiences and challenges regularly. This helps build resilience and a more open mindset towards change.

- **Practice Self-Compassion:** Be kind to yourself during the process of change. Understand that it's okay to feel uncertain or uncomfortable, and acknowledge your efforts and progress.

- **Learn from Past Experiences:** Reflect on previous experiences of change. Identify what strategies worked well for you and apply those lessons to the current situation.

- **Stay Open-Minded:** Approach the change with an open mind. Be receptive to new ideas, perspectives, and ways of doing things. A flexible mindset can make adapting to change more fluid.

- **Visualize Success:** Envision a positive outcome and success associated with the change. Visualization can be a powerful tool in reinforcing a constructive and optimistic mindset.

- **Seek Professional Guidance:** If the change is particularly challenging or overwhelming, consider seeking the guidance of a counselor, coach, or mentor who can provide valuable insights and support.

Remember that embracing change is a gradual process, and it's okay to take one step at a time. By incorporating these strategies, you can build a foundation that enables you to face change with greater resilience and a more positive outlook.

Let us repeat some affirmations together:

- I welcome change as a natural and essential part of my growth.

- Each change brings an opportunity for me to evolve into a better version of myself.

- I release the need for control and embrace the flow of life's transformations.

- Change is a catalyst for positive growth, and I welcome it with an open heart.

- I trust that every change is leading me towards a more fulfilling and authentic life.

- Resisting change only prolongs my journey to becoming the best version of myself.

- I let go of fear and uncertainty, trusting that change is a path to personal improvement.

- Change allows me to discover new strengths and capabilities within myself.

- Embracing change empowers me to create the life I truly desire.

- I release the need to cling to the familiar and welcome the opportunities that change brings.

- Change is an invitation to explore new horizons and expand my potential.

- I am resilient, and change only enhances my capacity for adaptability and growth.

- I trust that every change, big or small, is contributing to my continuous improvement.

- As I embrace change, I discover hidden aspects of myself that contribute to my wholeness.

- I release resistance and welcome the unfolding journey of becoming the best version of myself.

Repeat these affirmations regularly, especially during moments of uncertainty or resistance, to reinforce a positive and embracing attitude towards change.

The Best Moments in Life Are Lived and Not Just Captured

Perched at the back of my villa in this enchanting nature resort, I find myself in a symphony of tranquility. The villa seamlessly connects to a step-down pool, its cool azure waters mirroring the lush greenery surrounding it. Beyond the infinity pool stretches a pristine beach, where the ocean's waves ardently embrace the shore. It's 5:30 in the evening, and the sun, preparing to retire for the day, bathes the sky in a breathtaking palette of orange, pink, and gold.

As I absorb the serenity of this moment, the couple to my right, both in their late twenties, catches my attention. Engrossed in the screens of their phones, they seem present in body but miles away in spirit. Nature unfolds a picturesque sunset, an ephemeral masterpiece, and yet their gaze remains fixed on the digital glow, oblivious to the romantic spectacle unraveling just beyond.

The beauty of the moment is only slightly marred by the couple to my right who seem more captivated by their cameras than the unfolding spectacle. Their phones hover over their coffees, capturing meticulous shots of the steaming cups and, curiously, their feet beside them. Even the enchanting sunset becomes a mere backdrop for their incessant photo session.

As I observe them, my mind drifts into contemplation. I wonder, if only the lens of their cameras could convey the true essence of what their eyes are witnessing. Will looking back at those pictures conjure the same emotions, the missed chance at a romantic connection with the world around them?

The couple, ensnared in the digital documentation of their every move, appears to be experiencing this captivating evening solely through the screen. They click away, creating a visual chronicle of their coffee, their feet, and the sunset, but are they truly present in these moments? I imagine the subtle caress of the evening breeze, the distant melody of the ocean, and the fleeting warmth of the sun's embrace—experiences that escape the confines of a photograph.

As they meticulously frame each shot, I can't help but wonder if, in their quest to capture the scene, they're inadvertently missing out on living it. The lens, a mediator between reality and memory, has the power to freeze time, but can it encapsulate the emotions that surge when one truly immerses oneself in the present?

I ponder whether, years from now, they will sift through these images and feel the echo of what they missed—a chance to experience the quiet romance of a sunset, the subtle dance of shadows, and the shared warmth of a moment, unfiltered by the constraints of a camera lens. Will the pictures, meticulously framed and filtered, evoke the same emotions as the raw, unfiltered experience that eluded their digital documentation?

In this tranquil setting, as the sun inches closer to the horizon, I can't help but feel a tinge of sadness for the couple. They are preserving memories, yes, but at the expense of experiencing them in their entirety. The real-time romance of the sunset, I think, is not through the lens but in the unfiltered gaze of our own eyes, capturing moments that linger in our hearts long after the pixels have faded.

The air is hushed, interrupted only by the distant murmur of the ocean and the occasional laughter of seabirds. The infinity pool, reflecting the evolving canvas of the sky, becomes a liquid mirror capturing the transient beauty of the twilight.

It's a scene that might never be recreated again – a private villa merging with the horizon, an untouched beach, and a sunset aware of its own splendor.

In these final moments before the sun's departure, casting the sky in deeper shades of twilight, I decide to set aside my phone. Choosing to be fully present, I immerse myself in the fading warmth of the day, savoring the magical interplay of light and shadows. Grateful for the solitude and connection to nature, I bid a silent farewell to the sun. The couple beside me, however, remains engrossed in the digital realm, missing out on the romantic symphony playing just beyond their screens. Some moments, I reflect, are too precious to be forfeited to the allure of technology in a world captivated by its glow.

Where are we heading?

In the age of digital interconnectedness, social media has emerged as a ubiquitous presence in our lives, reshaping how we communicate, share information, and perceive our relationships. While the platforms promise enhanced connectivity, the paradoxical consequence of their overuse is the creation of a false sense of connection. As individuals immerse themselves in the curated realms of Instagram, Facebook, Twitter, and others, the illusion of being intimately connected to a vast network of individuals becomes increasingly pronounced.

One primary facet of the false connectivity fostered by social media is the curated self-presentation. Platforms encourage users to showcase the highlight reel of their lives, carefully selecting and filtering moments for public consumption. This curated representation often veils the nuances of reality, leading to a distorted perception of others' lives. Individuals, bombarded with images of seemingly perfect relationships, thriving careers, and enviable lifestyles, may feel a pervasive sense of inadequacy, as their own experiences pale in comparison to the meticulously crafted narratives of others.

Moreover, the incessant quest for validation through likes, comments, and shares amplifies the artificial nature of social media connections. The pursuit of social approval becomes a driving force, shaping behaviors and content to align with perceived audience preferences. In this pursuit, the authenticity of interpersonal connections is compromised, replaced by a transactional dynamic centered on accumulating digital affirmations. Individuals may find themselves tethered to the relentless cycle of seeking external validation, perpetuating a false sense of worth tied to online metrics.

The immediacy of communication facilitated by social media also contributes to the illusion of connection. While it allows for quick exchanges of information and updates, the depth and quality of communication often suffer. Emoji-laden reactions and brief comments replace nuanced conversations, leading to a superficial sense of engagement. The volume of interactions may increase, but the substance and intimacy of meaningful connections may erode, leaving individuals with a plethora of shallow exchanges that lack the depth inherent in face-to-face interactions.

Furthermore, the constant connectivity fostered by social media paradoxically breeds isolation. The digital realm, while ostensibly connecting individuals across vast distances, can contribute to a sense of disconnection from the immediate physical environment. The preoccupation with capturing moments for online consumption can detract from genuine, in-the-moment experiences. Individuals may find themselves physically present but emotionally absent, engrossed in the virtual world at the expense of authentic, real-time connections with those around them.

In conclusion, the overuse of social media has profound implications for the sense of connectivity in people's lives. The curated self-presentation, the quest for digital validation, the immediacy of communication, and the paradoxical isolation it may induce collectively contribute to a false sense of connection. As we navigate the digital landscape, it is essential to critically examine the impact of social media on our perceptions of relationships and cultivate a balanced approach that prioritizes authentic, meaningful connections over the allure of virtual validation.

What did that evening teach me?

In the midst of the pervasive culture of constant sharing, Instagram reels, and the relentless pursuit of the perfect picture, there lies a poignant question: How can we truly live and savor the present moment, unfiltered by the lens of our devices? As I sit at the back of my villa, surrounded by the beauty of nature, I can't help but reflect on the profound difference between experiencing reality and viewing the world through a screen.

The overuse of social media has subtly shifted our focus from living in the moment to capturing the moment. The couple to my right, engrossed in their digital documentation of coffee cups, feet, and the sunset, embodies this shift. The act of incessantly photographing their surroundings raises a critical question about the nature of our experiences: Are we truly living in the present, or are we crafting a curated version of our lives for the digital realm?

Experiencing reality is a multisensory, immersive endeavor. It involves not just the visual aspect but also the aroma, the texture, the sounds, and the emotions that weave together to create a rich tapestry of the moment. When we view the world through a lens, however, we inevitably filter and narrow our perception. The act of framing a photograph or recording a video fragmentarily captures the essence, often at the expense of the holistic experience.

Living in the present requires a conscious effort to disengage from the constant urge to document every instant. It beckons us to put down the camera, set aside the smartphone, and fully engage our senses in the unfolding reality. The touch of the evening breeze, the scent of the ocean, the warmth of the sun—these nuances can only be truly appreciated when we allow ourselves to be present, unburdened by the pressure to share.

The act of constantly seeking the perfect picture for social media, while offering a curated glimpse into our lives, can inadvertently rob us of the authenticity of the experience. It replaces genuine connection with the world with a performative engagement geared toward external validation. The memories we construct are often through the lens of our devices, and the emotional resonance may be sacrificed in the pursuit of the flawless shot.

To truly live in the present, we must break free from the digital trap, allowing ourselves to be immersed in the unfiltered beauty of reality. It involves putting aside the need for instant documentation and embracing the ephemerality of the moment. The joy of living is in the unscripted, unrehearsed interactions with the world around us—moments that are genuine, unfiltered, and uniquely ours.

As the sun sinks lower, casting its warm glow across the horizon, I make a conscious decision to put away my phone. I want to be present in this tranquil moment, experiencing the beauty of the sunset not through the lens but through my own eyes. The challenge, in a world inundated with social media pressures, is to rediscover the art of simply being—of living for the experience rather than the applause.

Let us repeat a few affirmations:

- I cherish the present moment, knowing that the best memories are created by fully experiencing them, not just capturing them.

- My joy is found in the richness of living each moment, not in the pursuit of the perfect picture.

- I release the need to document every experience, understanding that true fulfilment comes from living fully, not just from creating a curated digital record.

- The beauty of a moment is not confined to a photograph; it resides in the sensations, emotions, and connections I experience in real-time.

- I choose to be present and engaged, recognizing that the depth of an experience far surpasses the pixels of a captured image.

- Life's most precious moments are felt in the heart, not seen through a screen. I embrace the fullness of each moment.

- The best stories are lived, not just told through pictures. I am the author of my experiences, capturing them with my senses.

- I let go of the pressure to capture every detail, trusting that the essence of a moment resides in the living, not the documenting.

- My memories are etched in the canvas of my heart, not just stored in a digital album. I choose to live fully in each fleeting moment.

- The value of an experience is not measured by likes or shares but by the depth of connection and fulfilment it brings to my life.

- I am the curator of my own life, prioritizing the richness of experiences over the need for a picture-perfect record.

- I celebrate the impermanence of moments, recognizing that their fleeting nature adds to their beauty and significance.

- I release the pressure to capture every smile, sunset, and milestone. Instead, I relish in the joy of living it authentically.

- The real magic of life happens in the unscripted, unfiltered moments. I choose to be fully present to witness and enjoy them.

- I am mindful of the present, knowing that the true essence of life is experienced in the moments I fully live, not just those I capture.

Keep Your Plans Private, Your Move Silent; Live Life Low Key but Recite Your Prayers Aloud and Free

Chanakya, the ancient Indian strategist and philosopher, is renowned for his profound wisdom and strategic acumen, often encapsulated in the concept of "kootneeti." This term refers to the art of political maneuvering and diplomacy, emphasizing the strategic and calculated approach to achieving one's goals. The quote "Keep your plans private, your move silent; live life low key but recite your prayers aloud and free" embodies key principles of Chanakya's kootneeti.

The first part of the quote, "Keep your plans private, your move silent," underscores the importance of secrecy and discretion in strategic planning. Chanakya believed in the power of surprise and the advantage gained by keeping one's intentions concealed. This aligns with the idea that divulging strategic plans prematurely can lead to vulnerabilities and opposition.

"Live life low key" suggests adopting a modest and unassuming lifestyle. Chanakya believed in the strategic advantage of not drawing unnecessary attention to oneself. Maintaining a low profile can allow individuals to observe and understand the dynamics of their surroundings without becoming a target for undue scrutiny or opposition.

The concluding phrase, "but recite your prayers aloud and free," introduces a spiritual dimension to Chanakya's philosophy. Despite advocating for secrecy in worldly matters, he recognized the importance of expressing one's spiritual beliefs openly. This could serve both as a source of personal strength and as a means of connecting with others on a deeper level, fostering trust and understanding.

In essence, Chanakya's kootneeti, as reflected in this quote, encourages a balanced approach to life—one that combines strategic thinking, humility in personal conduct, and a genuine and open expression of one's spiritual convictions. This multifaceted approach aims to navigate the complexities of human interactions and attain success with prudence and integrity.

Why should you keep your plans private?

Keeping one's plans private can be a strategic and intentional choice for several reasons:

Avoiding Unnecessary Pressure: Sharing plans publicly may subject an individual to external expectations and pressures. Keeping plans private allows for flexibility and the ability to adjust without the weight of others' expectations.

Protecting Against Negativity: Unfortunately, not everyone may respond positively to one's plans. Some individuals might express doubt, scepticism, or negativity, which can be discouraging. Keeping plans private shields, them from unnecessary criticism.

Maintaining Focus: Publicizing goals can lead to constant discussions and inquiries, potentially diverting attention from the actual work required to achieve those goals. Keeping plans private allows for a more focused and concentrated effort without external distractions.

Preserving Privacy: Some plans may involve personal or sensitive matters. Keeping them private ensures the preservation of personal boundaries and privacy, especially when the details are not suitable for public consumption.

Preventing Sabotage: In competitive or professional environments, prematurely sharing plans could give others an opportunity to undermine or compete against those plans. Keeping strategic initiatives confidential until the right time can be a wise tactic.

Cultivating Independence: By keeping plans private, individuals can develop a sense of independence and self-reliance. This fosters personal growth and a reliance on internal motivation rather than external validation.

Minimizing Distractions: Sharing plans can sometimes lead to unsolicited advice or recommendations, which may not always align with the individual's intentions. Keeping plans private helps in avoiding unnecessary distractions and staying true to one's vision.

Preventing Overcommitment: Announcing plans may lead to an influx of requests for collaboration, assistance, or involvement. Keeping plans private allows individuals to manage their commitments and avoid overextending themselves.

Fostering Authenticity: Sharing plans publicly may sometimes lead to individuals crafting plans based on what they believe will be well-received rather than what truly aligns with their values and aspirations. Keeping plans private allows for more authentic goal-setting.

Enhancing Accountability: Paradoxically, some individuals find that keeping their plans private enhances their sense of accountability. This internal accountability can be a powerful motivator without the need for external validation.

Ultimately, the decision to keep plans private or share them publicly depends on individual preferences, the nature of the plans, and the specific circumstances. Some plans benefit from transparency, while others thrive in a more discreet environment.

The need for your moves to be silent:

The idea behind keeping one's moves silent, as advocated by Chanakya and many strategic thinkers, is rooted in the principles of secrecy, surprise, and strategic advantage. There are several reasons why it is often advisable to keep your moves silent in various aspects of life:

Avoiding Opposition Preparations: When you keep your plans and moves silent, you prevent others from anticipating or preparing for your actions. This element of surprise can catch opponents off guard, limiting their ability to counteract your strategies effectively.

Maintaining the Element of Surprise: Surprise is a powerful tactical tool. By keeping your intentions and plans private, you increase the likelihood of surprising others with the timing and nature of your actions. This surprise factor can lead to a more significant impact and can be advantageous in various scenarios, such as negotiations, competitions, or conflicts.

Minimizing Information Leakage: In a competitive or strategic environment, information is a valuable commodity. By keeping your moves silent, you reduce the risk of information leakage, ensuring that critical details about your plans do not reach competitors or adversaries prematurely.

Preserving Flexibility: Publicizing your plans may limit your flexibility to adapt to changing circumstances. By keeping your moves silent, you retain the ability to adjust your strategies and tactics without external pressure or interference.

Enhancing Personal Security: In certain situations, broadcasting your intentions may pose risks to your personal safety or the success of your endeavours. Maintaining discretion about your movements and plans can contribute to your overall security.

Building Trust and Relationships: In interpersonal relationships, keeping certain plans or actions private can contribute to trust-building. It demonstrates a level of discretion and reliability, as others come to know that you do not reveal sensitive information indiscriminately.

While the concept of keeping moves silent is often associated with strategic and tactical considerations, it's important to note that transparency and open communication have their places, especially in collaborative and trust-based relationships. The decision to keep moves silent or to communicate openly depends on the specific context and goals involved.

Why should you live life low key?

Living life low key, or adopting a modest and unassuming lifestyle, can be advantageous for various reasons, drawing from principles of discretion, humility, and strategic living. Here are some reasons why living life low key might be beneficial:

Reduced Attention and Scrutiny: Maintaining a low-key lifestyle helps you avoid unnecessary attention and scrutiny. It allows you to go about your daily activities with less interference, minimizing the risk of attracting unwanted attention from individuals or groups.

Enhanced Observational Skills: Living low key enables you to observe and understand your surroundings more effectively. By staying understated, you may be able to grasp the dynamics of your environment without becoming a focal point, giving you a strategic advantage in assessing situations and making informed decisions.

Preservation of Privacy: A low-key lifestyle contributes to the preservation of personal privacy. This can be particularly important in an era where privacy is increasingly valued. It allows you to safeguard aspects of your life that you prefer to keep private.

Cultivation of Humility: Living low key is often associated with humility. Humble individuals tend to be more approachable and collaborative, fostering positive relationships with others. This can be beneficial in personal and professional settings, contributing to a harmonious social environment.

Avoidance of Unnecessary Conflict: A low-key approach helps in avoiding unnecessary conflict or competition. By not seeking the spotlight or engaging in conspicuous behavior, you reduce the likelihood of provoking envy or rivalry, creating a more peaceful and cooperative atmosphere.

Focus on Substance over Appearance: Living low key emphasizes the importance of substance and character over external appearances. This approach values authenticity and genuine connections, fostering relationships based on shared values and mutual understanding.

Mitigation of Risks: In certain situations, a high-profile lifestyle may attract risks or unwanted attention. Living low key can mitigate these risks, contributing to personal safety and security.

Flexibility in Adapting to Change: A low-key lifestyle often implies a degree of flexibility. When you're not tied to a specific image or reputation, you have the freedom to adapt to changing circumstances and explore new opportunities without being constrained by preconceived expectations.

Reciting your prayers aloud and free:

The notion of reciting prayers aloud and free, as suggested in the quote, often aligns with the idea of expressing one's spiritual or personal beliefs openly. There are several reasons why reciting prayers in such a manner might be considered beneficial:

Personal Affirmation: Reciting prayers aloud can serve as a personal affirmation of one's beliefs and values. Speaking words of prayer aloud can strengthen one's connection with their spirituality and reinforce a sense of purpose and commitment.

Community and Shared Beliefs: Reciting prayers aloud can foster a sense of community and shared beliefs. When prayers are expressed openly, it creates an environment where individuals with similar faith or values can come together, share their convictions, and support each other.

Emotional Release: Speaking prayers aloud can be a cathartic and emotionally releasing experience. It allows individuals to externalize their thoughts and emotions, providing a form of emotional expression and connection with the divine or the sacred.

Building Trust and Connection: Openly reciting prayers can contribute to building trust and connection with others. It reflects a level of authenticity and transparency, which can be valued in interpersonal relationships, whether within a religious community or in personal interactions.

Inspiration for Others: When prayers are recited openly, it can serve as inspiration for others. Sharing one's spiritual journey and expressions of faith may encourage and uplift those who are facing similar challenges or seeking a deeper connection with their beliefs.

Public Worship and Rituals: In many religious traditions, communal prayer involves the collective recitation of prayers aloud. This practice is often part of religious rituals and ceremonies, enhancing the sense of unity and shared experience among worshippers.

Mindfulness and Focus: Reciting prayers aloud can be a form of mindfulness practice, helping individuals stay focused on the present moment and their spiritual intentions. The act of vocalizing prayers can serve as a tangible reminder of one's faith and values.

Cultural and Ritual Significance: In certain cultures, and religious traditions, the act of reciting prayers aloud is deeply rooted in ritual and tradition. It may be considered a way of honouring cultural practices and connecting with ancestral beliefs.

While reciting prayers aloud and free can have various benefits, it's important to recognize that individual preferences and cultural contexts play a significant role. Some individuals may find solace in private, silent prayer, while others may feel a greater sense of connection through vocalized expressions of faith. Ultimately, the choice of how to recite prayers is a personal one, guided by individual beliefs and preferences.

Drop the Baggage Before You Run

In the intricate tapestry of human existence, individuals are often confronted with challenges, conflicts, and uncomfortable situations. Curiously, it is not uncommon for people to exhibit a natural inclination to escape rather than confront these issues head-on. This instinct to evade difficulties is deeply rooted in human psychology and manifests itself in various aspects of life. While the impulse to run away can sometimes provide temporary relief, it also raises important questions about the long-term consequences of avoiding confrontation.

The allure of escapism is deeply ingrained in human nature. When faced with adversity, discomfort, or confrontation, the human mind often seeks the path of least resistance. It is a natural response, driven by the instinct for self-preservation. The desire to avoid conflict is, in part, a protective mechanism, a way to shield oneself from potential harm or emotional distress. However, this instinctual response can have complex implications for personal growth, relationships, and the overall well-being of individuals.

One primary reason people choose to run away from situations is the fear of the unknown. Uncertainty and the potential for negative outcomes can be paralyzing, prompting individuals to opt for the perceived safety of avoidance. This fear of the unknown often masks the opportunities for growth and learning that lie on the other side of confrontation. By evading challenges, individuals may inadvertently limit their personal development and miss out on valuable experiences that contribute to resilience and adaptability.

Avoidance is not solely a coping mechanism; it is also rooted in the desire for immediate relief from discomfort. Confronting issues head-on requires courage, introspection, and a willingness to endure short-term discomfort for the sake of long-term benefits. The prospect of facing unpleasant truths or dealing with uncomfortable emotions can be daunting, leading individuals to choose the seemingly easier path of escape. However, this avoidance may result in a perpetuation of unresolved issues, leading to deeper and more persistent challenges in the future.

In the realm of interpersonal relationships, the impulse to run away can strain connections and hinder effective communication. Whether in familial, romantic, or professional contexts, avoiding difficult conversations may provide a temporary reprieve but can erode trust and intimacy over time. Healthy relationships often necessitate open dialogue, honest expression, and a willingness to navigate through disagreements. Evading such discussions can lead to misunderstandings, resentment, and a gradual deterioration of the relationship fabric.

Furthermore, the prevalence of escapism in the face of challenges raises broader societal questions. In a world that demands resilience and collective problem-solving, a widespread propensity to run away from difficulties can impede progress. Societal issues, whether on a local or global scale, require individuals to confront uncomfortable truths, engage in constructive dialogue, and work towards sustainable solutions. The collective ability to face challenges head-on is essential for fostering positive change and building a resilient, empathetic society.

In conclusion, while the temptation to run away from situations rather than face them is a natural aspect of human behavior, it is crucial to recognize the potential consequences of this avoidance. Confronting challenges head-on requires courage, resilience, and a commitment to personal and collective growth. As individuals and as a society, embracing discomfort as an opportunity for learning and transformation can lead to more fulfilling and meaningful lives. It is through facing challenges that we discover our true strength and capacity for growth, ultimately shaping a future characterized by resilience, understanding, and progress.

What happens if you run away?

However, even if someone runs away from a situation, it is not likely to provide the respite they seek. The very issues they sought to escape continue to circulate in the recesses of their mind, casting a lingering shadow that fosters restlessness, persistent discomfort, and a pervasive sense of unease. The act of avoidance, while momentarily relieving, fails to eradicate the underlying causes of distress, allowing them to fester and potentially intensify over time. In essence, the mind becomes a battleground where unresolved conflicts skirmish for attention, disrupting the tranquility that eluded the individual in their attempt to evade the situation.

This internal turbulence, born from the decision to run away, can manifest in various ways, infiltrating both thoughts and emotions. The mind becomes a repository of unaddressed concerns, a turbulent sea where waves of doubt, regret, and unanswered questions relentlessly crash against the shores of consciousness. The initial relief sought through avoidance transforms into a persistent undercurrent of anxiety, subtly but steadily eroding the mental peace one hoped to attain.

Moreover, the unresolved situation often takes on a life of its own within the mind. Like an unwelcome guest overstaying its welcome, it stubbornly occupies mental space, refusing to be ignored. The more one attempts to push it aside, the more it demands attention, growing in significance and influence. This mental preoccupation can extend its tendrils into other aspects of life, affecting focus, productivity, and overall well-being.

In this psychological landscape, the decision to run away becomes a fleeting escape rather than a genuine resolution. The individual, haunted by the specter of unfinished business, may find it increasingly challenging to fully engage with the present. The unease generated by the unresolved situation permeates various facets of life, coloring experiences with an undertone of discontent.

Moreover, the internal strife resulting from avoidance can impact relationships. The restlessness and inner turmoil may spill over into interactions with others, leading to strained connections and misunderstandings. The very act of running away, intended to preserve peace, paradoxically contributes to the erosion of harmony in both personal and professional spheres.

In light of these reflections, it becomes evident that confronting situations, no matter how uncomfortable, holds the key to genuine resolution. Acknowledging and addressing the root causes of distress allows for the possibility of healing and growth. It is in facing challenges head-on that one can hope to reclaim mental tranquility and build the resilience necessary for navigating the complexities of life. While the allure of escape may seem enticing in the moment, the enduring peace that follows true confrontation far outweighs the fleeting relief of avoidance.

Are you moving forward or simply dragging yourself?

In the journey of life, the wisdom encapsulated in the notion that to move forward, one must let go of the past is both profound and transformative. Holding on to the baggage of bygone experiences, whether marked by triumphs or trials, can act as a weight that hinders progress and impedes the trajectory toward success.

The past, with its myriad memories and lessons, often exerts a powerful influence on the present and future. While reflection on past experiences can be a valuable tool for growth and learning, clinging to past grievances, regrets, or outdated identities can become a stifling force. Much like an anchor, the weight of the past can impede forward momentum, making the journey towards success an arduous and sluggish endeavor.

To truly move forward, it is essential to release the grip on what has already transpired. This act of letting go is not an erasure of the past but a conscious decision to disentangle oneself from its limiting shackles. It involves freeing the mind from the burdens of resentment, self-doubt, or the need for validation based on past achievements.

The analogy of baggage is apt in this context. Baggage, laden with old wounds or outdated narratives, not only consumes physical and emotional energy but also occupies valuable mental space. It creates a barrier between the present self and the limitless possibilities that the future holds. Success often requires a lightness of being, an unencumbered state that allows for nimble adaptation, resilience, and an openness to new opportunities.

The rate of success is intrinsically tied to the ability to embrace change and navigate uncharted territories. Clinging to the past constrains this ability, fostering a resistance to the very evolution that is essential for progress. Success is not merely the destination but a dynamic and ongoing process of growth and self-discovery. Releasing the hold on the past is, therefore, an act of liberation, paving the way for a more fluid and expansive journey toward success.

Letting go is not a dismissal of the significance of one's history; rather, it is an acknowledgment that the past does not define the entirety of who we are or limit what we can become. It is an empowering decision to reclaim agency over one's narrative and shape a future unencumbered by the constraints of yesterday.

In conclusion, the adage "to move forward, you need to let go of the past" carries a timeless truth. Success is often found in the space created by releasing the burdens of yesteryears. It is a conscious choice to embrace the present with all its possibilities and chart a course unburdened by the weight of what has been. In this act of letting go, there lies the freedom to shape a future marked by resilience, growth, and the unbridled pursuit of success.

Let us repeat a few affirmations:

I release the past and embrace the present with open arms.

I let go of old wounds and welcome healing into my life.

My future is not defined by my past; I am free to create a new narrative.

I forgive myself for any mistakes and allow myself to move forward with grace.

Every day is a new opportunity to let go of the past and start afresh.

I release the grip of yesterday's regrets and step into the light of a new day.

I am not bound by the chains of my history; I am liberated by the choices I make today.

I choose to focus on the present moment and build a positive future.

The past is behind me, and I am empowered to shape my destiny.

I am worthy of a joyful and fulfilling life, unencumbered by the weight of the past.

I release the need for approval from past experiences; I approve of myself in the present.

I am resilient, and I trust in my ability to overcome challenges and embrace new beginnings.

My past does not define my worth; I am worthy of love, success, and happiness.

I release any attachments to negative memories; my focus is on creating a positive future.

I am the author of my story, and I choose to write a narrative filled with love, growth, and joy.

I am at peace with my past, and I move forward with a light heart and a clear mind.

I let go of what no longer serves me and make room for positive experiences.

I choose to learn from the past without being burdened by it.

Each day is a new canvas, and I paint my future with vibrant and positive strokes.

I am a work in progress, and I embrace the journey of self-discovery and transformation.

Love Your Problems; They Make You the Solution Master

Problems are the enigmatic catalysts of personal growth and transformation, shrouded in the symbolic tapestry of life. Like the chisel to the sculptor, problems carve the contours of our character, pushing us to confront the depths of our resilience and unravel the hidden threads of our inner strength. They are not mere roadblocks but rather signposts on the winding path of self-discovery, urging us to pause, reflect, and evolve. Just as the lotus emerges from the murky waters, problems hold the promise of blooming into opportunities for enlightenment. They serve as cosmic invitations, challenging us to transcend our limitations and dance with the rhythm of life's intricate symphony. The significance of problems lies not in their inconvenience but in their power to propel us toward the sublime journey of becoming our best selves. Embracing problems as integral to the human experience is to unravel the secrets of our own existence, uncovering the profound wisdom that lies within the very fabric of our struggles.

In the realm of spiritual symbolism, problems are often seen as profound teachers, guiding individuals on their journey toward enlightenment and self-realization. Each challenge becomes a symbolic stepping stone, urging the seeker to delve deeper into the recesses of their soul. Problems are like mirrors, reflecting aspects of the self that may remain hidden during times of ease. They symbolize the transformative fires through which individuals must pass to refine their character, burn away the impurities of ego, and emerge as beings of greater wisdom and compassion. In this symbolic context, problems are not viewed as mere obstacles to be overcome, but as sacred opportunities for growth, self-discovery, and ultimately, spiritual evolution. They are the alchemical crucible in which the raw material of human experience is transmuted into the gold of awakened consciousness. Embracing and understanding the spiritual symbolism of problems invites a profound shift in perspective, encouraging individuals to see challenges as sacred gifts rather than burdens, each holding the potential for profound spiritual insight and evolution.

Why are problems necessary?

Problems play a crucial role in an individual's life, serving as essential elements in the tapestry of personal growth, resilience, and self-discovery. Several reasons highlight the necessity of problems in shaping an individual's journey:

Catalysts for Growth: Problems act as catalysts that stimulate personal and spiritual growth. Facing challenges requires individuals to stretch beyond their comfort zones, fostering adaptability, and enhancing their capacity to navigate diverse situations.

Learning and Wisdom: Problems offer invaluable lessons and opportunities for acquiring wisdom. Each challenge presents a chance to learn about oneself, others, and the world, contributing to the accumulation of knowledge and a deeper understanding of life.

Resilience Building: Confronting problems strengthens an individual's resilience. The ability to bounce back from setbacks and adversity is a crucial life skill that develops through facing and overcoming challenges.

Self-Discovery: Problems provide a mirror for self-reflection. Through adversity, individuals discover their strengths, weaknesses, and the depths of their character. Problems often reveal hidden talents, untapped potential, and areas for personal development.

Cultivating Empathy: Experiencing challenges fosters empathy and understanding. Those who have grappled with difficulties are often more compassionate toward others facing similar struggles, creating a sense of shared humanity.

Motivation for Change: Problems can serve as powerful motivators for positive change. The discomfort or dissatisfaction arising from challenges propels individuals toward seeking solutions, making necessary adjustments, and embracing personal or lifestyle transformations.

Building Character: Character development is intricately tied to the ability to confront and overcome problems. Challenges provide individuals with opportunities to exhibit virtues such as courage, perseverance, and integrity, shaping a strong and resilient character.

Balancing Life's Dynamics: Life is inherently dynamic, marked by ups and downs. Problems are a natural part of this ebb and flow, ensuring that individuals experience a range of emotions, circumstances, and opportunities for personal development.

Fostering Creativity: Problems often necessitate creative problem-solving. The need to find innovative solutions to challenges encourages individuals to tap into their creativity, expanding their thinking and problem-solving abilities.

Deepening Spiritual Connection: For those on a spiritual journey, problems are seen as opportunities for soul evolution. The struggles of life prompt individuals to connect with deeper spiritual truths, fostering a sense of purpose, resilience, and inner peace.

In essence, problems are not obstacles to be avoided but essential elements that contribute to the richness and complexity of the human experience. Embracing challenges with a positive and growth-oriented mindset allows individuals to harness the transformative power inherent in life's difficulties, ultimately leading to a more fulfilling and purposeful existence.

Why be the solution master?

The phrase "Love your problems; they make you a solution master" encapsulates a profound perspective on the nature of challenges and their transformative potential in an individual's life. At first glance, it may seem counterintuitive to love the very obstacles that create friction and adversity. However, beneath the surface lies a philosophy that acknowledges the inherent value of problems as catalysts for personal and intellectual growth.

To love one's problems is to embrace them with an open heart and a mindset that perceives challenges as opportunities rather than setbacks. Problems, in this context, are not viewed as burdens to be avoided but as essential components of a dynamic and evolving life journey. They serve as the raw material from which solutions, resilience, and wisdom are forged.

The concept of becoming a "solution master" implies a mastery over one's ability to navigate and overcome challenges effectively. Loving problems is an acknowledgment that, in the crucible of adversity, individuals have the chance to hone their problem-solving skills, deepen their self-awareness, and cultivate a mindset that is attuned to innovative solutions.

The transformative power of problems lies in the lessons they offer. Each challenge presents an opportunity for self-discovery, pushing individuals to explore the depths of their capabilities, confront their fears, and tap into hidden reservoirs of strength. It is through these trials that individuals develop the tenacity to persevere in the face of difficulty and emerge on the other side with newfound insights.

Moreover, loving problems is about fostering a positive relationship with adversity. Instead of resisting or resenting challenges, individuals who embrace this mindset approach them with curiosity and resilience. They recognize that problems, no matter how daunting, carry within them the seeds of growth and evolution.

The quote also implies a shift in perspective from a victim mentality to that of an empowered individual. Rather than feeling overwhelmed by problems, one learns to see them as stepping stones to personal and professional mastery. It is an invitation to adopt a proactive stance, viewing challenges not as insurmountable obstacles but as puzzles waiting to be solved.

In a world that is inherently uncertain and dynamic, cultivating a love for problems is a strategic mindset. It prepares individuals to be adaptable, innovative, and agile in the face of ever-changing circumstances. It encourages a continuous process of learning and evolution, where challenges become the fuel for progress rather than roadblocks to success.

In conclusion, "Love your problems; they make you a solution master" is a call to embrace the complexities of life with an open heart and a resilient spirit. It invites individuals to view problems not as adversaries but as valuable companions on the journey of self-discovery and mastery. In loving their problems, individuals unlock the transformative potential within adversity, becoming architects of innovative solutions and masters of their own destinies.

How to be a solution master?

Becoming a solution master involves developing a mindset and set of skills that enable you to navigate challenges effectively and creatively. Here are some key steps to cultivate the mindset of a solution master:

Embrace a Positive Mindset: Adopt a positive and optimistic outlook. See challenges as opportunities for growth rather than insurmountable obstacles. A positive mindset allows you to approach problems with resilience and creativity.

Cultivate a Growth Mindset: Embrace a growth mindset that believes in the ability to learn and develop. See challenges as a chance to acquire new skills, knowledge, and insights. A growth mindset fosters adaptability and a willingness to take on new challenges.

Develop Problem-Solving Skills: Hone your problem-solving skills. Break down complex issues into manageable parts, analyze them systematically, and generate creative solutions. Developing a systematic approach to problem-solving enhances your ability to find effective solutions.

Enhance Critical Thinking: Cultivate critical thinking skills. Analyze situations objectively, consider various perspectives, and evaluate the potential outcomes of different solutions. Critical thinking helps you make informed decisions and anticipate potential challenges.

Build Resilience: Strengthen your resilience to bounce back from setbacks. Understand that setbacks are a natural part of the journey. Resilience enables you to persist in the face of adversity and maintain a solution-oriented mindset.

Stay Adaptable: Be adaptable and flexible. The ability to adapt to changing circumstances is crucial for finding solutions in dynamic environments. Embrace change and view it as an opportunity for innovation.

Seek Continuous Learning: Foster a commitment to continuous learning. Stay curious and open-minded, always seeking to expand your knowledge and skills. A curious mind is more likely to discover novel solutions to complex problems.

Effective Communication: Develop strong communication skills. Being able to articulate ideas clearly, listen actively, and collaborate with others enhances your ability to implement and communicate solutions effectively.

Collaborate with Others: Recognize the power of collaboration. Solutions often emerge through collective intelligence. Engage with others, share ideas, and leverage diverse perspectives to arrive at comprehensive and effective solutions.

Practice Emotional Intelligence: Cultivate emotional intelligence to understand your own emotions and those of others. Emotionally intelligent individuals can navigate interpersonal challenges more effectively, leading to better collaborative problem-solving.

Learn from Failure: Embrace failure as a learning opportunity. Analyze failures to understand what went wrong, extract lessons, and use that knowledge to refine future solutions. Failures are often stepping stones to success.

Set Clear Goals: Clearly define your goals and objectives. Having a clear vision allows you to align your efforts and resources toward achieving specific outcomes, making it easier to identify and implement solutions.

Innovate and Be Creative: Foster creativity and innovation. Think outside the box, explore unconventional solutions, and challenge the status quo. Creative thinking often leads to breakthrough solutions.

Maintain a Solution-Oriented Attitude: Cultivate an attitude of focusing on solutions rather than dwelling on problems. Train your mind to naturally seek opportunities for resolution and improvement in every situation.

Becoming a solution master is an ongoing journey that involves continuous self-improvement, learning, and a commitment to approaching challenges with a positive and proactive mindset. It's about developing the skills and habits that empower you to not only solve problems but to innovate and thrive in the face of adversity.

Let us repeat some affirmations together:

- I embrace challenges as opportunities for growth, knowing that they are the stepping stones to becoming a solution master.

- Every problem is a puzzle waiting to be solved, and I am ready to unlock the solutions within me.

- I love my problems, for they are the canvas on which I paint the masterpiece of my resilience and ingenuity.

- Challenges are my allies; they mold me into a solution master, shaping my character and refining my abilities.

- I welcome difficulties with open arms, knowing that each one is a teacher guiding me toward mastery over life's complexities.

- In the face of challenges, I remain calm and centered, confident in my ability to find creative and effective solutions.

- I view problems not as roadblocks but as invitations to showcase my problem-solving prowess and resourcefulness.

- Every challenge I encounter is an opportunity to prove to myself that I am a solution master in the making.

- I see beyond obstacles, recognizing them as the raw material for constructing the bridge to my success.

- I am a solution-oriented thinker, and I effortlessly navigate through challenges with a positive and resilient mindset.

- Challenges do not define me; my adeptness in solving them does. I am the master of my solutions.

- With love and gratitude, I welcome each problem as a guide leading me to greater wisdom, strength, and mastery.

- I am the architect of my destiny, and every problem I encounter is an opportunity to build a brighter future.

- As I face challenges, I tap into my inner well of creativity and innovation, emerging as a true solution master.

- I love my problems because they propel me towards self-discovery, making me more resilient, wise, and solution-oriented.

The Journey Towards Smart Work Is Hard Work

The dichotomy between hard work and smart work has been a perennial subject of contemplation in the realm of personal and professional development. At first glance, the two concepts might seem at odds, but a deeper exploration reveals that they are complementary approaches to achieving goals. Hard work is often associated with sheer effort, diligence, and persistence—the tenacity to invest time and energy relentlessly. On the other hand, smart work transcends the brute force of labor and focuses on efficiency, strategy, and innovation. Understanding the nuances between the two is pivotal in navigating the complexities of modern life.

Hard work, the traditional and time-honored approach, has its merits. It is a testament to discipline and dedication, often characterized by long hours, repetitive tasks, and a willingness to grind through challenges. Hard workers demonstrate resilience and an unyielding commitment to their objectives. They believe in the principle that effort, when sustained, can lead to success. The sweat equity invested in hard work is undeniable, often forming the bedrock of accomplishment in various fields.

However, hard work, when divorced from strategic thinking and adaptability, can become a treadmill of exertion with diminishing returns. It risks falling into the trap of quantity over quality, where the sheer volume of work takes precedence over its impact. Burnout becomes a potential hazard, as individuals may find themselves drained, yet not necessarily progressing at an optimal pace.

This is where smart work emerges as a paradigm shift. Smart work is characterized by an astute allocation of resources, a focus on high-impact activities, and the integration of innovation and efficiency into one's approach. It is about working intelligently, not just arduously. Smart workers leverage their strengths, prioritize tasks based on impact, and continually seek ways to optimize processes. They are not afraid to embrace technology, delegate tasks, and pivot when necessary.

The essence of smart work lies in understanding the 80/20 principle, where a significant portion of results comes from a minority of efforts. Smart workers identify and concentrate on the critical tasks that yield the most significant outcomes. They are adept at time management, identifying the most efficient ways to achieve their objectives without unnecessary toil.

In a rapidly changing world, the importance of adaptability and innovation cannot be overstated. Smart work thrives in dynamic environments, where individuals are not just working hard, but working intelligently to stay ahead of the curve. It involves strategic thinking, continuous learning, and a proactive approach to challenges.

The synergy between hard work and smart work is the key to holistic success. A judicious blend of both ensures a robust work ethic that is not only industrious but also strategic. While hard work lays the foundation with its unwavering commitment, smart work adds the finesse that propels individuals towards greater efficiency, effectiveness, and ultimately, success.

In conclusion, the dichotomy between hard work and smart work is not a choice between one or the other; it's about striking a balance. It's recognizing that effort, when coupled with strategic thinking and innovation, can yield optimal results. The most successful individuals are those who understand when to exert sheer effort and when to apply intelligence, creating a synergy that propels them towards their goals with vigor and sagacity.

Why is smart work preferred over hard work?

Hard work forms the bedrock upon which the edifice of smart work is constructed. It serves as the essential foundation, providing the discipline, resilience, and work ethic necessary for success. Hard work is the embodiment of dedication, a commitment to putting in the hours and effort required to build a strong work ethic. It is through the crucible of hard work that individuals develop the tenacity to persevere in the face of challenges, cultivating a mindset of persistence and grit.

However, hard work is not an end in itself but a means to an end. It sets the stage for the evolution towards smart work. The lessons learned through dedicated effort become the stepping stones for a more strategic and efficient approach to tasks. Hard work instills the value of discipline, time management, and the importance of consistent effort.

Smart work, in essence, is the natural progression from hard work. It involves a shift in mindset, where individuals leverage not only their labor but also their intellect, creativity, and strategic thinking. By incorporating efficiency, innovation, and adaptability into their approach, individuals can optimize their efforts and achieve greater results with less exertion.

In this narrative, hard work is not overshadowed or replaced by smart work; rather, it acts as the scaffolding upon which the elegance and efficiency of smart work are built. The diligence, commitment, and perseverance cultivated through hard work are essential attributes that individuals carry with them as they transition to a more strategic and intelligent mode of operation. It is the fusion of hard work and smart work that propels individuals towards sustainable success, allowing them to navigate challenges with both resilience and ingenuity.

The preference for smart work over hard work stems from a recognition that efficiency, strategy, and innovation can often yield more significant results than sheer effort alone. While both hard work and smart work have their merits, several factors contribute to the growing preference for a strategic and intelligent approach in various domains:

Optimal Resource Utilization: Smart work emphasizes the efficient use of resources, including time, energy, and expertise. By identifying high-impact tasks and focusing efforts on them, individuals can achieve more with less, leading to optimal resource utilization.

Adaptability to Change: In today's fast-paced and dynamic world, adaptability is crucial. Smart work encourages individuals to stay agile, embrace change, and adjust strategies based on evolving circumstances. It allows for quick pivots and adjustments in response to shifting environments.

Emphasis on Quality over Quantity: Smart work prioritizes quality over quantity. Rather than measuring success solely by the volume of work completed, it focuses on delivering high-quality results. This approach is particularly relevant in knowledge-based and creative industries.

Strategic Time Management: Smart work involves strategic time management, where individuals identify and prioritize tasks that contribute the most to their goals. This prevents the exhaustion and burnout that can result from prolonged periods of hard work without a clear strategy.

Innovation and Creativity: Smart work encourages innovation and creative problem-solving. It involves thinking outside the box, exploring alternative approaches, and leveraging technology and new methodologies to enhance productivity and effectiveness.

Work-Life Balance: While hard work can lead to burnout and an imbalance between professional and personal life, smart work considers the importance of work-life balance. It allows individuals to achieve their goals without sacrificing their overall well-being.

Continuous Learning and Improvement: Smart work involves a commitment to continuous learning and improvement. Individuals who work smart are open to acquiring new skills, staying informed about industry trends, and refining their approaches based on feedback and experience.

Effective Problem-Solving: Smart work places a strong emphasis on effective problem-solving. It involves analyzing challenges, identifying root causes, and devising innovative solutions. This approach is particularly valuable in complex and rapidly changing environments.

Strategic Delegation: Smart work includes the strategic delegation of tasks. Rather than attempting to do everything independently, individuals identify tasks that can be delegated to others, allowing them to focus on higher-priority activities that align with their strengths.

Long-Term Sustainability: Smart work is often more sustainable in the long term. It reduces the risk of burnout and fatigue associated with relentless hard work. Individuals who work smart are more likely to maintain consistent productivity over an extended period.

While hard work remains fundamental, the preference for smart work reflects a growing understanding that success is not solely determined by effort but by the strategic application of that effort. Smart work leverages intelligence, innovation, and adaptability to navigate the complexities of the modern world, resulting in more efficient and sustainable paths to achievement.

Why do we fail to understand the contribution of hard work towards smart work?

The understanding that hard work lays the foundation for smart work can be elusive for various reasons, often rooted in misconceptions, biases, or a lack of awareness. Here are some common factors that contribute to people failing to grasp this foundational relationship:

Instant Gratification Culture: In a culture that often values instant gratification, the idea of investing time and effort in hard work for long-term benefits may seem counterintuitive. The allure of quick success can overshadow the recognition that sustainable success often requires a solid foundation built through hard work.

Misconception of Smart Work: Some individuals might mistakenly perceive smart work as a shortcut or an alternative to hard work. This misconception can lead to a belief that working smart means avoiding the diligence and perseverance associated with hard work, rather than integrating strategic thinking into a foundation of dedicated effort.

Overemphasis on Efficiency Alone: People may equate smart work solely with efficiency and optimization, neglecting the recognition that efficiency gains are most effective when built upon a foundation of hard work. Without the diligence and discipline established through hard work, attempts at efficiency may lack depth and sustainability.

Lack of Awareness and Education: A lack of awareness or education about the interconnectedness of hard work and smart work can contribute to the misunderstanding. Individuals may not have been exposed to the idea that success often involves a progression from laying a strong foundation through hard work to refining strategies for optimal outcomes.

Fear of Burnout: The fear of burnout can lead some individuals to seek shortcuts or avoid the perceived strain of hard work. In attempting to prioritize well-being, they may overlook the fact that hard work, when balanced and strategic, can be a source of fulfilment and accomplishment.

Cultural Influences: Cultural influences can shape perceptions of work. In cultures that emphasize immediate results or place a high value on specific outcomes, the importance of the gradual process of building a foundation through hard work may be overlooked or undervalued.

External Pressures and Expectations: External pressures and expectations, such as societal norms or comparisons with others, can drive individuals to seek quick solutions rather than appreciating the step-by-step progression from hard work to smart work.

Lack of Personal Experience: Some individuals may not have personally experienced the transformative journey from hard work to smart work. Without firsthand knowledge of how dedication and diligence can pave the way for more strategic and efficient approaches, the concept may remain abstract.

Addressing these factors requires a shift in perspective and a nuanced understanding of success as a dynamic and multifaceted process. Encouraging education on the principles of hard work and smart work, promoting a balanced view of efficiency, and highlighting real-life success stories that reflect this progression can contribute to a more comprehensive understanding of the interconnected nature of these two approaches.

Let us repeat some affirmations:

- I embrace the journey towards smart work, understanding that it is paved with the dedication and perseverance of hard work.

- As I work diligently, I am laying the foundation for smarter and more strategic approaches to achieve my goals.

- Every effort I invest in hard work is a step forward on the path to mastering the art of working smart.

- I trust the process of growth and evolution, recognizing that the challenges of hard work are shaping me into a more strategic and efficient individual.

- In the crucible of hard work, I find the resilience and determination needed to navigate the complexities of working smart.

- My commitment to hard work is a testament to my dedication to continuous improvement and the pursuit of excellence in all that I do.

- As I toil with purpose, I am refining my skills, honing my abilities, and preparing myself for the intelligent and strategic endeavors that lie ahead.

- I view the challenges of hard work as valuable lessons, equipping me with the skills and mindset required for successful smart work.

- With each task I undertake diligently, I am building a strong foundation that will support my endeavors to work smarter in the future.

- The effort I invest today is an investment in the innovative and efficient approaches that will characterize my journey towards smart work tomorrow.

- I honor the process of growth, recognizing that the fusion of hard work and strategic thinking is the key to unlocking my fullest potential.

- As I tackle challenges head-on, I am gaining the experience and knowledge needed to navigate complex situations with wisdom and efficiency.

- My commitment to excellence involves both hard work and smart work, creating a synergy that propels me towards unparalleled success.

- I trust that the lessons learned through hard work are shaping me into a master of my craft, ready to navigate the nuanced landscape of smart work.

- I celebrate the journey, understanding that the fusion of hard work and smart work is the dynamic force propelling me towards my goals and aspirations.

Bad Day ≠ Bad Life

First day of office:

The shrill blare of my alarm clock cut through the haze of my dreams, signaling the beginning of what would turn out to be an unrelenting day. I fumbled with the snooze button, desperately trying to cling to the remnants of sleep. Little did I know that the malfunctioning alarm had set the tone for a day that seemed destined for chaos.

In my groggy haste, I stumbled through the morning routine, a cacophony of missed opportunities and unfortunate events. The tiffin box lay forgotten on the kitchen counter, and my clothes, unpressed and crumpled, mirrored the disarray of my morning. The clock mocked me as I realized I had overslept and missed the company bus, the lifeline for a newcomer like me. Public buses were on strike, a twist of fate that added to my misery.

A paid lift to the office turned out to be a silver lining, albeit tarnished. The late arrival garnered the ire of my boss, a storm of criticism and insults raining down on me before the entire office. The workload escalated to an overwhelming crescendo, accompanied by the cruel symphony of a pay deduction, a financial punch to the gut.

The cafeteria, my refuge in times of stress, offered no solace. Sold out and barren, it mirrored the emptiness in my stomach. Gum and water became my meager sustenance as I battled through the deluge of assignments, each one more daunting than the last.

By the time the clock's hands signaled the end of the torturous day, I found myself penniless and at the mercy of the rain-soaked streets. Forgotten wallet, weary legs, and frustration were my only companions on the long walk back home. Every step echoed my discontent, curses at the universe punctuating the sound of raindrops hitting the pavement.

Home, a sanctuary turned battleground, welcomed me with darkness. In a fit of frustration, I kicked a table, and the sharp pain in my injured foot became the cruel reminder of my wretched day. Exhausted, hungry, and battered, I collapsed on the couch, defeated by the relentless torrent of misfortune.

Morning arrived on a Saturday, a holiday unbeknownst to my malfunctioning alarm. The remnants of the disastrous day clung to me like a shadow. Yet, something had shifted. My body, once battered and bruised, felt refreshed. As I opened my eyes, my dog's wagging tail greeted me—a loyal companion unfazed by the trials of my human existence.

The doorbell rang, and my neighbor, a beacon of unexpected kindness, handed me a steaming vegetable casserole. The aroma filled the air, dispelling the remnants of despair. In the warmth of shared food and unexpected compassion, the trials of the previous day began to fade. Life, it seemed, had a way of balancing its scales, offering unexpected moments of solace in the wake of relentless storms.

As the aroma of the vegetable casserole enveloped my senses, my neighbor, Mr. Johnson, stood there with a warm smile. His eyes crinkled at the corners, betraying the sincerity of his friendly demeanor. It seemed the universe, in its mysterious ways, had sent me a guardian in the form of a benevolent neighbor.

Mr. Johnson, a portly man with a graying beard, was the epitome of neighborly kindness. His simple gesture of bringing over the casserole spoke volumes about the compassionate soul residing next door. He explained that he noticed my hasty departure yesterday and, concerned for my dog, had taken it upon himself to ensure that my furry companion wasn't left hungry in my absence. My heart swelled with gratitude for the unsolicited act of kindness.

As we shared a meal at the kitchen table, Mr. Johnson couldn't help but praise the sweet disposition of my dog. He recounted how, despite the chaotic events of yesterday, my canine companion had greeted him with wagging tail and warm eyes, a stark contrast to the tumultuous day I had endured. His words resonated, and I couldn't help but smile at the thought of my dog, a steadfast friend who had weathered the storm with unwavering loyalty.

Over the shared lunch, Mr. Johnson and I exchanged stories and laughter, a stark contrast to the isolation and frustration of the previous day. In his presence, the weight of my misfortunes seemed to lift, replaced by a sense of community and the realization that even in the midst of life's storms, there were beacons of kindness that could illuminate the darkest corners of our existence. The vegetable casserole, a simple dish, became a symbol of shared humanity and the power of neighborly bonds to heal wounds inflicted by life's capricious nature.

The weekend that followed the tumultuous workday unfolded in stark contrast—a gentle reprieve from the chaos that had defined the week's outset. With the calming cadence of raindrops against my window as a lullaby, I found solace in the simplicity of an uneventful Saturday and Sunday.

On waking up naturally without the jarring buzz of a malfunctioning alarm, I was greeted by the subtle rays of sunlight filtering through the curtains. It was a gentle awakening, a luxury denied to me on the preceding weekdays. As I stretched and felt the absence of stress, I marveled at the rejuvenating power of uninterrupted sleep.

The weekend, a canvas of restful moments, provided the perfect opportunity to address the misadventures of the alarm clock. Armed with patience and a small toolkit, I dismantled and reassembled the temperamental device. The rhythmic ticking of a properly functioning clock signaled a small victory over the technological glitches that had haunted me. With newfound satisfaction, I marveled at the simplicity of a well-functioning alarm and the impact it could have on the quality of my mornings.

The tranquility of the weekend extended to the meticulous organization of my wardrobe. Every piece of clothing found its designated place, and the chaos that had characterized my frantic search for an ironed shirt on that dreadful first day was replaced by a sense of order. The week ahead stood before me, a neatly arranged array of possibilities, devoid of the disarray that had marred my initial entrance into the new workplace.

In the calm cocoon of the weekend, I reveled in the luxury of quiet moments, appreciating the value of rest and reflection. The uneventfulness of those two days became a sanctuary, a deliberate choice to distance myself from the whirlwind of the workweek. As the weekend sun dipped below the horizon, I felt a quiet satisfaction—an affirmation that sometimes, the most restorative moments are found in the stillness of uneventful days.

As Monday dawned, a renewed sense of purpose accompanied the soft glow of morning light. The alarm, now dutifully repaired, coaxed me out of sleep at the intended hour, allowing for a leisurely start to the day. The morning routine unfolded seamlessly; chores that had once felt like insurmountable obstacles were now conquered with ease. Dressed in freshly ironed clothes from an orderly wardrobe, I stepped out, ready to face the week with a newfound determination.

The work bus, once missed and now a symbol of punctuality, awaited me at the designated stop. As I boarded, the air hummed with the quiet efficiency of a well-timed morning routine. The commute, once a frantic race against time, became a calm journey to the office, setting the tone for a day that promised redemption.

Arriving at the office before the clock struck the official start of the workday felt like a small triumph. The dark clouds of the disastrous Friday were beginning to dissipate, replaced by the anticipation of a fresh start. Opening my work email, a pleasant surprise awaited—a client's appreciation for the efforts put in on that fateful Friday. The accolades were a salve for the wounds inflicted by the boss's harsh words, a reassurance that hard work did not go unnoticed.

The cafeteria, once a desolate place, now beckoned with the promise of a free lunch, a token of recognition for outstanding work. The tables, once solitary islands, transformed into communal gathering spots as colleagues extended invitations to share a meal. The camaraderie that had been momentarily fractured by Friday's ordeal began to mend.

And then, the pièce de resistance—a few colleagues, sensing the need for a collective exhale, joined me and my best friend at the table. Laughter and camaraderie flowed freely, erasing the lingering shadows of the dreadful Friday. As we shared anecdotes and exchanged smiles, the sense of normalcy returned like the gentle tide reclaiming the shore after a storm.

The dreaded Friday, a chapter best forgotten, faded into the recesses of memory. In its place stood a Monday that unfolded like a well-orchestrated symphony, each note resonating with a harmonious balance of diligence, recognition, and camaraderie. As the day unfolded, it became evident that the echoes of past challenges were mere ripples in the vast sea of potential and possibility that lay ahead.

What do we learn from this?

The narrative, with its rollercoaster of a week, from a disastrous Friday to the tranquillity of the weekend and the redemption of Monday, encapsulates the timeless wisdom embedded in the quote, "A bad day does not equal a bad life." Life is an intricate tapestry woven with threads of both triumphs and tribulations. The protagonist, navigating through the challenges of a new workplace, experienced the ebb and flow of fortune, from the chaos of a malfunctioning alarm to the tranquillity of a peaceful weekend.

The overarching moral of the story is a profound reminder that individual moments of adversity, no matter how distressing, do not define the entirety of one's existence. The narrative beautifully illustrates the impermanence of difficulties and the potential for positive change. The protagonist, despite enduring a dreadful Friday, found solace and rejuvenation in the simplicity of an uneventful weekend. The subsequent Monday brought a series of small victories, turning the tide and restoring balance.

In essence, the story encourages the recognition that life is a continuum, an ever-evolving journey marked by peaks and valleys. A single challenging day, or even a series of them, does not encapsulate the entirety of a person's life. It's a call to resilience, an invitation to weather storms with the understanding that, like the changing seasons, life holds the promise of renewal and brighter days ahead. By persevering through adversity, embracing moments of rest, and finding joy in the ordinary, the protagonist navigates the complexities of life, ultimately demonstrating the profound truth that a bad day, no matter how formidable, does not equate to a bad life.

People often fall into the trap of extrapolating the challenges of a single bad day to define the entirety of their lives. It's a common human tendency to let a particularly difficult or disappointing day cast a shadow over our broader perspective. In moments of frustration, stress, or despair, individuals may be prone to magnifying the impact of immediate setbacks, allowing the emotional weight of a bad day to color their perception of life as a whole.

However, it's crucial to remember the profound truth embedded in the wisdom that "a bad day does not signify a bad life." Life is an intricate journey, a mosaic of diverse experiences that encompass both highs and lows. A single challenging day, no matter how tumultuous, is just one pixel in the larger canvas of existence.

By succumbing to the inclination to attribute the weight of an entire life to the struggles of a bad day, individuals risk overlooking the inherent ephemerality of such moments. Life is a dynamic tapestry, subject to constant change, growth, and renewal. Just as joyful days do not guarantee a lifetime of happiness, challenging days do not condemn an individual to a perpetually difficult existence.

This perspective encourages resilience and a broader outlook, urging individuals to navigate through bad days with the understanding that they are transient, impermanent facets of the human experience. Rather than letting the shadows of a challenging day obscure the entirety of life's potential, it's essential to recognize that adversity is a part of the human journey and can often pave the way for growth, learning, and eventual triumph.

In essence, the wisdom behind "a bad day does not signify a bad life" serves as a powerful reminder to approach setbacks with perspective, acknowledging them as isolated incidents rather than defining moments. By cultivating resilience and maintaining a broader view of life's tapestry, individuals can weather the storms of difficult days and embrace the ever-unfolding narrative of their existence.

The Start Always Takes Care of the End

Owing to the richness of the quote let us begin the chapter with a story.

In the picturesque coastal village of Silten ave, where the azure sea kissed the cerulean sky, lived an adventurous fisherman named Aiden. With the sea in his veins and dreams as vast as the horizon, Aiden inherited his father's modest fishing boat, the "Sea Serenity." Aiden was born into a family of fishermen who had cast their nets into the same shimmering waters for generations. Their small cottage, weathered by the sea's salty embrace, stood as a testament to their modest existence.

From a young age, Aiden was initiated into the family trade. His father, a weathered seafarer with calloused hands and a heart of gold, taught him the art of fishing. They would rise before dawn, their breath mingling with the cool, salty breeze as they set out in their trusty but weather-beaten fishing boat, the "Sea Serenity." Though life in Serenity Cove was peaceful, yet it was far from opulent. The modest catch from each day's labor was barely enough to make ends meet. The village, though close-knit and resilient, was like a pearl in the rough—its beauty hidden beneath the layers of simple living.

Aiden's family, while bound by love and tradition, often found themselves in the clutches of financial hardship. Yet, despite the scarcity that surrounded them, they shared their meager possessions with open hearts. Aiden's mother, a woman with eyes that mirrored the sea's depth, would prepare hearty meals for her family and offer the same to those in need. Their home, though small and weather-worn, was a haven for warmth and generosity.

One bright morning, a thrill rippled through Silten ave, carrying with it the promise of adventure. An announcement echoed through the village square, proclaiming a grand fishing competition that had captured the villagers' collective imagination. The prize? None other than the elusive Silverfin, a shimmering marvel said to bring boundless riches. The townsfolk cheered with excitement, but it was Aiden who felt a deeper, more profound call.

In the early hours before dawn, as the first light of morning painted the sky in soft pastel hues, Aiden stood on the weathered dock of Serenity Cove, his heart and mind a canvas of determination and purpose. The sea breeze ruffled his salt-sprayed hair, and the distant sound of waves crashing against the shore echoed in his ears. Aiden's eyes, a reflection of the depths of the ocean, held a quiet intensity that spoke of reverence for the journey ahead.

In those solitary moments of preparation, he meticulously inspected his fishing gear, ensuring every line, hook, and net was in perfect order. Each tool held significance, a connection to generations of seafaring wisdom that coursed through his veins. Aiden's small boat, the "Sea Serenity," bobbed gently in the harbor, a loyal companion awaiting another adventure. It was a vessel that had weathered storms and danced with the waves, an embodiment of resilience.

His attire was practical, bearing the telltale signs of a life spent at sea—a weathered hat to shield his face from the sun's relentless glare, and well-worn boots that had touched countless shores. But it was the look in Aiden's eyes that revealed his true preparation—an unwavering resolve to honor the sea, to pay homage to the creatures that called it home, and to embark on a quest not driven by greed but by the profound connection he shared with the ocean.

As he cast his gaze out onto the vast expanse of water that stretched before him, Aiden took a deep breath, inhaling the scent of salt and adventure. In that moment, his heart and soul were primed for the journey, and his readiness was not measured in equipment alone but in the profound respect and reverence he held for the sea and its mysteries.

With the twinkle of a seafarer's eye and the steady hum of the "Sea Serenity," Aiden set sail into the endless blue, guided by a simple creed: **"Show mercy to the sea, and the sea shall show mercy to you."** Aiden was not merely pursuing wealth; he sought a connection with the sea, a communion with the world beneath the waves.

Days melted into weeks as Aiden confronted the unforgiving trials of the sea. But the Silverfin remained as elusive as a sigh on the breeze. Doubts, like shadows on the sea's surface, cast their veil over Aiden's spirit.

"Is this quest in vain, Sea Serenity?" Aiden muttered, gazing out at the expanse of water that stretched to infinity.

Yet Aiden pressed on, determined to honor the sea and its creatures. He rescued stranded turtles and dolphins, cleaned up litter that marred the pristine waters, and treated fellow fishermen with kindness and respect. His actions bore testimony to a profound reverence for the ocean, and the sea, like a wise elder, watched in silent approval. One enchanting evening, as the setting sun painted the sea in shades of molten gold and rosy pink, Aiden felt an irresistible tug on his line. The line sang with tension, and Aiden's heart echoed the rhythm of waves crashing on the shore.

"Could it be? Is this really the Silverfin?"

With one final, ardent pull, he brought the Silverfin to the surface.

"It's the Silverfin! I've found it!"

Aiden stood breathless, gazing upon a creature of unparalleled beauty. The Silverfin's scales gleamed like polished gemstones, its eyes held secrets of the depths, and its fins moved like poetry in motion. It was the embodiment of nature's splendor, a living testament to the majesty of the sea.

"But what if I catch it and secure my family's future?"

"What if I let it go and regret it for the rest of my life?"

"Think of the wealth, the fortune that awaits!"

But Aiden recalled the essence of his journey—it was not about capturing the Silverfin for personal gain.

"The Silverfin is a creature of beauty and wonder."

"The sea has given so much to us; it deserves my respect."

"The Silverfin is a part of this intricate ecosystem."

With great care and profound respect, Aiden lowered the Silverfin back into the sea. The fish, as if acknowledging his sincerity, swam away with a regal flick of its tail.

"I embarked on this journey to show reverence to the sea."

And this final thought left behind a sense of fulfilment that transcended any treasure.

As Aiden sailed back to the villagers gathered on the shore, their eyes filled with curiosity and admiration. Aiden recounted his extraordinary encounter with the Silverfin, emphasizing the transformation he had undergone.

"It wasn't the Silverfin that was the ultimate prize," Aiden explained to the captivated audience. "It was the connection

I forged with the sea and the profound lessons it taught me. That, my friends, is the true treasure."

The villagers applauded Aiden's wisdom, and his story spread like ripples on the sea. He became known as the fisherman with a heart as deep as the ocean, and his journey inspired countless others to seek their own adventures with hearts full of reverence.

Months drifted by, and one day, while casting his net, Aiden made an astonishing discovery—a bed of luminous pearls, each one glowing like a miniature moon. Aiden realized that by showing mercy to the sea, he had received a gift more profound than wealth—an enduring connection with the ocean and the knowledge that sometimes, the greatest prize is not material riches but the wisdom gained along the way.

Let us reconnect to our culture to justify this:

The significance of auspicious beginnings is revered, celebrated, and deeply intertwined with spirituality. At the heart of these traditions lies the belief that making a good start is paramount, for it is in the commencement that we set the course for the journey ahead.

In India, the essence of auspicious beginnings finds expression in myriad rituals and ceremonies. One of the most revered is the Ganesh Puja, a time-honored tradition that marks the initiation of any significant venture or office opening. Lord Ganesha, the beloved elephant-headed deity, is invoked as the remover of obstacles and the harbinger of good fortune. His divine grace is sought to ensure a propitious start, one that paves the way for success and prosperity. As we delve deeper into the significance of these rituals, we discover a profound wisdom rooted in the belief that the start takes care of the end. It is a concept that transcends religious boundaries and resonates with universal truths.

Consider the image of Lord Ganesha, the deity with a broken tusk and a formidable form. His broken tusk is a symbol of sacrifice and humility, reminding us that every beginning requires us to relinquish something of ourselves. In this act of letting go, we make space for new possibilities, unburdened by the weight of the past. The Ganesh Puja teaches us that before embarking on any journey, we must first clear the path of obstacles. Just as Lord Ganesha is worshipped for his ability to remove impediments, we too must identify and overcome the barriers that obstruct our progress. These barriers may be external, such as logistical challenges, or internal, such as self-doubt and negativity. By seeking the blessings of Lord Ganesha, we acknowledge the need to confront these obstacles head-on, with faith and determination.

Moreover, the rituals surrounding auspicious beginnings emphasize the importance of mindfulness. The lighting of the lamp, the offering of flowers, and the recitation of sacred verses—all are acts of reverence that cultivate a sense of presence and intention. When we begin with mindfulness, we set the stage for a journey marked by conscious awareness, where every step is purposeful and every decision is made with clarity.

In Indian culture, the concept of "Shubharambh" (auspicious beginning) is not limited to religious or ceremonial contexts. It extends to every facet of life, from starting a new job to commencing a business venture, from entering into a marriage to embarking on a creative endeavor. It is a reminder that the quality of our beginnings profoundly influences the outcomes we achieve. The wisdom of auspicious beginnings underscores the interconnectedness of our actions, intentions, and results. It is a reminder that the energy we invest in the start ripples through the entirety of our journey, shaping our experiences and outcomes. In this way, we come to understand that making a good start is not merely about securing a favorable outcome; it is about aligning ourselves with the rhythms of the universe and infusing our endeavors with purpose and grace.

As we reflect on the profound teachings of Indian culture and rituals like the Ganesh Puja, let us carry with us the wisdom that the start takes care of the end. With each auspicious beginning, we honor the potential within us, seek the divine blessings that guide us, and step onto a path illuminated by the light of purpose. May our beginnings be filled with positivity, our journeys be marked by resilience, and our endings be celebrated as the culmination of a well-begun voyage.

Let us repeat these affirmations!

- "I trust that my positive and purposeful beginnings will lead to fulfilling and successful outcomes."

- "With every new venture, I embrace the belief that a strong and noble start sets the stage for a prosperous end."

- "I release fear and doubt, knowing that my intentions and actions at the beginning of any journey pave the way for triumph."

- "In every challenge, I find the courage to start with hope and determination, knowing that the start will guide me to victory."

- "I recognize that the energy and effort I invest at the outset of any project determine its ultimate success."

- "I welcome each day as a fresh start, a new opportunity to align my actions with my aspirations for a brighter future."

- "I am the author of my own story, and I begin each chapter with positivity and purpose, confident that it will lead to a fulfilling ending."

- "I trust that the universe conspires in my favor when I start with intention and authenticity."

- "I release the need for perfection and embrace the power of a genuine and heartfelt beginnings."

- "I believe that every small step I take towards my goals is a powerful beginning that will ultimately take care of the end I desire."

About the Author

Kaushik is an Award-winning international speaker, a Top-selling Author, Asia's most promising Corporate Coach and Trainer, Leadership Coach, Business & Career change coach, Renowned Mindfulness & Neuroscience Guru, Spiritual Teacher and an Emotional Health Educator in Asia.

🎯 He has been mentored by the World's Best Leaders - John Mattone - World's No.1 Executive Coach & Steve Jobs Coach) and Tony Robbins - World's No. 1 Speaker and Motivator), Blair Singer - The Master of Masters, Jack canfield - The man who modernized formulas for success, Gurudev Sri Sri Ravi Shankar - Most sought after Spiritual Leader and Founder of Art of Living, Deepak Chopra - Meditation Guru & Breath Science Expert and Wim Hof - The Iceman.

🎯 Kaushik founded Indian Leadership Academy(ILA), and serves as the president with over 150,000 Alumnus in Multiple countries. These certified coaches, Leaders and trainers have created a leadership movement within their own communities. He also works as an advisor to Skill Central UK - a leading learning organization in UK. His motto is to Lead with Wisdom and create oneness in the world through unconditional sharing and wisdom.

🎯 27 years of rich experience in running multi million business units as a Leader. As a Facilitator and a Coach, he has worked with 100000 + leaders in world-class companies, including IBM, Amazon, Bosch, Deutsche, Ericsson, PayPal, Flipkart, Softcrylic, DHL (Philippines), Amadeus(France), Unity(Dubai), Virtusa (US), MASHREQ Bank (UAE), Makino (Japan).

🎯 Specializations: Leadership Interventions, Leadership Coaching, Inclusive Leadership, Quantum Leadership, Millennial Leadership, Leadership development through Sports, Career Switch Coaching, CXO coaching, Ontological Coaching, Emergenetics, Neuroscience, Neuroleadership, Neurosales, Neuroeconomics, Coach the Coach Programs, Emotional Wellness, NLP & Mindfulness, Corporate Spirituality, Agile, Design Thinking, DISC, Thomas DISC Assessments, Retreats, Worldcafe facilitation, Keynote Speaking.

"Are we Leading" (TOP SELLER), "Minibook of Mindfulness", Coffee Tea or Coaching.

Recipient of Philipe Award for community leadership by GE.

Visit him at www.kaushikmahapatra.com

His Dream Project - ILA - Indian Leadership Academy International Venture - KMG - Kaushik Mahapatra Global Global Voluntary Organization : Inspire a Billion Education Venture : The Popcorn School- Life beyond education

Social Venture: 60+ - India's first play school for senior citizens, The Female Founders Program

🎯 His Workshop Locations: India, Singapore, UK, UAE, Philippines, Vietnam, Spain, Indonesia, Mauritius, Qatar